First edition – 1996, Spring Green Wisconsin

Second edition – 2001 Houston, Texas

Third edition – 2008, Houston, Texas

Fourth edition – 2014, Houston, Texas

Fifth edition – 2025, Roanoke, Virginia

The Bemis Family Cookbook

A collection of favorite recipes from the Bemis Family.

Original cover art by Sandy Bemis

I dedicate this edition to my loving wife Ridley for inspiring me to try new things and my mom and dad for starting this journey as well as contributing many recipes and experiences.

Introduction

First off, a couple of items of note to keep in mind as you read this edition

- All the comments in this edition are mine (John) unless noted otherwise, several people have contributed commentary in various places and I have tried to attribute them as much as possible.

- When the measurements are available in units of weight, use those if possible, as they will be more accurate. Some recipes, especially bread ones, are only in grams. A kitchen scale is your friend for any serious baking.

This cookbook began as the compilation of recipes collected and created by the Bemis family over the years. My father began this effort over 30 years ago with the intent to preserve the recipes that he and my mom had developed and perfected over the years, but had never been committed to paper. In my hands, the collection and book has grown considerably expanded with recipes from our daily menu in Houston and Roanoke, drawing much inspiration from our travels, most notably numerous trips to New Orleans, and from the local seafood of the Gulf of Mexico.

Some of the recipes are handed down from previous generations, others are modifications from other cookbooks and many times combination of two or more recipes Some are inspired by dishes encountered in restaurants. I have tried to recognize sources where possible. As usual and as it should be, the recipes evolve over time with healthier and tastier innovations. Some effort has been made to retain the original with optional modifications/variations as annotations where ever possible.

Cooking and food have been a central part of my life since I was a small child. Some of my earliest memories are of growing, harvesting and preparing food from the many gardens, both flower and vegetable, in the 1 acre yard of my childhood years in Naperville, IL. We worked as a family to grow much of the produce that we consumed during those years.

We grew a wide variety of produce ranging from staples to more exotic varieties. From leafy greens like lettuce spinach and chard to members of the cabbage family, broccoli, kohlrabi, Brussels sprouts, and sometimes cabbage itself. Annual staples included spring peas, winter squashes, green beans both pole and bush, cucumbers, zucchini, tomatoes, bell and banana peppers, and some more exotic vegetable like celeriac, asparagus, sun chokes. Included in the mix were many types of herbs including basil, sage, thyme, dill, mint, chives, Egyptian onions and rosemary. While most were annuals, there were a few perennial vegetables in the mix, including asparagus, Jerusalem artichokes (sun-chokes) and rhubarb. Less frequently included but at least some summers I remember we included cabbage, cauliflower, carrots, beets, kale, fava beans, yellow onions, leeks, and chili peppers.
Although we had a few fruit trees including apples, pears, peaches. The only fruit I remember harvesting in large quantity were the wild plumbs we used to make plumb jelly, which on at least one occasion was affectionately known as sticky stuff, having been perhaps cooked down a little too far.

This bountiful variety of produce was a blessing that I did not appreciate until later in life, but even so, gardening, especially vegetables was a big influence growing up and has stuck with me.

There are many memories for me in the garden, some fun like trying to find and harvest all the zucchini before they grew to the size of baseball bats, throughout the summer we would invariable miss at least one which would be destined for zucchini bread. Some not so fun, like fighting to protect our hard work from groundhogs, chipmunks Some that seemed like a chore at the time but today would not like picking produce for dinner, or harvesting Brussels sprouts from under the snow for thanksgiving. Often we would go harvest direct for dinner including green beans, broccoli, chard, lettuce, etc. It was a rare meal in which we did not have a salad of some sort on the table, usually a green salad with what ever fresh produce we had at the time. What at the time was just another chore, now would seem like a privilege.

Most vegetables were prepared very simply, letting the freshness do the work. For example the most common way we ate zucchini was to slice it with some onions and peppers and saute until lightly browned. Many others would be simply blanched or eaten raw.

In particular, tomatoes are a vegetable where, until I moved to other areas of the country, I did not have the perspective to understand how much difference homegrown can make. Today, finding ripe tomatoes such a challenge that I look back nostalgically on those tomato plants. Two memories come immediately to mind when I think about growing tomatoes; One is of planting tomatoes on memorial day. In northern Illinois the first day you can be confident to avoid a frost is memorial day so we would plant tomatoes and peppers. A a child I remember having the Indy 500 race on the radio as we all worked in the gardens. The second is standing at the kitchen counter running tomatoes through a food mill so we could put them up in jars.

While we canned a lot of things, when I was growing up, three things seemed to dominate, tomatoes, pickles, and jellies including wild plumb jelly and Apple butter. Later on after moving to Texas and planting a couple of lemon trees, I would make and preserve Meyer lemon marmalade, preserved lemons and artichoke pickle relish.

Growing up, cooking with vegetables straight from the garden instilled in me an expectation for fresh produce. Not that I understood at the time how good we had it. Later in life I have seen just what a challenge it is to find fresh produce. It gives me a new appreciation for the hard work we did and the benefits we reaped.

I began helping out in the kitchen very much as soon as I was able. First in harvesting and cleaning the produce. From there, my participation grew with my capabilities. Holidays were often a time where I was able to do new things as they were usually all hands on deck type events.

One day while I was in middle or high school stands out in particular contrast because it was, to my recollection, the first time I prepared an entire family meal by myself unsupervised. That meal was spaghetti with meat sauce. That meal kicked off a lifetime of cooking both everyday and special meals.

I hope that the recipes in this volume inspire you to try something new and to share it with your friends and family.

Contents

Special Occasion Menus

New Years Day

Collards
Black eyed peas
Corn bread (page 113)

New Years day is typically a low key day for us, even if we don't usually stay up until midnight the night before. Black-eyed peas and collards are traditional favorites, especially in the south as symbols for good luck in the coming year. Typically these are made as a mid-day sort of meal and we try to get out of the house weather permitting.

Easter

Jerked Ham (page 182)
Potatoes gratin (page 89)

A big Easter meal is usually only in the cards if we have company joining us. Often this was the best time of the year in Houston. We would often take weekend or day trips to do something outside to enjoy the weather. In Roanoke, you can spring is on it's way so on good days we enjoy the sun and start thinking about summer.

Texas BBQ

Brisket (page 239)
Pickles
Onions
BBQ Sauce (page 242)
Cole slaw (page 66)
White bread

When in Texas, at least once a summer I would break out the big smoker and cook a brisket. While there are a ton of place around Houston you can get a decent brisket, there is something about doing it yourself that can't quite be captured.. This is an all day affair as the smoker needs tending throughout. A great activity to do while lounging in the pool or doing yard work. Not to say that BBQ can't be done outside Texas, but it is not as much part of the culture, not to mention the price of brisket has made BBQ a luxury.

Fourth of July

Main
Barbecued Spare Ribs *(page 255)*

Sides
Corn on the Cob
Coleslaw *(page 66)*
Watermelon

Dessert
Homemade Ice Cream *(page 291)*

I have fond memories of hot summer fourth of July with barbecued ribs, corn on the cob and ice cream. Throwing lawn darts in the back yard, for those of you who remember them as I am sure lawn darts are no longer on the market for reasons that become obvious when you picture a regular dart blown up to 20 times the size and weight. We only occasionally had fireworks but always had a fun party.

Sandy- BBQ ribs always remind me of the 4th of July, when the kids were young. Alan's mom, John's grand-mom, was born on the 4th of July, very fitting for such an independent lady. Also Alan's brother Phil was born on the third of July, but only because the Doctor did not want to work on the 4th! So it was Birthday Party time. The outdoors rib operation (in front of the garage) would start early, and go on a long time with lots of talk of politics, and cabbages, and kings with games for the kids. In the kitchen, the BBQ sauce was made, but also with lots of talk. In the afternoon, the ice cream making began, also in front of the garage. This was a lot messier than the new electric machines, because of the salt and ice, and overflows of brine. For a few years, we had a peach tree in the back yard, and at least once it made a nice batch of wonderful peaches. The years with peaches were especially memorable. Such wonderful tasting ice cream.
The Birthday Cake may have been done the day before, but still candles and presents had to be rounded up. I do not remember the side dishes we served. Probably baked potatoes, certainly a green salad, and some vegetables. What a feast! We would later walk through the woods to the fireworks.

9

Oktoberfest

Grilled Bratwurst *(page 252)*

Braised Red Cabbage *(page 73)*

Apples *(page 252)*

Sauerkraut

Beverage Pairing
Oktoberfest Craft Beer

This menu is not really attached to a specific holiday, but during early fall we like to get in the mood by having a German inspired meal. Of course grilled bratwurst are a must have for a solid Oktoberfest menu. Good artisan mustard is a great condiment for the sausage. Nothing goes better with brats as a side than braised red cabbage and a good craft beer. Ridley prefers a pilsner style while I lean more toward IPA or Oktoberfest style. Sauerkraut is a nice tart pairing with this meal, but is very time consuming to make that I just pick up a quality brand from the store. Apples are the autumn fruit and go equally well in a side like sautéed apples, or as a dessert like pie or baked apples

Traditional Thanksgiving

Roast Turkey (*page 187*)
Stuffing/Dressing (*page 188*)
Holiday Knot Rolls (*page 120*)
Cranberry Sauce (*page 74*)
Sweet Potato Souffle (*page 91*)
Brussels Sprouts (*page 76*)

Optional/New Extras
Cranberry Chutney (*page 75*)
Mashed Potatoes
Butternut Squash and Red Pepper Casserole (*page 83*)
Caramelized Pearl Onions (*page 80*)

Dessert
Apple Pie (*page 279*)

Beverage Pairing
Medium Dry White Wine *e.g.,Sancerre*
Medium Light Red Wine *e.g., Pinot Noir*

Alan- As you will see, it takes most of the day to make the stuffing and roast the turkey. In addition, the sweet potatoes, Brussels sprouts, salad, and rolls have to be made. The chutney is always made in advance. The rolls are homemade (naturally) and are timed so that their final rising after being shaped is done when the turkey is taken out of the oven, so that the rolls can now be baked. There is plenty of work for 3 or 4 people in getting everything ready, including the table setting and opening a bottle of nice medium dry white wine. Eating this feast takes quite a while, and when everyone has been satisfied, or the stuffing runs out (usually there is at least a little left over) it's time to relax. Only CAT is still talking, and sometimes we save some of the turkey liver for this time just to quiet her!

John-I will devote some time here to a topic near and dear to the chef's heart; that is time management. Many of us however so much as we love the Holidays and even the cooking that goes along with it, get frustrated by the lack of time to socialize with our guests. There is a two pronged approach to mitigating this issue. One is to draft your guests into the kitchen staff. This works fine as long as they are foodies. The other approach is time management, that is do everything you can ahead of time. Many side dishes and relishes can be easily made one to several days before with no noticeable loss of quality, in fact some like the cranberry sauce and chutney improve with a couple of days in the fridge. The onions and celery can be chopped the night before. I usually do not cook the sausage and onions and celery ahead as I worry they might get waterlogged. Regardless there is nothing you can really do about the compromise between quality and time and if you want to do Thanksgiving right, you have to accept the giant whack out of your day.

Traditional Christmas

Appetizers with cocktails and/or wine include typically
Chicken Liver Pâté *(page 48)*
Pickled Herring
Pickled Shrimp *(page 44)*

Dinner
Roast prime rib of beef *(page 153)*

Roast Potatoes (John's recipe) *(page 153)*
Roast Parsnips
Brussels Sprouts *(page 76)*
Cranberries Sauce *(page 74)*
Cranberry Chutney *(page 75)*
Holiday Knot Rolls *(page 120)*
Green Salad with citrus fruit and apples *(page 61)*

Desert / Midnight / after church snacks
Assortment of Christmas Cookies *(page 295)*
Mincemeat *(page 274)*
Fruit Cake *(page 276)*

Beverage Pairing
A nice hearty red wine, usually a Cabernet Sauvignon or red Bordeaux

The Traditional Bemis Family Christmas Dinner

Alan- Actually, since when the kids were small, we have always had our Christmas dinner on Christmas Eve. One of the reasons for this was that we could go to the midnight church service and open our presents in the morning after a rather short night's sleep (very short when the kids were young!!) and no big cooking had to be done on Christmas (Sandy could celebrate Christmas by not spending the whole day in the kitchen). Of course the theory that there would be NO cooking on Christmas never quite worked out since everybody got hungry for some real food by evening (after a day of snacking on bread, cookies, candy, eggnog, some other good stuff).

Cocktails

Bemis Eggnog

Alan- This recipe was created by me in an attempt to duplicate the eggnog that my Dad made at Christmas. I (Alan) didn't have his recipe, so I read several cookbooks and then guessed what ingredients and proportions to use. After some adjusting, this is the result which we have been using for years.

  4 Eggs, separated
  1/2 cup Sugar
  2/3 cup Liquor, preferably Bourbon whiskey, but rum or brandy can be used
  1 cup Whipping Cream
  2 cups whole Milk
  1/4 teaspoon Vanilla
  a whole Nutmeg

Separate the eggs into yolks and whites. Put the whites into a bowl suitable for whipping and allow to warm (to room temperature) while carrying out the next step.

Put the yolks into a mixing bowl, and blend with the sugar at slow speed until smooth.

Slowly add the liquor while stirring at slow speed, and allow to "cook" for a minute.

Add the cream, milk, and vanilla and stir just until all of these ingredients are mixed.

At this point the bowl often has some sticky egg on the bottom or sides, so I transfer the mixture into a clean bowl.

Chill this milk mixture over ice or in the refrigerator.

Whip the egg whites until stiff.

Fold them into the milk mixture so that all of the whites are well coated with the milk mixture.

Grate fresh nutmeg over the eggnog.

Makes 8 small servings--too small for real eggnog lovers!

Mint Julep

Copper julep cups are not a requirement here, but lend a note of atmosphere to this late spring/ early summer drink. An old recipe from Kentucky goes as follows; Carefully pick the freshest possible mint, prepare a simple syrup, and measure out a half tumbler of your best bourbon, then pour the whiskey into a well frosted glass and throw the rest away and enjoy your bourbon. While I have some sympathy with the enjoyment of unblemished bourbon, the mint julep is a refreshing change.

Classically:

    5-6 Mint Leaves
    2 Sugar cubes
    3 ounces Bourbon
    Crushed ice

Place 4-5 mint leaves in the bottom of a chilled glass, add sugar cubes and muddle gently. Add crushed ice and 3 ounces of bourbon.   The bourbon should melt enough of the ice to create the proper strength but optionally you can dilute with spring water to the strength desired. Garnish with a mint leaf.

Whiskey Sour

I was looking around for a way to use all my surplus Myers lemons and this classic cocktail fits the bill and is tasty to boot.   Also it is really easy to make.

Classically:

    1 oz lemon juice
    1 ounce simple syrup
    2 ounces good bourbon whiskey
    Crushed ice

Fill a large tumbler with crushed ice and transfer to a shaker.   Add the lemon juice, syrup, and bourbon and shake well .... Pour back into the tumbler and serve.

Rum Punch

The classic recipe for true Caribbean rum punch in rhyme...

One of Sour;	(Lime Juice)
Two of Sweet;	(Grenadine Syrup)
Three of Strong;	(Rum)
Four of Weak.	(Water)

This is a drink we first encountered in the Grenadine islands. The best one ever from a small bar overlooking Clifton harbor on Union Island. The recipe below is as close as I can get to reproduce this relief from the tropical heat. The recipe diverges slightly from the ditty, but remains generally true to the spirit of the formula. Finding very ripe fruit is key to making this drink.

1 Banana, sliced in chunks
1 Mango, peeled and seeded and roughly chopped
1 Orange, halved and sliced in ¼ slices
Juice from two limes
2 cups Rum (can be a combination of light and dark)
Some combination of Pineapple, Orange, Mango juices

In a ½ gallon pitcher, add fruit chunks, lime juice, and rum to pitcher, fill the pitcher with an equal parts mixture of the fruit juices you have. Allow to marinate in the fridge for at least an hour, overnight is better.

To make the drinks

½ ounce of Grenadine Syrup
Angostura bitters
Nutmeg, fresh grated

To a tall glass of ice, add the aged rum and then fill most of the way up with the cold fruit mixture including a chunk or two of fruit as desired. Top with Grenadine syrup and a dash of bitters and finally grated nutmeg, garnish with one of the half slices of orange.

Sword of Orion

I tried this drink first at Seven Lamps restaurant in Atlanta, Georgia. I decided to try to replicate it.

2 oz. Pyrat XO Rum
Juice of ½ medium/small Lime
1 ounce Grilled Pineapple Szechwan Peppercorn Syrup

Shake with crushed ice, strain and serve neat in a cold martini glass

Grilled Pineapple Szechwan Peppercorn Syrup

½ fresh Pineapple, sliced in ½ inch slices (~5 slices)
1 Tablespoon Szechwan Peppercorns roughly crushed
½ cup Water
½ cup Sugar

Grill pineapple until well caramelized on both sides

Chop pineapple roughly and combine all ingredients in a vacuum seal bag. Cook at 150°F sous vide for at least 4 hours

Strain through a fine mesh

Commodore 64

This pre-dinner drink is an orange-infused variation on the Commodore No. 2 (bourbon, crème de cacao, lemon juice and grenadine) from the 1935 Waldorf-Astoria Bar Book. I could not resist adding this one because the name alone reminded me of the first computer I had as a child, setting a direction for my whole career.

Ice
1 1/3 ounces Bourbon
2/3 ounce white Crème de Cacao
2/3 ounce fresh Lemon Juice
2/3 ounce fresh Orange Juice
1/2 ounce
Dash of Bitters

1 Orange Wedge, for garnish

Fill a cocktail shaker with ice. Add all of the remaining ingredients except the garnish and shake well. Strain into an ice-filled rocks glass and garnish with the orange wedge.

Old Fashioned

2 oz Bourbon
1 oz Simple Syrup
Orange bitters
Orange slice

Measure bourbon and simple syrup over cubes add a couple dashes of bitters, stir and garnish with orange slice.

Jungle Bird

1 1/2 ounces dark or blackstrap rum
3/4 ounce Campari
1 1/2 ounces pineapple juice
1/2 ounce lime juice, freshly squeezed
1/2 ounce Demerara syrup
Garnish: pineapple wedge

Add the rum, Campari, pineapple juice, lime juice and demerara syrup into a shaker with ice and shake until well-chilled.

Strain into a rocks glass over fresh ice.

Garnish with a pineapple wedge.

Breakfast

Apple Pancake

Alan- This is a delicious alternative to scrambled eggs or an omelet. When Karen and John were kids, they and I would always ask Sandy to make this for us on Saturday or Sunday morning. I don't know where Sandy found or invented the recipe, but it was a great stroke of luck for us!

John- Later on, doing some research I have found similar recipes where this is called a dutch baby. I make this from time to time and find that twice as many apples is not out of line.

1 and 1/2 apples, preferably Jonathan
5 tablespoons Sugar
1 teaspoon Cinnamon
2 tablespoons Butter
3 tablespoons Flour
1/4 teaspoon Baking Powder
dash of Salt
2 Eggs, separated
3 tablespoons Milk

Peel, core, and slice the apples. In an oven usable fry pan melt the butter, add 2 tablespoons of the sugar, the cinnamon, and the apples and cook the apples until they are soft and lightly browned and the sugar is lightly caramelized.

Mix together the flour, baking powder, salt, the yolks of the eggs, and the milk.

Separately, whip the egg whites with 3 tablespoons (the rest) of the sugar until this makes soft peaks.

Fold the egg whites into the flour mixture, and pour over the apples.

Bake at 400° F for 10 minutes, or until the filling is set and brown on top.

Corn Meal Pancakes

Alan- These are a great breakfast with a little mild maple syrup. Other syrups or jams are OK, but these corn meal pancakes have such a nice, delicate, yet distinctive taste that it seems a shame to put strong flavorings on them. Anyway, I like them a lot. They are a bit of work, not too much, but more than normal so we have them as a special occasion. The recipe originate, as do so many, in Mama Rombauer.....although in this case it has been so modified that you can't blame Mama if you don't like it! It is supposed to make 12 four inch cakes, I guess it does, but that doesn't go very far! I would hazard a guess that if you have more than 3 people who like to eat, this recipe isn't big enough.

    1 cup Cornmeal (white or yellow)
    1 teaspoon Salt
    1 cup boiling Water
    1 Egg
    1/2 cup Skim Milk
    1 tablespoon Vegetable Oil
    1/2 cup All-purpose Flour
    2 teaspoons Baking Powder

Mix in a bowl the cornmeal and salt. Add the boiling water. Depending on the kind of cornmeal you have, you may need more water. Cover the cornmeal mixture, and allow to stand 10 minutes or longer.

Separately, beat together the egg, milk, and oil. Add this to the cornmeal mixture.

Sift together the flour and baking powder. Then add these to the cornmeal mixture. Stir together briefly.

Fry in a hot skillet. In this case, a hot skillet will cause drops of cold water to bounce and sputter. If you use a non-stick skillet, no grease should be necessary. Fry until the bubbles in the first side firm, then turn. The second side will be done in about half the time that the first side took.

Silver Dollar Pancakes

After testing a number of recipes looking for the perfect recipe to make little pancakes that are not heavy and cake-like. This one that makes surprisingly light pancakes that are best when made small, hence the silver dollar moniker.

4 Eggs
½ teaspoon Salt
½ teaspoon Baking Soda
½ cup Cake and Pastry Flour
2 cups Sour Cream
3 Tablespoon White Sugar

In a blender, mix the eggs until blended. Add the salt, baking soda, flour, sour cream, and sugar. Blend until well mixed and slightly bubbly.

Heat a griddle or frying pan to medium-high, then lightly grease with vegetable oil or butter (not necessary if you have a good non-stick surface).

Pour the batter into little silver dollar sized circles. Cook until bubbles appear on the top and the bottom is golden brown, then flip and continue cooking until the second side is also golden brown, about 2 minutes.

Eggs Benedict

This is Ridley's favorite breakfast. The most important aspect of making this is to find the freshest eggs possible. Our best experience is with eggs from a farmer's market, but reasonably fresh supermarket eggs will do, the brown or free range variety are usually the best bet.

For Hollandaise Sauce
1/2 cup Butter
2 Egg Yolks
1 teaspoon fresh Lemon Juice
1/4 cup boiling Water
Dash Salt
Dash ground Cayenne Pepper

For poaching water
Juice from ½ of a Lemon,
1 tablespoon Salt

Multiply by the number of diners:
2 Eggs
1 English Muffin, split, toasted, and buttered

Hollandaise Sauce

In the top of a double boiler, whisk egg yolks and lemon juice together. Add 1/3 of the butter, about 3 tablespoons. Place double boiler over simmering water. Cook, beating constantly, until butter melts and sauce begins to thicken. Add 3 more tablespoons of butter, stir until butter melts, then add remaining 2 tablespoons of butter. Slowly whisk in boiling water. Continue cooking over simmering water, stirring, until mixture thickens, about 2 to 3 minutes. Remove from heat; stir in salt and cayenne pepper.

Poached eggs

Pour about 2 inches of water into a large skillet. Lightly salt water; bring to a simmer. Add the juice of ½ a lemon to acidify the water. Carefully break each egg first into a small bowl keeping the yolk intact, and then gently slipping it into the water. Simmer eggs, while basting with the water, for 3 to 4 minutes or until the whites are set. Remove with slotted spoon; drain on a towel.

On warm serving plates, place English muffins, 2 halves to each plate. Top with poached eggs. Spoon a little sauce over the egg.

Breakfast Sandwich

I make these a lot and I have gotten pretty good at putting them together quickly. The most important part is to keep the egg yolk runny.

English Muffin (Biscuits will work well too, bread is ok)
Butter
egg
Cheese sliced
Sausage, ham or bacon, pre cooked

Butter the muffin and start in the toaster

Meanwhile warm the desired meat in microwave

Heat a small non-stick pan over medium heat. Add a small pat of butter. Once the butter is foaming and spread around the pan, crack the egg into the center.

Cook the egg on one side until the white is almost all cooked, flip and cover with cheese. Turn the heat off.

Retrieve the muffin from the toaster and assemble

Muffin bottom
Egg w/cheese
meat
Muffin top

Sourdough Waffles

When I was a kid, one of my favorite weekend memories is making sourdough waffles. This had to be started the night before, then I would get up early and start the preparation early the next morning. Just the smell of these cooking would probably wake me from a deep sleep even today.

Sourdough Starter (1-2 cups) *(page 96)*
2 cups All-purpose Flour
2 cups Water

2 tablespoons Granulated Sugar
1 teaspoon Salt
1/2 teaspoon baking powder
3 tablespoons Canola Oil
2 Eggs, well beaten
1/2 teaspoon Baking Soda, dissolved in about 2 teaspoons water

The night before, combine starter, flour and water in a bowl. Mix until smooth. Cover with a towel and leave on counter overnight.

The next morning, return 1 cup of the mixture along with ½ cup flour and ½ cup water to refrigerator.

Combine the rest of the starter you made the night before with the sugar, salt, baking powder, oil and eggs. Mix well. Gently stir in baking soda dissolved in water.

Each waffle will use about ½ cup of batter depending on you waffle iron and take from 4-7 minutes to cook, get to know your iron.

Ridley's variation on this is to add fresh or frozen blueberries to the batter. These will cook in the iron creating pockets of blueberry throughout the waffles. The caveat is that the waffles will take significantly longer to cook, especially if frozen berries are used, but they are worth the wait.

Sticky Bun Bread Pudding

This is an amazing decadence, so rich you can't make it often and stay alive.

4 large Eggs
2 cups plus 2 tablespoons (or more) Half and Half
1 teaspoon Vanilla extract
1 cup chopped Pecans
1/2 cup (packed) Golden Brown Sugar
2 1/2 teaspoons ground Cinnamon
Butter, room temperature
8 (1-inch-thick) slices from day–old large loaf of Challah Bread, crusts removed
Powdered Sugar

Blend eggs, 2 cups half and half, and vanilla; reserve. Stir pecans, brown sugar, and cinnamon in small bowl to blend; reserve.

Butter bread on both sides and well butter a 9x5x3-inch loaf pan

Layer bread, pecan mixture, and egg mixture in thirds starting with the bread

Allow to sit for 30 min to 1 hour to fully saturate the bread with the egg mixture while the oven preheats to 350°F

Place loaf pan in center of 13x9-inch baking pan; set in oven. Pour enough hot water into baking pan to come halfway up sides of loaf pan. Bake until pudding is set, about 45 minutes.

Remove pan from water; cool slightly. Turn loaf out. Slice warm bread pudding thickly and transfer to plates.

Dust bread pudding slices with powdered sugar and serve.

Blueberry Biscuits

I made this when we had guests over and it was such a hit we now make it for most visitors.   The mini biscuits came about for a treat at Winnie Sommer's christening party.

Biscuits
1 tablespoon unsalted butter, melted,
10 tablespoons unsalted butter, frozen
3 cups (15 ounces) all-purpose flour
½ cup (3½ ounces) sugar
2 teaspoons baking powder
½ teaspoon baking soda
1 ¼ teaspoons table salt
1½ - 2 cups blueberries,
1 ⅔ cups buttermilk, chilled
Honey Butter (optional)
2 tablespoons unsalted butter
1 tablespoon honey
Pinch table salt
Lemon Glaze(optional)
3 tablespoons lemon juice + zest of one lemon
½ cup Powdered sugar, more as necessary

Adjust oven rack to middle position and heat oven to 425 degrees. Brush bottom and sides of 8-inch square baking pan with melted butter.

Whisk flour, sugar, baking powder, baking soda, and salt together in large bowl. Grate frozen butter into flour mixture toss to coat butter with flour . Add blueberries and toss with flour mixture. Gently stir in buttermilk until no dry pockets of flour remain.

Using rubber spatula, transfer dough to prepared pan and spread into even layer and into corners of pan. Using bench scraper sprayed with vegetable oil spray, cut dough into 9 equal squares (2 cuts by 2 cuts), but do not separate. Bake until browned on top and paring knife inserted into center biscuit comes out clean, 40 to 45 minutes.

Meanwhile, combine butter, honey, and salt in small bowl and microwave until butter is melted, about 30 seconds. Stir to combine; set aside.

Remove pan from oven and let biscuits cool in pan for 5 minutes. Turn biscuits out onto baking sheet, then flip biscuits onto wire rack. Brush tops of biscuits with honey butter (use all of it). Let cool for 10 minutes. Using serrated knife, cut biscuits along scored marks and serve warm.

Variation - Mini biscuits

Extra Equipment - mini muffin pan (24 mini muffins) Paper inserts are recommended

As above except Increase the amount of buttermilk to 2 ½ cups and spoon batter into muffin cups. Bake as above but check early starting at 30 minutes as they will cook faster.

Biscuits and Gravy

Biscuits and gravy is my number one breakfast craving and a traditional southern specialty. This is also closely related to the cream dried beef we had when I was young.

  biscuits or toast
2 Tablespoons Fat (butter or sausage drippings)
2 Tablespoons flour
2+ Cups milk
Salt
Black pepper
Cooked meat, crumbled sausage or shredded dried beef

The first step is to make the biscuits, traditionally in the south sausage gravy is served on a split buttermilk biscuit (see page 129). However when I was young, we served it over drop biscuits (see page 128). I have found that in a pinch even toast is ok.

The best time to make gravy is when you are cooking breakfast sausage. Once you are done cooking the sausage, remove the sausage and add the flour to the pan, You can scale the flour depending on how people are being served, just make sure to have equal amount of fat, adding butter if necessary. If you are starting with a clean pan, simply add equal amounts butter and flour. Whisk the flour around making sure it does not burn.

Once the flour is lightly browned, add cream or milk whisking in a small amount at a time until the desired consistency is reached. Bring this mixture to a simmer, adding more milk to maintain the desired thickness as it will further thicken as it cooks. Season this with salt and lots of fresh ground black pepper.

Now is the time to add your (already cooked) meat if desired, either crumbled breakfast sausage or dried beef that has been curt into thin strips.

Once the gravy has simmered enough that the added meat is hot, serve over biscuits.

Cinnamon Buns

One half a batch of brioche dough (page 125)
¾ cup raisins
1 tsp cinnamon
½ cup sugar

Using ½ a batch of brioche dough, roll out to a 12 x 16 inch rectangle (~1/4 inch thick)

In a small bowl stir cinnamon and sugar together and then spread evenly over the dough. Sprinkle raisins evenly across the rectangle

With a short side toward you, roll away from you, trying to keep the roll as tight as possible.

Cut roll into even pieces about 1 ½ inches wide (~8-10 pieces)

Butter a 9x13 baking pan, place the buns with a cut side down evenly spaced into the pan

Proof for about 2 hours or until the dough is puffy, pillowy and soft

Bake at 350 for 35 to 45 minutes until golden brown.

Pecan sticky buns

One half a batch of brioche dough (page 125)
Topping
    ¾ cup butter
    1 ½ cups light brown sugar
    1/3 cup honey
    1/3 cup heavy cream
    1/3 cup water
    ¼ tsp salt
    ½ cup pecan haves, toasted, chopped

filling
    ¼ cup light brown sugar
    ¼ cup granulated sugar
    1/8 tsp cinnamon
    ½ cup pecans, toasted , chopped

To make the topping, melt butter in a small pan, add brown sugar and wisk until dissolved. Remove from heat and stir in honey, cream, water & salt. Allow to cool

Using ½ a batch of brioche dough, roll out to a 12 x 16 inch rectangle (~1/4 inch thick)

In a small bowl stir filling ingredient together and then spread evenly over the dough

With a short side toward you, roll away from you, trying to keep the roll as tight as possible. Cut roll into even pieces about 1 ½ inches wide (~8-10 pieces)

Pour topping into a 9x13 baking pan, sprinkle pecans evenly across the entire surface.

Place the buns with a cut side down evenly spaced into the pan

Proof for about 2 hours or until the dough is puffy, pillowy and soft

Bake at 350 for 35 to 45 minutes until golden brown.

Remove from oven and allow to cool about 20 minutes on a rack. Invert onto a serving rack and spoon any remaining topping over the buns

Appetizers

Shrimp–Snapper Ceviche

For this recipe it is of the essence to get only extremely fresh fish and shrimp, in fact if I can't get shrimp and snapper which are basically straight out of the water I won't bother. Luckily which living on the Texas coast they are readily obtainable.

 1/2 pound medium-small Shrimp, peeled and de-veined
 1/2 pound Gulf Red Snapper, cut into ½-1 inch pieces
 2 Tablespoons Salt
 1-1.5 cup Lime Juice (juice from 4-6 limes) some lemon juice can be substituted
 1 cup finely chopped Red Onion
 1 Serrano Chile, ribs and seeds removed, minced
 1 cup chopped Cilantro
 1 Cucumber, peeled diced into 1/2-inch pieces
 1 Avocado, peeled, seed removed, cut into 1/2-inch chunks

Place red snapper in a glass or ceramic bowl. Mix in the lime juice. Cover and refrigerate for a half hour.

In a large pot, bring to a boil 4 quarts of water, salted with 2 Tablespoons salt. Add the shrimp and cook for 1 minute to 2 minutes max, depending on size of shrimp. (Over-cooking the shrimp will turn it rubbery.) Remove shrimp with a slotted spoon and place into a bowl of ice water to stop the cooking.

Drain the shrimp. Cut each piece of shrimp in half, or into inch-long pieces. Mix the shrimp, chopped red onion and Serrano Chile into the marinating snapper. Refrigerate an additional half hour.

Right before serving, add the cilantro, cucumber, and avocado.

Pickled Shrimp a la Commander's Palace

Alan- The basis for this recipe came from the Commander's Palace cookbook. It is highly recommended that every food lover eventually visit this foodie Mecca in New Orleans. Even months after Hurricane Katrina, Commander's Palace was in fine form. This shrimp make an irresistible appetizer which if you leave it to your guests.

3 pounds of medium Shrimp peeled with tails removed

1 medium Red Onions, finely diced
1 bunch Green Onions, thinly sliced
½ tsp Crushed Red Pepper
6 cloves Garlic, minced fine
¼ cup coarse Mustard
2 Tb Sugar
Salt and fresh ground Black Pepper to taste
¾ cup Cider Vinegar
1¼ cups Olive Oil
2 Bay Leaves

Bring a large pot of water, 8-10 quarts, to a boil. Add a bay leave and ¾ cup shrimp boil mix if desired. If you do not use shrimp boil add four tablespoons salt. Add the shrimp and lower the heat to a simmer. Cook the shrimp for 3½ to 4 minutes drain and put in ice water.

While shrimp are cooling, mix the onions, peppers, garlic, mustard, sugar, salt and pepper and vinegar in large bowl. Whisk oil in slowly to create an emulsion. Add the bay leave and taste for seasoning. Toss shrimp in the marinade and refrigerate at least overnight.

Ridley's Edamame Hummus

This recipe comes from Tanya Boyd via Ridley; she adapted it from *Cooking Light* magazine. It is a great alternative to using chick peas and has a brighter more fresh taste..

¼ cup Parsley
2 tablespoon Onion, chopped
2 tablespoon Tahini
2 tablespoon Rice Vinegar
2 teaspoon Soy Sauce
1-2 cloves Garlic
1 teaspoon Dijon Mustard
¼ teaspoon Cumin
¼ teaspoon Ginger
¼ teaspoon Coriander
¼ teaspoon Turmeric
¼ teaspoon Paprika
¼ teaspoon Salt
Pepper
12-14 ounces frozen Edamame, shelled
¼ cup Orange Juice

Thaw edamame in microwave on low power.

Meanwhile add everything except edamame and orange juice into a food processor and blend until smooth.

Add the edamame slowly adding small amounts of orange juice if the mixture gets too thick. Once the edamame is all added, orange juice is added until desired consistency is reached.

Serve with pita or crackers

Deviled Ham

Alan- Our starting point for this recipe was the *March 1993 Gourmet*, but we made a lot of changes in it. Perhaps it needs more, because it was less popular than the Swiss Cheese and the Celeriac appetizers.It certainly is less unusual.

    3/4 pound Baked Ham
    1/4 cup Gray Poupon Mustard
    1 tablespoon Honey
    1/4 teaspoon ground Cloves
    3 tablespoons minced Onion
    3 tablespoons homemade Pickle Relish (sweet)

Julienne the ham into thin sticks, about 2 inches long.Mix the remaining ingredients and then combine thoroughly with the ham until it is well coated.Serve with crackers.Makes about 2 cups. This should serve 4 to 12 people as an appetizer.It is good, although it admittedly tastes mostly like baked ham.

Swiss Cheese With Walnuts And Mustard

Alan- This is a nice appetizer which we found in the *March 1993 Gourmet* and modified slightly. Our gourmet group seemed to like it.

  2 tablespoons Gray Poupon mustard
  3 tablespoons Nonfat Yogurt
  1/4 teaspoon dry Tarragon
  1/2 cup minced Green Onion
  1/2 pound Swiss Cheese
  1/2 cup chopped Walnuts

In a bowl mix the mustard, yogurt, tarragon, and green onion together thoroughly.Coarsely grate the Swiss cheese (I suggest you use a good quality such as Baumgartners' Aged Swiss).Toast the walnuts lightly and cool them to hand comfortable temperature.Combine the cheese and walnuts with the mustard mixture and mix until the cheese is well coated.Serve with crackers or French bread.This recipe makes 2 and 1/2 cups,for 4 to 12 people as an appetizer depending on what else is being served, etc.

Pâté

Alan- This is wonderfully rich appetizer that we used to make at the Holidays. It is not exactly a heart healthy recipe given the amount of butter, but on a good piece of rye crater it is delicious.

½ pounds Chicken Liver
2 Tablespoon Onion, roughly chopped
1 teaspoon Dry Mustard
1 teaspoon Salt
½ cup Butter
½ teaspoon Cloves, ground
½ teaspoon Cayenne
1/8 teaspoon Nutmeg

Cover the livers with water in a small saucepan and bring to a boil. Simmer for 15-20 minutes until tender. Drain and add a blender, add the rest of the ingredients and allow butter to soften somewhat. Blend until smooth and pour into a crock or bowl and chill until set. The flavors benefit from a day or two of aging in the fridge.

Guacamole and Salsas

The key here is freshness and ripeness of the ingredients both of these are at their peak within minutes of preparation and so ideally should not be made ahead. Serve with any kind of chips or as a relish with a main course. When selecting avocados for this recipe, ripeness is especially critical to get the right balance of flavor. After some research on onions and Mexican cooking, I found the proper onion to use for raw food is white onion.

Guacamole
   1 ripe avocado (Hass type with black wrinkled skin preferred)
   1/2 medium Tomato, diced
   ¼ - ½ cup white Onion, finely diced
   1 medium Jalapenos, seeded and finely diced
   2 Tablespoons Parsley or Cilantro
   Lime Juice
   Paprika
   Hot Sauce (Tabasco)
   Black Pepper
   Salt

Mix everything together, you can roughly chop avocado or mash it smooth according to how you like it. There is a lot of tinkering with ratios and preparation and generally all turn out good.

Add salt last to taste and remember that typically this will be eaten with salty chips.

Allow to sit for a few minutes before serving to allow flavors to mellow, but it does not long so make only as much as will be consumed immediately.

Pico de Gallo or Salsa Bandera

   1 Medium Tomatoes medium dice
   ¼ medium white onion, fine dice
   1 Jalapenos, fine dice
   About 1 tablespoon Lime Juice (about ½ of a lime)
   2 tablespoons cilantro leaves, copped fine
   Salt
   Fresh ground Black Pepper

Mix all ingredients together and serve, it's just that easy. Vary ratios to taste.

Salsa Verde

3 small Tomatillos
½ small Red Onions
1 Avocado
Juice of Lime
3 medium Jalapeños, halved and seeded
Salt
Pepper
Cayenne

Remove skins from tomatillos. Char tomatillos on all sides and the skin side of the jalapeños. Gently brush the charred skin off and core the tomatillos. Add all the ingredients except the spices to a food processor. Process until just smooth. Add a dash of cayenne a few grinds of fresh ground black pepper. Start with a ½ teaspoon salt. Stir and season to taste.

Lettuce Wraps

These are a fun appetizer or light meal for small groups allowing one to adjust to appetite.

1 tablespoon Sesame Oil
1 pound Ground Meat (Chicken, Turkey Beef, Lamb, Pork, etc.)
1 large Onion, chopped
2 tablespoons Garlic, minced or pressed

1 tablespoon Soy Sauce
1/4 cup Hoisin Sauce
2 teaspoons fresh Ginger, minced
1 tablespoon Rice Wine Vinegar
3 teaspoons Sriracha sauce
1 can (8 ounces) sliced Water Chestnuts, drained and finely chopped
1 small bunch Green Onions, sliced
Roasted Peanuts, chopped (optional)
2 teaspoon Sesame Oil
Salt to taste

Bibb or butter lettuce leaves, rinsed and drained

Soy sauce, hoisin, spicy mustard sauce for dipping

Sauté onions, garlic and ground meat in 1 tablespoon sesame oil until onions begin to brown. Remove from heat.

Stir in the rest of the ingredients and fold until completely coated and well combined. Salt to taste.

Serve deconstructed, with filling, lettuce, and dipping sauces in separate bowls, allow diners to construct to taste.

Potstickers

With this recipe, I would say that making your own dumplings is optional. There are a number of brands of frozen dumplings that are quite good, the one we prefer is the mini-dumplings by BiBiGo. Traditionally served as an appetizer, we often do this for a meal.

Dumplings

Filling
½ lb ground pork(you can substitute chicken, shrimp or even mushrooms)
1 baby bok choy,or nappa cabbage diced (about 1 1/4 cups, diced)
6 water chestnuts, diced
2 green onions, thinly sliced
2 garlic cloves, crushed
2 teaspoons fresh ginger, minced
1 teaspoon sesame oil
2 teaspoon salt
½ teaspoon cracked black pepper
1 egg, lightly beaten
Assembly
1 egg, lightly beaten
40 round wonton wrappers

Mix all filling ingredients together making sure they are thoroughly combined.

Brush the edges of a wonton wrapper with the beaten egg and fill center with 1 heaping tablespoon of filling.

Fold wonton in half over filling.

Starting at one end of the fold, push small pleats onto one side of the wrapper, pressing and sealing with the hand holding the potsticker until the dumpling is sealed.

Repeat until all filling has been used.

Potsticker

1 Tablespoon oil
½ cup chicken stock

Heat a skillet over medium heat, add oil, when oil is hot, place dumplings in the pan making sure not to crowd them too much. Each should have a flat side down on the pan.

Cook until potstickers are deeply brown on the bottom, pour the chicken stock over the dumplings and cover.

Cook for 2-3 more minutes until the dumplings are cooked and most of the chicken stock is evaporated. Uncover and continue to cook until no stock remains.

Serve with dipping sauce

Potsticker Dipping Sauce

Scale this recipe according to how many people will be sharing

> Equal parts Hosin Sauce and Oyster Sauce
> 2 parts Soy Sauce
> 1 part Rice wine vinegar
> 1 teaspoon Dijon mustard
> 1 teaspoon Sriracha(optional)

Wisk together all ingredients and divide into small bowls for dipping

Szechuan Wonton Sauce

Caution, depending on the heat of the peppers you use, this one can be spicy.

> 4 to 8 whole arbol chile peppers, stems removed
> 2 teaspoons sichuan peppercorns
> 1/4 cup (60ml) vegetable oil
> 1 tablespoon roasted sesame oil
> 2 tablespoons rice vinegar
> 1 tablespoon balsamic vinegar)
> 2 tablespoons soy sauce
> 1 tablespoon sugar
> 1 tablespoon minced fresh garlic (about 3 medium cloves)
> 1 tablespoon toasted sesame seeds

Place chilies and Sichuan peppercorns in a bowl and microwave on high until toasted and aromatic, about 15 seconds.

Process in a food processor until it's about the texture of crushed red pepper flakes. Transfer to a heat proof bowl.

Heat oil to shimmering hot and pour over the pepper flakes. Allow to cool.

Add the rest of the ingredients and wisk until sugar is dissolved

Buffalo Chicken Dip

1 pound Chicken shredded
12 ounce Frank's Red Hot or Buffalo Wing sauce
1 1/2 cups chopped Celery
2 T Olive Oil
2 8 ounce packages Cream Cheese
1 small bottle of good quality Blue Cheese Dressing
8 ounces shredded Cheddar Cheese

Preheat oven to 350°F

Heat olive oil in a sauté pan over medium to medium-high heat. Add celery and sauté just until tender. Take pan off of heat. Add chicken mixture and combine.

In large bowl, whip cream cheese until fluffy (adding a tablespoon or two of milk can sometimes help to loosen up the cream cheese if it's very cold and firm). When cream cheese is creamy, add blue cheese dressing and stir to combine. Add chicken/celery mixture and mix thoroughly.

Place dip in large casserole dish. Bake uncovered for 20 minutes. Add cheddar cheese and stir to combine. Bake for another 20 minutes or until heated through.

Serve with celery, and sliced French bread or tortilla chips.

Buffalo Cauliflower

Cauliflower

 1 cup milk
 1 cup flour
 1 teaspoon garlic powder
 pepper to taste
 1 tablespoon olive oil
 1 head of cauliflower
 2/3 cup Panko bread crumbs

Buffalo sauce

 1/3 cup butter, melted
 1/3 cup Franks Hot Sauce
 Dash of garlic powder

Preheat oven to 450 degrees F.

Cut cauliflower into bite sized pieces discarding the core.

Combine milk, flour, garlic powder, pepper and olive oil in a large bowl. Place batter and cauliflower in a large Ziploc bag and toss until cauliflower is coated.

Pour cauliflower into a large strainer letting any excess batter drip off. Sprinkle with Panko breadcrumbs and gently toss.

Place on a foil lined pan and bake 15 minutes. Remove from the oven and gently toss with buffalo sauce. You want the cauliflower coated but not soaked.

Place back on the pan and bake an additional 5-10 minutes or until cauliflower is tender crisp.

Ham and Cheese Sliders

This a great way to use up some of the jerked ham from page 182

   1 package (12) sweet Hawaiian rolls
   ½ pound of thin sliced ham
   ½ lb thin sliced Swiss cheese
   4 Tbs Mayonnaise
   1 Tbs Poppy seed
   ½ cup Butter
   2 ½ Tbs Mustard divided
   1 Tsp Worcestershire sauce
   1Tsp onion powder

Without separating the rolls, carefully remove from the foil tray and slide horizontally.

Mix 1 Tbs mustard with the mayo and spread mix on inside of both halves

Put the bottom ¼ of the buns back in the tray and layer ham and cheese followed by the top half of the buns.

Mix 1 ½ Tbs of mustard with the poppy seeds, melted butter, Worcestershire sauce and onion powder and pour evenly over the buns

Cover with foil and rest for 10 minutes.

Bake in a 350 degree oven for 15-20 minutes until hot and melty.

Salads and Sides

Traditional Dinner Salad

This is the traditional dinner salad which I make as a side to most any dinner. Sliced steak, chicken or shrimp can be added to make it a complete meal. As you will see from my notes this salad can be made in almost infinite different combinations, all delicious.

Dressing

My preference is for the vinaigrette on page 63, however a good homemade Caesar (page 62) is good for a change up or with spinach, a warm bacon dressing (page 64) poured over the salad to partially wilt the salad.

Greens, torn into small/medium pieces

The greens used primarily depend on what you can get that is freshest and your personal preference. I am most partial to Bibb lettuce, but spinach, romaine, leaf, etc. all work perfectly well.

Tomatoes, cut into chunks

Fresh, ripe tomatoes make this salad, so get as good quality as you can. Heirlooms when possible. Cherry tomatoes work especially well, you can throw them in whole, however I prefer to halve them

Cucumbers, large dice

Any type of cucumber will work, however if using salad or English cucumbers, the seeds and tough skin should be removed.

Onions, diced fine

Either green onions sliced, sweet or red onions diced work fine.

Bell Pepper, large dice

Any color will do

Cheese, small dice

My preference is for Blue if you want a more wedge salad feel, Swiss for classic, or feta for more a Greek touch.

Bacon, crumbled

Good with spinach and a small amount of the hot bacon grease can be used to slightly wilt the spinach for a really nice warm winter salad.

Other optional ingredients include: avocado, ham, hard boiled egg, olives, fruit like strawberries, chopped apples, or sliced oranges

Caesar Salad

3 ounces day-old Bread cut ½ inch cubes
1 ½ tablespoons Olive Oil

1 tablespoon Red Wine Vinegar
1 tablespoon Lemon Juice
2 Garlic cloves, pounded to a puree (or put through a garlic press)
2 teaspoons chopped Anchovies, about 2-3 fillets
Salt and freshly ground Pepper
1 Egg Yolk
¼ cup Olive Oil
¼ cup Parmesan, freshly grated

¼ cup Parmesan, freshly grated
1 heads Romaine Lettuce, dark outer leaves removed, roughly chopped
2 medium Tomatoes cut into wedges

Toss the bread cubes with olive oil and a generous amount of salt. Bake at 350 F for 10-12 minutes, stirring occasionally so they toast evenly. Don't let them cook too long—they're best crispy on the outside but still chewy on the inside. You can also put them into a large skillet over medium-low heat, tossing occasionally until they are golden and chewy.

Meanwhile, wash the lettuce well, tearing the larger leaves into bite-size pieces and leaving the small light interior leaves whole. Dry well in a salad spinner and chill until ready to serve.

In a small bowl, mix together the acids, garlic, anchovies, and a good pinch of salt and pepper. Whisk in the olive oil very slowly to make an emulsion. Then whisk in the egg yolk and about half of the Parmesan cheese. Taste for seasoning and acidity with a piece of the lettuce.

In a large bowl, add the lettuce, tomatoes, and croutons and pour over about a third of the dressing, tossing well, adding more dressing to taste.   Top with any remaining cheese and serve with a twist of black pepper.

Salad Dressings

Vinaigrette

This is a recipe I have adjusted over the years to my taste, please feel free to alter the proportions to suite your own tastes.

2/3 cup Extra Virgin Olive Oil
1/3 cup Red wine vinegar
1/3 cup White wine or Rice vinegar
3 cloves garlic, crushed
1 teaspoon. Balsamic Vinegar
1 tablespoon. Oregano
1 tablespoon. Basil
2 teaspoons Thyme
1 Tsp Black Pepper
2 teaspoons Salt
1 tablespoon. Mustard
1 tablespoon. Honey
1 teaspoon Paprika
½ tsp Cayenne

Measure all ingredients into a pint size mason jar. Seal with lid and shake to combine well. Allow to sit at least 30 minutes at room temp to allow dried herbs to re-hydrate before applying to salad. Best after an overnight sit in the fridge. Keeps a few weeks at least in fridge, it will solidify in the fridge as good olive oil has a relatively high melting point.

Peppercorn Buttermilk

¼ cup mayo
¼ cup buttermilk
2 Tbs sour cream
½ tsp black pepper
2 tsp horseradish
½ tsp Dijon mustard
¼ tsp salt

Combine and whisk together, ideal let sit in refrigerator for at least an hour for flavors to combine.

Warm Bacon Dressing

This is a great dressing for a spinach salad

3 strips of Bacon
3 tablespoons Red Wine Vinegar
1 teaspoon Mustard
1 teaspoons honey (optional)
Fresh ground Black Pepper

Cook bacon until all fat is rendered and the bacon is crisp, remove from heat and reserve the bacon to crumble over the salad. Drain all but 3 tablespoons of the bacon grease and put over low heat. Wisk wine vinegar, mustard, and a couple of grinds of black pepper into the grease. Pour over the salad while still warm to slightly wilt the spinach.

Celeriac Salad

By Alan & Sandy

Celeriac, sometimes called celery root or knob celery, is an interesting, delicious vegetable. It can be eaten raw or cooked. Raw celeriac is particularly delicious, and can often be found in grocery stores. For many years we grew it, but it takes 5 or 6 months to mature, and when harvested has lots of small roots and is usually caked with mud. Now we buy it, but still enjoy eating it.

1 cup Yogurt
2 tablespoons Apple Cider Vinegar
½ teaspoon Salt
½ teaspoon Sugar
1 tablespoon finely minced Onion

For the salad:
1 Celeriac, about 4 inches in
1-2 Apples
2 tablespoons freshly chopped Italian Parsley

Sandy started making this dish in the autumn when we grew celeriacs, and they were ready to be harvested, after a frost in October or November. Because raw celeriac will quickly turn brown unless coated with dressing, do not cut up the celeriac until the dressing is made.

The first step, therefore, is to mix the dressing. Simply combine all the ingredients and mix well. Then cut the celeriac into quarters. Take one quarter, and peel and rinse it. Coarsely grate it, mixing each batch of gratings immediately into the dressing. It will usually take two iterations of grating to do each quarter. Repeat for the other 3 quarters. At this point, Sandy usually has a short rest break and cleans up the mess! Cut up the parsley next and mix with the dressing/celeriac. Last, cut each apple into quarters, remove core, and cut in half lengthwise, then into 1/4 inch slices. Rapidly mix into celeriac/parsley/dressing mixture. (Remember that apple turns brown without dressing also) Unless you hate peel, leave it on because the red looks pretty.

This dish can be refrigerated for at least one day without harm. I think it's quite good, and a nice change from other salads. Serve with crackers or French bread.

Vinegar based Coleslaw

This is my favorite coleslaw, it is bright and summery, and with no mayo it keeps longer. It is best made 2-3 days up to a week ahead of the event you are planning, which is most cases is a plus too. I like to use a small green savoy cabbage and a small purple cabbage for color, but any cabbages should work, even Napa cabbage, although I can't remember if I have tried it.

For the Dressing:
1 cup Apple Cider Vinegar
1 cup Sugar
3 tablespoons Extra-Virgin Olive Oil
1 teaspoon crushed Garlic (about 1 large clove)
1 teaspoon freshly ground Black Pepper
1 teaspoon Celery Seeds

For the Slaw:
1 large head Green Cabbage (about 3 1/2 pounds), finely shredded (1/2 inch pieces)
4 large Carrot, grated
1 medium Red Onion, diced
2/3 cup sugar
1/3 cup Salt
2 Medium to large Granny Smith Apples, peeled and diced

For the Dressing:

Whisk together vinegar, sugar, oil, garlic, black pepper, and celery seeds in small bowl.

For the Slaw:

Combine shredded cabbage, grated carrot, and diced onion in a large bowl. Sprinkle with 2/3 cup sugar and 1/3 cup salt and toss to combine. Let stand 1 ½ to 2 hours, then transfer to a large colander and rinse thoroughly under cold running water.

While waiting for the cabbage mixture to stand, peel and dice the apples. Toss them with a couple tablespoons of the dressing to prevent browning until you are ready to mix. Transfer the rinsed and drained cabbage mixture in batches to a salad spinner and spin dry. Alternatively, transfer to a large rimmed baking sheet lined with a triple layer of paper towels or a clean kitchen towel and blot mixture dry with more towels. Return to large bowl.

Pour dressing over vegetables and toss to coat. Adjust seasoning to taste with salt, pepper, and/or sugar.

Now comes the hard part! Wait 2-3 days, tossing twice a day. This allows the cabbage time to absorb the dressing.

Mustard Coleslaw

I researched around and came up with this recipe after a trip through Memphis, this pairs really well with barbecued ribs.

For the dressing:
1/4 cup yellow mustard
1/4 cup cider vinegar
1/2 cup freshly squeezed lemon juice
1 1/2 cups sugar
Kosher salt and freshly ground pepper
For the salad:
½ large cabbage rough chopped
1 large carrot grated
1/2 green bell pepper, seeded and finely chopped
2 tablespoons celery seed
Hot sauce, to taste

In small bowl whisk together the mustard, vinegar, lemon juice, and sugar until the sugar has dissolved.

Season with salt and pepper to taste.

In a large salad bowl toss together the cabbage, carrot, green bell pepper, and celery seed.

Add the dressing to taste and gently toss until well combined.

Season with the hot sauce to taste.

Improves with a night in the fridge.

Pickled Carrot Salad

Sandy- I find this a great stand-in for entertaining as it can be made ahead. Also, you can add extra veggies liked blanched zucchini if you want.

  1 pound Carrots, sliced into thick rounds
  1 medium Red Onion, julienned
  1 Green Pepper julienned
  1/2 cup Olive Oil
  1/2 cup Cider Vinegar
  1/3 cup Water
  1 tablespoon Sugar
  2 Garlic cloves, minced
  2 teaspoons dried oregano
  1 teaspoon Salt
  1/2 teaspoon Pepper
  1/2 teaspoon Ground Mustard

In a saucepan, cook carrots in a small amount of water until crisp-tender; drain.

Transfer to a serving dish.

Combine remaining ingredients in a jar with a tight-fitting lid; shake well.

Pour over carrots; cover and refrigerate for several hours or overnight.

Serve with a slotted spoon.

Cucumbers and Dill Salad

This is apparently a Hungarian or Polish originating dish, we had it often during the summer when cucumbers were plentiful and the biggest challenge was finding them and picking them before they grew to be yellow bellied monsters.

2 large Cucumbers, peeled (optional) and thinly sliced
1 small Red Onion, thinly sliced
Optional
4 Radishes, sliced paper thin

Dressing
2 tablespoons Fresh Dill, finely chopped
½ cup Sour Cream (or yogurt, plain)
2 tablespoons Cider Vinegar
½ teaspoon Salt
pinch of finely ground Black Pepper
1 teaspoon Sugar
1 teaspoon Celery Seed

Mix the dressing ingredients until well combined. Toss the sliced vegetables with the dressing and refrigerate for at least 1 hour, overnight is better.

Barb's Pasta Salad

Alan- Our friend Barb found this recipe in a small paperback Betty Crocker cookbook and brought it to the Wisconsin Woods. Everybody liked it. Sandy made her version for the Great Huie-Notre Dame golf outing, and it was a success. Sandy thinks that it's the Lime Vinaigrette that gives it its unusual and distinctive character. I also think that the Anaheim chili adds a nice flavor, but of course also some bite. The original recipe had cilantro in it, which we omitted because we think it's a yuppie trend to put cilantro into everything, and anyway I don't like cilantro all that well! In any case, use whatever good fresh veggies you have, the list below is only a guide.

1 pound of Farfalle (bow-tie pasta)
8 Green Onions
4 large Tomatoes (about 4 cups after cutting up)
2 large Cucumbers (3 cups)
2 cups of sliced small Zucchini
2 Red Pepper
2 Yellow Pepper
1 green Anaheim Chili (optional)
6 ounces whole pitted Kalamata Olives (optional)

Lime Vinaigrette
1 cup Tomato Juice
1/2 cup Olive Oil
1/2 cup Lime Juice
1 teaspoon Salt
1/2 teaspoon Black Pepper
4 cloves Garlic

Cook the pasta as directed on the package, drain, and rinse in cold water. Pasta for this salad should not be overcooked and mushy. Clean and wash the veggies, slice the onions into 1/2 inch lengths, slice the tomatoes into eighths, slice the zucchini (which should be the small ones about 6 inches long) into 1/2 inch thick rounds, slice the peppers into 1/2 inch wide strips, and cut the strips into about 2 inch lengths. Remove the seeds from the Anaheim chili and chop into small pieces about 1/4 inch long. Add the olives. Make the Lime Vinaigrette by peeling the garlic cloves, crushing them, and then mixing the garlic with the other ingredients. Assemble the pasta salad by putting the pasta and veggies together, pouring the Lime Vinaigrette over the pasta mixture, and mixing it all by hand until the ingredients are well mixed. Chill the salad for a couple of hours before serving, stirring once or twice during that period. We have found that the salad keeps very well in the refrigerator:

we have eaten it over three days without it losing any flavor or texture. Note: red and yellow bell peppers are often quite expensive. You can substitute green bell peppers without losing any taste, but the salad will be less colorful. Also, I do not recommend substituting other chili peppers for the Anaheim chili unless you are a chili pepper expert. In any case, be careful when handling the chili pepper, since even Anaheim chili peppers are sometimes quite hot and can irritate eyes if you rub them with hands that have touched the chilies.

Egg or Tuna Salad

This is one of those recipes that came from the conclusion that egg salad or at least the way its made in all the recipes I looked at, is boring.   So I decided lets put some more tasty interesting stuff in.

   6 eggs, hard boiled and diced
   2/3 cup diced celery (about 2 stalks)
   ½ cup dice red onion
   ¼ cup diced red bell pepper
   ¼ cup diced dill pickle
   1 Tablespoon finely chopped fresh dill
   ½ Tablespoon finely chapped fresh parsley
   1 Tablespoon Dijon mustard
   ¼ cup mayonnaise
   1 teaspoon salt
   ¼ teaspoon pepper or to taste

Simply mix all together and chill

Potato Salad

1 lb white potatoes
2/3 cups of diced celery
1 Tablespoon finely chopped fresh dill
1 Tablespoon pickle relish
1 Tablespoon mustard
3 Tablespoons Mayonnaise
1 teaspoon salt
½ teaspoon pepper
¼ cup diced jalapenos

You can cook your potatoes using what ever method you prefer, I think that boiling them in salted water is best since it allows you to get some seasoning into the middle of the potato.

While still warm, cut the potatoes into 1-1½ inch chunks

Mix all the other ingredients together first, then fold in the potatoes, taking care to not smash them up too much.

Adjust seasoning to taste

This can be serve warm or cold, but I think it is better after a night in the fridge.

Braised Red Cabbage

By Alan and Sandy

This recipe came from a Swedish cookbook *Smorgasbord and Scandinavian Cookery* by Florence Brobeck and Monika Kjellberg. But it has been revised and clarified by Sandy.

1 large head of red cabbage, about 2 pounds
1 small onion, about 6 ounces
1 tablespoon butter
3 tablespoons wine vinegar
3 tablespoons water
1 teaspoon salt
½ teaspoon pepper
4 apple

Chop the onion and sauté it in the butter. Reserve it. Wash the cabbage, drain, cut in quarters, and slice into 1/8 to 1/4 inch thick slices and then half again the other way. Put in a heavy pot with the reserved onion, and other ingredients except the apples. Cover tightly and cook over low heat for 2 and ½ hours or longer.   Core, and dice the apples into ½ inch thick pieces. Add to the cabbage mixture after 1 hour. Cover the pot and continue the slow cooking. This dish should be served warm.

Cranberry Sauce

We used to make the cranberry sauce according to the directions on the bags of fresh cranberries. But in recent years they have reduced the size of the package and not change the amounts of the other ingredients. So here is a recipe I prefer. It is a little tarter than the bag recipe. Also is makes a sauce and not a jelly, so if you want to slice your cranberries, you will have to resort to the can.

    1 pound Cranberries
    1 cup Water
    1 cup Sugar
    Juice of ½ Lemon

Bring the water to a boil and dissolve the sugar, add cranberries and lemon juice. Simmer until the berries have all burst. Simmer for another 5 minutes and allow to cool.

Cranberry Chutney

By Alan

I (Alan) acquired this recipe from the Chicago Tribune's food pages where it was attributed to Julia Child. We often make it for Thanksgiving and Christmas. While I enjoy it and find it a good complement to heavy dishes, it is not universally liked and has a strong ginger/curry flavor. Note that this recipe is for a 16 ounce package of cranberries. Today, most packages of cranberries are 12 ounces. The cook can either buy 2 12 ounce packages of cranberries or adjust the quantities of other ingredients—somewhat awkwardly for some of them.

1 cup Onions
1 cup Water
3/4 cup Dark Brown Sugar
1/2 cup Sugar
3/4 cup Cider Vinegar
2 tart Apples
1/2 teaspoon Salt
1 teaspoon fresh Ginger
1/2 teaspoon ground Mace
1/2 teaspoon Curry powder
2 Oranges
1 pound fresh Cranberries
1/2 cup dried Currants

Slice onions thinly (not critical how thin) before measuring, then add to water and both sugars in a 3 quart saucepan and simmer for 30 minutes. While onion/sugar mixture is simmering, peel, seed, and dice apples. Reserve them for the moment. Take a piece of fresh ginger and grate it until a teaspoon has been obtained. Add this to the diced apples. Grate the rind of the oranges and reserve it also. Take the remainder of the oranges and squeeze them to obtain the juice. Strain the juice and save it for later. When the onions have completed their 30 minute simmer, add the diced apples and grated ginger, the vinegar, the orange rind, the grated ginger, the salt, the mace, and the curry powder. Simmer for another 30 minutes. Now add the cranberries, currants, and reserved orange juice. Boil gently until cranberries burst, about 10 minutes. Taste and add sugar if too sour. Makes 1 quart, which is quite a few servings unless you have some chutney addicts like some of us!

Brussels Sprouts

I (John) love Brussels sprouts. My favorite way to make them is to cook as follows.

1-2 pound Brussels Sprouts cleaned
1 slice Bacon, diced
1 tablespoon Extra-Virgin Olive Oil.
Salt and Pepper to taste

Cook sprouts in boiling heavily salted water until they are just beginning to get tender. Then remove them from the water and slice in half. Meanwhile sauté bacon until crispy and drain most of the fat. Add the olive oil and sprouts and sauté until the sprouts are well coated. Remove from heat and season with salt and pepper.

Smashed Brussels Sprouts

I tried these as an interesting alternative, they are great when first made, but do not keep well in the fridge as the cheese does not stay crisp.

~1 lb Brussels sprouts, cleaned and trimmed

~ 6 oz grated Parmesan cheese

Salt and pepper

Pre-heat the oven to 400 degrees Fahrenheit

Bring a pot of heavily salted water to a rolling boil. Add sprouts and cook until just tender.

Remove sprouts, drain, season with salt and pepper and allow to cool.

Meanwhile on a parchment lined sheet tray, make as many small piles of Parmesan cheese as you can fit, leaving around 2 inches of space between piles.

Place in oven and bake until the Parmesan just melts and spreads but does not brown.

Remove from oven, taking care with the hot pan, place a sprout on each pile of cheese and press the sprout down into the cheese with a flat object, a meat pounder works great

Sprinkle a little more cheese on top of each sprout.

Return the tray to the oven and bake until the cheese is crisp

Dry Cauliflower Curry

By, Alan, Karen, and Sandy

We got this recipe from Karen. She said, "This is a dish from Singapore, or at least so it says in the book we got it from. It's pretty in a glass bowl, good warm or cold, and even pretty good if overcooked. By adjusting the amount of cayenne, you can make it whatever heat you like. Sandy says "I have modified this really good cauliflower dish to use ingredients that I have at hand, and leave out the carb- rich potatoes. But leaving out the potatoes is a small effect, so if you like potatoes, just add some, and leave out the equivalent amount of cauliflower."

1 large Poblano Pepper, already roasted, skinned, and seeded
1 medium-large Onion, cut into 2 inch chunks
2 tablespoons Olive Oil
1 teaspoon Cumin Seed
¾ teaspoon Salt
½ teaspoon ground Turmeric
2 dashes of Cayenne
2 tablespoons of minced, fresh Ginger Root
1 Cauliflower—28 ounces, or about 6-7 inches in diameter, cut into florets (if some are large, divide into smaller pieces)
1-2 tablespoons Water
1 and ½ cups of frozen Peas
1 large Tomato diced, or ½ cup canned diced drained Tomatoes
½ teaspoon Garam Masala
(optional—1 lightly packed cup of Cilantro)

Note: We do not particularly like cilantro, so I leave it out!

Cut Poblano into roughly ½ inch squares. Mince ginger. Prepare other vegetables and spices. Heat oil in a deep skillet (I use an electric wok with a cover which makes mixing easy). Add cumin and fry 30 seconds. Stir in salt, turmeric, and cayenne. Add ginger root, Poblano, onions, and cauliflower. Also potato if using. Stir until vegetables are coated with seasonings. Add 1 tablespoon of water. WATCH! RESIST THE TEMPTATION to add more water—it can get too soupy. Reduce heat, and simmer until the cauliflower is getting just tender. But also, check often to make sure the mixture is not getting too dry. Adjust the heat as necessary, and/or add water. Add peas and tomatoes. Cook until peas are done. At this point, you can turn off the heat, and hold until time to serve. When ready to serve, sprinkle with the Garam Masala and heat until bubbling. If you use cilantro, stir it in just before serving. If you really like Garam Masala, or your Garam Masala is a little old, you can add another ½ teaspoon.

Smashed Cauliflower

By Karen

This recipe was motivated by a desire to eat mashed potatoes but a need to reduce the carbohydrate levels in my diet. So cauliflower is substituted for all or part of the potato. The resulting smashed cauliflower serves as a direct substitute for mashed potatoes; the flavor is distinct but mild enough not to draw the focus away from gravies or sauces. The recipe below uses a proportion that yields a texture fairly similar to mashed potatoes. But you can use any ratio you want. All cauliflower will give you a rice-like texture. No liquid is added in the basic recipe due to the greater moisture of cauliflower compared to potatoes.

> 1 Cauliflower (or 1/2 if it's really big)
> 2 medium Potatoes (you want about a quarter as much potato as cauliflower measuring by volume)
> 1/2 teaspoon each Salt and Black Pepper (or to taste)
> 2 tablespoon Butter
> Optional: Milk, Cream, or Soft Cheese and Herbs

Cut the cauliflower into florets. The size of the florets will control how long they need to cook to be soft; I generally go for 1.5-2in pieces. Also, the stem does not mash as easily so I often trim more off than I would if making a different dish (like roasted cauliflower or a curry). Cut the potato into similar sized chunks.

Put both cauliflower florets and potato chunks into a large pot. Cover with water -- enough that the cauliflower starts to float. Heat water to a boil and continue to boil for about 20 minutes until the cauliflower is very soft. The cauliflower needs to be fully cooked or it will not mash.

Drain and put the cauliflower and potato back into the pot. Let them steam a bit to lose the remaining moisture. Add butter, salt and pepper to taste. I usually put about 2 tablespoons butter and 1/2 teaspoon each of salt and pepper. It is a good idea to put in a little less than you think you need and then taste after the mashing. You can always add more later.

Mash the cauliflower and potato together after the butter has mostly melted. I have an egg-shaped handle with a stem and "feet" that works well -- a traditional masher or ricer should also work. Keep mashing until the remaining lumps disappear or are small enough. If you get a rice-like texture and want a smoother one, you will need more potato (make a note to yourself so you remember the next time). Once mashed, taste and add salt (and pepper) if needed. Cauliflower is damper than potatoes (especially boiling ones) so milk or cream is not needed, but could be added if you want a richer dish. Sometimes, I will turn the burner back on for a few minutes after mashing if the result is damper than I want -- this is the advantage of mashing in the cooking pot -- but you need to watch this or it may stick to the pan or burn.

I serve the basic version when I have a sauce or gravy planned, such as with roast chicken or turkey. A little parsley sprinkled on top or stirred in makes a prettier version. I've also used it as a topping for Sheppard's pie or other casseroles (with grated cheese on top). If I'm serving smashed cauliflower with steak and green beans, I sometimes add soft cheese (1/4 - 1/2 cup) and chopped herbs (1-5 tablespoons of basil, sage, dill, chives, parsley or a mix thereof) for a more interesting side dish. Cheddar cheese or roasted garlic could also be stirred into the basic version. Have fun and experiment!

Roasted Cauliflower

This recipe was inspired by chef Jose Andres and his vegetable cookbook.

2 1/2 cups dry white wine
1/3 cup olive oil
1/4 cup kosher salt
3 tablespoons fresh lemon juice
2 tablespoons unsalted butter
1 tablespoon crushed red pepper flakes
1 tablespoon sugar
1 bay leaf
1 head of cauliflower, leaves removed

Preheat oven to 475°F.

Bring wine, oil, kosher salt, juice, butter, red pepper flakes, sugar, bay leaf, and 8 cups water to a boil in a large pot.

Add cauliflower, reduce heat, and simmer, turning occasionally, until a knife easily inserts into center, 15-20 minutes.

Using 2 slotted spoons or a mesh spider, transfer cauliflower to a rimmed baking sheet, draining well as you do so.

Roast, rotating sheet halfway through, until brown all over, 30-40 minutes.

Caramelized Pearl Onions

I love onions of all sorts cooked and raw and these are no exception. This is e a good way to cook the onions for beef bourguignonne (page 166)

20 ounces (1-1/4 pounds) Pearl Onions
3 tablespoons Butter
1 tablespoon Olive Oil
Salt and Pepper to taste
1/2 cup Tawny Port Wine
1 tablespoon chopped fresh Sage (less if using dried)

To peel onions, blanch in boiling water for 2 minutes if small, 3 minutes if larger; rinse with cold water to stop cooking. Trim off just a little of the root end and skin should peel off.

Heat a large skillet over medium-high heat. Add the butter and olive oil. When hot, add the onions. Sprinkle with the salt and pepper.

Stirring often, sauté onions until browned and starting to caramelize, about 7 minutes.

Add the port wine. Reduce heat to medium-low and continue to cook until onions are tender and liquid has evaporated, less than 10 minutes. Add the sage and sauté for 2 more minutes. (If using dried sage, add with the salt and pepper.)

Roasted Baby Carrots with Pesto

This recipe was developed after we found a load of baby carrots at the farmers market and wanted to do something special for Thanksgiving.

Baby carrots with tops if possible
Curry powder
Sal and pepper
Avocado oil

Clean the carrots removing and reserving the leafy tops. If you like the visual look, you can leave an inch or two of the top on the carrot.

Drizzle enough oil over the carrots to coat them well.

Sprinkle with curry powder, salt and pepper

Roast at 400 degrees for about 20 minutes until the carrots are slightly tender. You may do this on the grill or in the air fryer as well.

Serve with Carrot Top Pesto as a condiment

Carrot Top Pesto

This is a great, fresh pesto and the use of carrot tops has the beneficial side effect of retaining it's vibrant color where regular pesto will oxidize and brown quickly,

2 Cups Carrot tops, washed and stems removed
1 teaspoon salt
¼ cup walnuts
(Optional) 1-2 tablespoons chopped basil
2-3 large Garlic cloves
3 tablespoons Parmesan cheese
3 tablespoons Olive oil plus more as needed

Add all the ingredients to a food processor or blender and process to a paste, adding more oil as needed to reach the desired consistency.

Roasted Cabbage

I adapted this recipe from several on the inter-webs to use some extra cabbage.

¼ medium Cabbage
Juice from ½ Lime
1 tablespoon fresh ginger, grated
Salt
1-2 tablespoons Avocado oil

Cut the cabbage into wedges, leaving part of stem on each to help hold wedges together

Add lime juice, ginger and oil to a bowl and wisk together.

Add the cabbage wedges and gently toss to fully coat with marinade. Allow to marinade for at least an hour or as much as overnight.

Roast the cabbage at 400F for about 20 minutes or until tender. You can do this on a grill or in an air fryer also.

Serve with creamy sauce if desired

Creamy Cabbage Sauce

½ cup heavy cream
½ cup Monterrey Jack cheese, grated
2 green onions, chopped
½ cup white wine
Salt & Pepper

Saute green onions in olive oil until lightly browned

Deglaze with white wine

Add heavy cream and stir in cheese

Season to taste

Butternut Squash and Red Pepper Casserole

3 1/2 pounds Butternut Squash
1 large Red Bell Pepper, cut into 1-inch pieces
3 tablespoons Olive Oil
3-4 large Garlic Cloves, minced
3 tablespoons minced fresh Parsley leaves
1 1/2 teaspoons minced fresh Rosemary leaves
freshly ground Black Pepper to taste
1/2 cup freshly grated Parmesan (about 2 ounces)

Preheat oven to 400°F.

With a sharp knife cut squash crosswise into 2-inch-thick slices. Working with 1 slice at a time, cut side down, cut away peel and seeds and cut squash into 1-inch cubes (about 9 cups).

In a large bowl stir together squash, bell pepper, oil, garlic, herbs, black pepper, and salt to taste.

Transfer mixture to a 2- to 2 1/2-quart gratin or other shallow baking dish and sprinkle evenly with Parmesan. Bake casserole in middle of oven until squash is tender and top is golden, about 1 hour.

Alan " Sandy and I first ate this dish when John made it for us, and we liked it so much that we have added it to our list of vegetable dish choices."

Bacon Feta Beans

8 slices Bacon, diced
1 pound fresh String Beans, cleaned
3 cloves Garlic, crushed
4 ounces crumbled Feta Cheese, reserving 1/4
Salt and fresh ground Black Pepper to taste

Steam the beans until al dente, set aside.

Place bacon in a large, deep skillet. Cook over medium high heat until evenly browned but only slightly crisp. Drain as much grease as possible. Add garlic and green beans and sauté on medium heat for a couple minutes. Sprinkle one half of the feta cheese and stir until mostly melted. Remove from heat and season with salt and black pepper. Transfer to a serving dish, and toss with remaining feta. Serve hot.

Tarragon Beans

1 pound fresh String Beans, cleaned
3 tablespoons Tarragon chopped
1 tablespoon Butter
¼ - ½ cup sliced Almonds (optional)
Salt and fresh ground Black Pepper to taste

Steam the beans until al dente, while beans are cooking melt butter with tarragon and almonds and sauté briefly until almonds and tarragon begin to release their aromas. Toss the cooked beans in the butter mixture, salt and pepper to taste and serve.

Toastwiches(a lunch or light supper)

By Alan

I LOVE toastwiches. I don't know who invented them, but Sandy has been making them for years. We would eat them all of the time, but they have too much fat and carbs. They are particularly nice for a late light supper. This makes 6 toastwiches, theoretically enough for 6 people, but I would probably sulk if told I could only have one.

6 Eggs
about 2 tablespoons Butter
12 slices of good thick sliced Bacon
12 pieces of good quality Homemade Bread, medium thick
Salt and Pepper
3 tablespoons Mayonnaise
1/4 cup Sandy's Homemade Sweet Pickle Relish

Hard boil the eggs. Cut the bacon into 1/2 inch by 1 and 1/2 inch pieces. (Bacon is about 1 and 1/2 inches wide so you are cutting the bacon strip every 1/2 inch) Fry the bacon crisp and drain well on paper towels, patting both sides. Discard drippings. Brush one side of each piece of bread lightly with melted butter. Cool eggs, peel, and coarsely chop. Mix the eggs with the bacon, salt, pepper, mayonnaise, and pickle relish. Spoon 1/6th of egg mixture on unbuttered side of each of six slices of bread. Top with slice of bread, buttered side up. Place on baking sheet, and put under broiler for about 3 minutes until golden brown, remove sheet, turn over toastwiches, and broil the other side until it also is golden brown, about 3 more minutes.

NOTE: You can substitute store bought for the bread and relish, but the bread should have some substance to it. I can hardly stand to finish writing this recipe without running to the kitchen to make some!

Tian I

By Alan

We were introduced to Tian by Diane Kennedy's book, "Nothing Fancy". It's really a nice way to use zucchini and corn, but we often make it with other veggies. It's nice with Poblanos, but can also be made with other peppers either chili or bell, depending on your liking for hotness. I think Poblanos are just about right on the hotness scale. This recipe is quite similar to Kennedy's, but with less oil, no unusual Mexican veggies, and considerably simplified procedure. We think it's very good. Note: before beginning this recipe, make sure that you have the necessary Poblano peppers that have been charred and peeled and deseeded.

1 tablespoons Extra Virgin Olive Oil
1/2 small Onion
3 cloves Garlic
3 Poblano Chili Peppers, charred, peeled, and deseeded
1 pound Zucchini
1 and 1/2 cups frozen Corn
1/4 teaspoon Salt
1 cup cooked Rice
3 tablespoons Parmesan cheese
Topping:
5 tablespoons Bread Crumbs
1 tablespoon Parmesan Cheese
1 tablespoon olive oil

Chop the onion and garlic and sauté' in the olive oil in a frying pan until they are limp and clear, not brown. Chop the peppers into large pieces and add to the onions and sauté' for one minute. Cut the zucchini into about 1/2 inch cubes, and add to the onions and peppers. Without thawing, add the corn and the salt (you may need more, but it depends on taste). Cook the veggies on medium heat until zucchini is just tender, but still crisp.. Remove from stove and allow to cool for 5 minutes. Stir in the rice and the 3 tablespoons of cheese. Put the veggies in an oiled one quart casserole dish; they should be about 2 inches deep. Sprinkle the bread crumbs and freshly grated Parmesan cheese on top, and bake in a preheated 375°F oven for 30 minutes until it is hot and bubbling throughout and lightly brown on top. This makes a great side dish for dinner, say with ham, and is nearly as good warmed up in a microwave a day later. You can certainly substitute other veggies for the zucchini or corn, but this combinations is particularly good, and in the summer we ALWAYS seem to have zucchini! Green beans or Lima beans in place of zucchini works well. Note: you can use frozen zucchini, but if you do, sauté the zucchini and onions until excess moisture is gone, then add the garlic and peppers.

Tian II

By Alan

It was fascinating that shortly after discovering Tian in Kennedy's book, we happened to get a cookbook (this is not surprising, we often get cookbooks!) called *The Savory Way* by Deborah Madison which contained SEVERAL recipes for Tian. Madison also explained that in France the oval red-glazed earthenware dishes they use to bake this food in are called tians. I guess that this recipe and Tian I could easily be translated as Casserole I and II! This particular recipe is an interesting example of a rice-less Tian. Sandy developed it based on reading both books, and on our growing fondness for Tians.

  1 tablespoon Extra-Virgin Olive Oil
  1 large Onion
  2 Garlic cloves
  1 and 1/2 teaspoons of Fresh Rosemary
  2 Sage Leaves
  1 teaspoon Thyme Leaves
  Salt
  Pepper
  1 pounds Zucchini
  1/2 pound of fresh Plum Tomatoes
  4 tablespoons Bread Crumbs

Chop the onions and garlic coarsely and sauté' in the oil in a frying pan with half of the herbs until the onions are soft and transparent. Remove the onions and garlic (leaving the oil), and place in a 1 quart oiled baking dish. Put the zucchini in the frying pan with the rest of the herbs and a pinch of salt, and sauté' until they are lightly browned, about 10 minutes. Layer the zucchini over the onions in the baking pan. Slice the tomatoes, and place on top of the zucchini. Lightly grind up the bread crumbs and sprinkle over the tomatoes. Drizzle a teaspoon of olive oil on top, and bake at 375°F for 30 minutes covered, and an additional 10 minutes uncovered.

Taters'(a vegetable side dish)

By Alan

The inspiration for this recipe was a column in the Chicago Tribune by Peter Kump with the recipe for "Tomato Casserole Provencal". Sandy has considerably simplified the recipe, including the elimination of cheese with each potato layer. It's very good if you use really ripe tomatoes. It's a nice simple dish, not too much effort to prepare, but it does take a long time in the oven.It's worth the time.

> 2 medium Yellow Onions
> 1 teaspoon Olive Oil
> 5 medium Red Potatoes
> 3 ripe Tomatoes
> Salt and Pepper

Chop onions (you should have about 2 cups of chopped onions) and sauté' in the oil until transparent and beginning to lightly brown. Slice the uncooked potatoes (you can leave the skins on if you like) about 1/2 inch thick. You should have about 5 cups of sliced potatoes. Slice the tomatoes about 1/2 inch thick.(You need about 3 and 1/2 cups of sliced tomatoes) In a 2 and 1/2 quart casserole dish, put a layer of potatoes on the bottom, salt them. Next put in a layer of onions, and then a layer of tomatoes. Salt the tomatoes lightly.(Also pepper if you wish). Continue layering in this order until all the veggies are used, but arrange to end with a tomato layer on top.Microwave for 5 minutes on high to get it hot, and bake covered in a preheated 375°F oven for 1 hour, then reduce temperature to 300°F for another 1/2 hour. You can put freshly grated Parmesan cheese on top before baking if you like.I don't think it's really needed if you have ripe tomatoes.

VARIATION: TATERS N' MATERS TARRAGON

This variation is particularly nice if you have some fresh tarragon. Use the same ingredients and directions as above, except omit the Parmesan cheese, use new potatoes with their skins on, and sprinkle chopped tarragon on each tomato layer. About 2 tablespoons total of tarragon.

Onion Fennel Potato Gratin

This recipe is a combination of various recipes inspired by what we had leftover.

4 medium Yukon Gold Potatoes
2 medium Onions
½ Fennel Bulb

Butter
3 Tb thyme
Salt
Pepper
6-7 cloves Garlic
2 medium Tomatoes
½ cup Cream or half &half
Cheese

Slice potatoes, onions, fennel, and tomatoes as thin as possible with mandolin 1/16 to 1/8 inch thick if possible.

Reserve tomato slices

Divide potatoes and thyme into 4 equal portions and onions, garlic and fennel into thirds.

Butter the casserole.

Create a layer of potatoes followed by onions, followed by fennel, sprinkle garlic and thyme. Season each layer with salt and pepper.

Repeat twice more until onions, fennel and garlic are used up.

Make a final layer of potatoes and sprinkle with thyme.

Pour cream over the top

Layer on tomatoes and season with salt and pepper.

Bake for 45 minutes covered at 375

Add cheese and bake for 15 minutes until cheese is bubbly

Mac & Cheese

This dish was inspired when we were craving comfort food and hit the internet in search of some fun food. This is a serious modification of the Luna Café recipe.

12 ounces, Macaroni or other short, dried, tubular Pasta
Topping
6 tablespoons Butter, melted
2 cups stale Bread Crumbs, coarsely crumbled, we use home made Whole Grain Bread Crumbs
2-3 cloves Garlic crushed
Cheeses (5 cups total cheese)
2 cups grated, aged Cheddar Cheese
1 cup grated Swiss Emmantal or Gruyere
1 cup grated, mild-flavored melting Cheese, such as Jack
1 cup grated Parmesan or Romano
Béchamel Sauce
2 tablespoons Butter
1 large Onion, minced
2-3 cloves Garlic, crushed
½ cup All-purpose Flour
4 cups Milk (or a mixture of half Milk and half Cream or Sour Cream, or a mixture of half Cream and half Chicken Stock)
1 cup Poblano Chili, roasted, peeled, seeded, diced
Salt and freshly ground Black Pepper, to taste

Prepare the baking dish: Coat a 6-cup capacity, ovenproof casserole with vegetable spray or a dab of butter.

To make the breadcrumb topping: In a small mixing bowl, combine the melted butter, bread crumbs, and garlic, reserve.

For the pasta, bring a large pot of water with two tablespoons of salt to a rapid boil, and add the pasta. Cook until al dente. Remove from heat and drain. Toss the pasta in a large, larger than you think need, bowl with all of the cheeses

To make the béchamel sauce: In a medium saucepan, melt the butter, add the onions, and slowly cook until onions are softened but not browned. Add the garlic and stir to combine.

Stir in the flour, and cook without browning for two minutes.

Slowly pour in the milk and whisk constantly while bringing the sauce to a simmer. Simmer, whisking continuously, for 2 minutes. Stir in chopped chilies.

Pour the sauce over the pasta and cheeses in the bowl and fold to combine. Spoon into the prepared baking dish, mounding slightly at the center. Sprinkle on the breadcrumb topping.

Bake at 350° for 1 hour until heated through and bubbling. Broil for a minute or two to finish browning the top, not usually necessary

Sweet Potato Soufflé

One Thanksgiving I was looking for a different way to do sweet potatoes, one that was a bit fancier than just mashed or candied. This recipe is from Emiril Lagassi. This recipe quickly became a frequent request. The only draw back is that making this as part of a holiday dinner significantly complicates the meal as the souffle has to served immediately when done cooking.

    1 1/2 pounds sweet potatoes
    1 tablespoon vegetable oil
    3/4 teaspoon plus one pinch salt, plus more for seasoning
    1/2 teaspoon freshly ground black pepper, plus more for seasoning
    8 tablespoons unsalted butter
    2 tablespoons light brown sugar
    1/4 cup all-purpose flour
    1 1/2 cups whole milk
    5 eggs, separated, plus 1 egg white
    Nonstick cooking spray
    1/4 teaspoon cream of tartar

Cook Sweet potatoes: Preheat oven to 350 degrees.

Rub sweet potatoes with oil, season with salt and pepper, and set on a baking sheet. Roast in oven for 1 to 1 1/2 hours or until soft. Remove from oven and set aside.

Increase oven temperature to 425 degrees.

Prepare Soufflé base(This base can be set aside at room temperature until ready to bake the souffle; you may cover and refrigerate it if done in advance, but it must be brought to room temperature before proceeding.)

Melt half the butter in a small skillet set over medium-high heat. Season with 1/2 teaspoon salt and 1/4 teaspoon pepper. Cook for one minute until butter is foamy and lightly browned. Remove from heat and stir in brown sugar.

Peel potatoes and measure out 1 cup roasted potato. Transfer to a food processor or blender and process on high. Drizzle in butter mixture and process until smooth, about 1 minute.

Melt remaining butter in a small pot set over medium heat. Whisk in flour and cook for 2 to 3 minutes, until light brown in color. Add 1/4 teaspoon salt and 1/4 teaspoon pepper, then whisk in milk, stirring as necessary and cooking until thickened, about 3 minutes.

Remove from heat and transfer to a large bowl. Whisk in yolks, one at a time, until incorporated. Whisk in sweet potato mixture.

Final Soufflé prep

Wrap aluminum foil around a 7-cup souffle dish to about 3 inches above the rim. Grease the inside of the dish and aluminum foil with nonstick cooking spray. Set it onto a rimmed baking sheet for easier handling.

Whip egg whites on low with a handheld electric mixer until foamy. Add a pinch of salt and cream of tartar. Whip on high until stiff peaks form.

Gently fold about 1/3 of the beaten whites into sweet potato mixture until uniform. Repeat with remaining egg whites. Transfer mixture to prepared souffle dish and place in oven. Reduce heat to 375 degrees and bake until souffle has risen 2 to 3 inches above the top of the dish and is nicely browned, about 1 hour. Remove from oven and allow souffle to sit no longer than 5 minutes before serving .

To serve, plunge two large serving spoons back to back in the middle of the souffle -- this will help prevent the souffle from falling. Serve immediately.

Wild Rice Salad

This recipe is best made the day before to allow the flavors to blend. Also unless you are making for a crowd, scale down the amounts by at least 50%

2 cups wild rice
1 cup long grain rice or brown rice
5 cups chicken stock
3 Tb butter, divided
2 bay leaves
1 tsp Salt
Several grinds black pepper
½ cup onions, diced
½ cups celery, diced
1 lb mushrooms, chopped
½ cup dried cranberries

Add wild rice, stock, salt, pepper, 2 tablespoons of butter and bay leaves to a sauce pan and bring to a boil.

Lower heat to simmer and cook for 45 minutes

Drain rice and reserve liquid

Cook long grain or brown rice in reserved liquid, adding water as needed

Saute onions, celery and mushrooms in 1 tablespoon butter until soft

Combine both rices, vegetable mixture and cranberries

Serve warm or chilled

Soups

Shrimp and Corn Stew

There are a couple of restaurants in one our favorite cities, New Orleans. Cochon and Peche, both are run by Chef Donald Link. This recipe is adapted from a recipe in his book *Real Cajun*.

2 pounds Shrimp, (head on preferred, 2 ½ pounds if so)
Olive Oil
2 medium Onions, diced
4 Celery stalks, diced
1 Bell Pepper, diced
4 cloves Garlic, chopped fine
3 cans diced Tomatoes
2 ½ cups fresh Corn Kernels
2 teaspoons Salt
2 Bay Leaves
1 ½ teaspoon Basil
½ teaspoon Thyme
Black Pepper
½ teaspoon Paprika
5 cups Shrimp stock
4 tablespoon Butter
½ cup All-purpose Flour
½ cup Parsley
½ cup Green Onions

Peel the shrimp reserving the shells and set aside. A short cut to shrimp stock is to put shells and heads in a quart of chicken stock with 2 cups of water and simmer while you prep the rest of the recipe.

Sauté Onions, Celery, and Bell Pepper until they are translucent and begin to brown. Add garlic and sauté for a minute longer. Add tomatoes corn and spices. Add the seafood stock, straining to remove any shells. Simmer for 20 minutes. Make a medium roux by cooking the flour in the butter until tan in color. Temper the roux by whisking a couple coups of the liquid from the stew into the roux before adding it back to the stew. Simmer for another 5 minutes. Add the Shrimp and parsley and simmer until shrimp are cooked. Serve with Green onions sprinkled on top.

Gumbo

Gumbo has become a staple soup for the fall as the days get chillier. This recipe was inspired by many recipes and examples from restaurants throughout New Orleans. These days we generally make it with chicken and sausage because that freezes better than the seafood versions. However if making for a crown, the seafood version is excellent.

For Seafood Gumbo
　2 pound large Shrimp
　1/2 pound (about 1 cup) fresh lump crab-meat
　(optional)1 cup shucked Fresh Oysters, with their liquor
　(optional)1 lb firm fleshed fish (Snapper, etc)

For Chicken Gumbo
　2 pound cooked and chopped Chicken

Gumbo Base
　2 tablespoons olive oil

　3 stalks Celery chopped
　2 medium Onions chopped
　1 Bell Pepper seeded and chopped
　3-4 Jalapenos seeded and chopped
　1 pound Okra, sliced

　1 pound Andouille Sausage sliced ¼ inch

　½ lb Tasso ham, diced
　4 cloves Garlic smashed and chopped

　1 tablespoon Salt
　4-6 turns freshly ground Black Pepper
　6 bay leaves
　1 tablespoon minced fresh Basil
　1 teaspoon minced fresh Oregano
　1 teaspoon fresh Thyme Leaves
　1 tablespoons Paprika
　1 teaspoon Cayenne

　1 28 ounce can Whole Tomatoes,

　2 tablespoons all-purpose Flour
　2 tablespoons Butter

　1 quart Shrimp Stock
　1 quart Chicken Stock
　1 teaspoon Worcestershire sauce
　1 teaspoon Filé powder

For Serving
1/2 to 3/4 cup chopped Green Onions
Hot Pepper Sauce if desired
4 cups cooked Long-Grain White Rice, warm (optional)

Using the same pan and splitting the olive oil between them, saute the vegetables separately until they are lightly browned. Brown the andouille sausage and reserve; drain excess grease. Add the garlic and tasso to the pan and saute until garlic begins to soften, add the salt, pepper, bay leaves, basil, oregano, thyme, paprika and cayenne and cook until spices are fragrant (2-3 minutes) Reserve with vegetables and sausage. Cook the tomatoes, smashing with a potato masher until the tomatoes deepen in color.

In a large stock pot, create the roux using the flour and butter. Cooking over medium heat and stirring constantly until the roux is dark toasty brown but not burnt.

Slowly add half of the stock, whisking constantly to avoid lumps. Use the rest of the stock to deglaze the saute pan into the pot. Add all the previously cooked, reserved ingredients. Add Worcestershire and bring to a simmer cook for 30 minutes.

Gently add shrimp, oysters, crab-meat, fish, and/or chicken and bring back to a simmer for 15 minutes. Slowly sprinkle in the filé powder, stirring to incorporate it thoroughly, and simmer, stirring, for 2 minutes. Remove from the heat.

To serve as a first course, ladle 1 cup of the gumbo into each of 12 gumbo bowls or soup plates, and add 1/3 cup of the rice to each; for a main course, allow 1 1/2 cups gumbo and 1/2 cup of rice. Sprinkle each serving with 1 tablespoon of the green onions. Provide your favorite hot sauce to spice things up as desired.

Gumbo Z'herbs

This is a different gumbo than any other. Traditionally a dish served on Good Friday, I read about this in a book about New Orleans and decided to give it a shot.

For the greens:
5 assorted bunches of greens, such as spinach, collards, dandelion greens, mustard greens, turnip greens, spinach, watercress, chicory, beet tops, carrot tops, or radish tops, washed, rinsed and chopped (enough to equal about 3 pounds or 12 cups)
1 ham hock, about 2 pounds, with several 1/2-inch slits cut into it
3 cups Chicken Broth

For the gumbo base:
3 slices Bacon, chopped

1 tablespoons Olive Oil
1 yellow Onion, medium dice
1 large Green Bell Pepper, medium dice
4 Celery stalks, medium dice
4 cloves Garlic, minced

2 Bay Leaves
4 sprigs fresh Thyme
½ tablespoon Black Pepper, freshly ground
2 whole Cloves
3 Allspice Berries
1 tablespoon minced Marjoram leaves
2 teaspoons salt
1/2 teaspoon Cayenne Pepper

2 quarts Chicken Broth

4 tablespoon Flour
2 tablespoon Butter
File Powder

1 bunch Parsley, chopped
1 bunch Green Onions, chopped
Cooked White Rice for serving with gumbo
Green Tabasco

In a large pot bring 2 cups of stock to a boil, add the ham hock add greens. Cook at a simmer over low heat while preparing the gumbo base.

In a large sauté pan cook bacon until rendered and crisp, remove the bacon to the greens pot. Drain the grease retaining 2 tablespoon and add a tablespoon of olive oil. Sauté the onion, celery, bell pepper and garlic until translucent and slightly browned. Add to the greens along with spices and additional stock. Simmer until greens are tender. In the sauté pan make a roux by browning flour in butter until tan. Temper the roux by whisking in a couple cups of the greens liquid before adding back into the gumbo. Add file powder and simmer for another 15 minutes.

Serve with parsley and green onions sprinkled on top and hot sauce to taste.

May be served optionally with rice or as a soup.

French Onion Soup

This soup is a regular for cold fall and winter nights. The most impactful ingredient in this is not onions but rather the beef stock in my opinion. I feel that if you are unwilling to make your own stock or obtain scratch made stock them make something else.

3 tablespoon Butter
3-4 pounds or about 8 Onions (5 yellow, 3 red), thinly sliced
1 teaspoon Salt
1 clove Garlic, crushed
1/2 teaspoon freshly ground Pepper
1/2 cup Dry White Wine or Dry White Vermouth
2 quarts boiling homemade Beef Stock
1 Bay Leaf
4 sprigs of Thyme
3 tablespoon Cognac
Salt and Pepper to taste
Roux (optional)
2 tablespoons Butter
3 tablespoons All-purpose Flour
To Serve
Croutons
1 to 2 cups grated Swiss or Parmesan Cheese

Croutons
8-10 slices of French bread, cut 3/4 to 1 inch thick
½ cup Olive oil or Beef Drippings if possible
1 clove of Garlic, crushed

In a heavy-bottomed, 4 quart covered saucepan melt butter and add onions and salt. Cook on low heat, stirring often, until onions are deeply browned. Be patient, this could take quite a while.

Add garlic and cook briefly. Add wine to deglaze, followed by the stock. Add herbs. Simmer for 30 minutes.

Depending on how thick you like the soup, In a separate sauté pan, make a roux with the butter and flour. Stir a ladle or two of soup liquid into the roux until smooth and then transfer to soup and stir until combined. We usually skip the roux as the homemade beef stock gives the soup plenty of body.

Add cognac. Simmer for another 10 minutes.

To make the Croutons, combine the oil and garlic, brush both side of the bread and toast under low broil flipping once until lightly browned on both sides.

To serve, place some soup in a bowl, top with a crouton and grated cheese. Broil on high until cheese is melted and starts to brown.

102

Potato and leek soup

This recipe was inspired one time when we went to the Grandin Village Farmers' Market and one of the vendors was selling leeks at a big discount because it was the end of the season. The most important part of this recipe is cleaning the leeks, clean them until they can't possible have any grit and then clean them again.

6-7 Leeks, trimmed but green tops <u>not</u> discarded

3 tablespoons Butter

1 large russet Potato, peeled and chopped into ½ inch cubes

2 cups Chicken stock (homemade if at all possible)

1 cup Buttermilk (whole milk if possible)

1 cup heavy Cream

Thyme (Fresh if possible)

8 cloves Garlic, divided

1 tablespoon whole Black Pepper.

Salt and Pepper

First chop the dark green portions off the leeks, cut in half lengthwise and chop into 2 inch pieces.

Put the leaves into a large bowl full of cold water and toss to rinse out any grit., Using a slotted spoon or your hands lift the greens out and drain in a colander, repeat

In a large put put the leek leaves, several sprigs of thyme (2 teaspoons dried), 3-4 Garlic cloves, smashed, and the whole peppercorns.

Add water to cover plus 2 inches, bring to a boil and simmer for 45 minutes

Strain the stock into a container and reserve

Meanwhile, cut the leeks in quarters lengthwise, chop into ½ inch pieces.

Wash them as you did with the above green tops using your fingers if necessary to separate all the layers, except repeat at least 4 times, the leeks must be absolutely free of grit.

Once the leeks are clean and drained, saute in 3 tablespoons of butter, adding 1 teaspoon salt, until soft and almost started to brown.

Remove about ¾ of the leeks to a bowl and reserve.

Add the chopped potato, several grinds of pepper and a pinch of salt, the chicken stock and 1-2 cups of the reserved leek stock.

Bring to a boil and simmer until the potatoes are very tender.

Remove about ½ the potatoes (it's ok if some of the remaining leeks come with.) to the bowl with the leeks and reserve.

Using an immersion blender, blend up the rest of the mixture into a smooth puree

Add the reserved leeks and potato back in along with 4 cloves of garlic, crushed. Add 2 cups more of the leek stock along with the buttermilk and cream. Add 2-3 sprigs of thyme (1 teaspoon dried) Bring to a simmer on medium-low heat.

Simmer for 10 minutes, adding more leek or chicken stock, if necessary, to thin to desired consistency.

Serve with crusty french bread

Blue Crab Chowder

One of our favorite restaurants when we lived in Houston, La Lucha, serves a dish called Chowder Fries. The recipe that follows is my closest approximation.

1 lb crab
Juice of ½ lemon
Zest of ½ lemon
1 ½ cup carrots diced
2 cups potatoes diced
1 cup onion diced
3 Tbs Old Bay seasoning
3 Tbs AP flour
3 Tbs butter
1 cup milk
2 cups ½ and 1/2
2 cups cream
2 cups chicken stock
2 tsp black pepper
1 ½ tsp salt

Saute carrots, onions and potatoes separately in olive oil or butter until just tender

Combine the flour and butter and cook over medium heat to a medium roux

Add cooked vegetables, dairy, stock and seasonings, bring to a simmer.

Add crab and lemon juice and zest

Bring to a. Simmer, adjust seasoning to taste.   If the chowder is thicker than desired, you can add. More milk or stock to thin.

Stocks

Many of the recipes from this book require as one of their ingredients, some sort of stock. Whether it is beef, chicken or seafood, stock is not hard to make once you have gathered the ingredients.

Chicken is probably the easiest, many cuts of chicken come bone in and you can save up the bones either before or after cooking. The carcass of a whole roast chicken works great. I save the wing tips every time we make hot wings and these are a great source of collagen.

Beef bones are harder to come by since not as many cuts come bone in these days. I will usually end up buying some. Either soup/stock bones from a butcher or a combo of short rib and ox tails.

I used to make stock in a big pot simmering for endless hours, then I found pressure cooking. This technique will not result in a perfectly clear broth, but will give you very rich gelatin rich stock for including in all kinds of recipes without the time consuming simmering for many hours.

Do not add salt under any circumstances, this is an ingredient and should be seasoned as part of the final dish.

3 lbs of bones / shells / scraps
1 small onion, quartered
2 carrots, halved
2 stalks celery, halved
1 Tb whole black peppercorns
3-4 Bay leaves
Water

For any raw bits, spread them on a baking sheet and broil, turning once until they are well browned

Place all the ingredients in a pressure cooker and enough water to cover at least, more is ok up to the max fill of your cooker.

Pressure cook for 90 minutes

Allow to cool and strain into another container.

Optionally remove the fat if needed

Cool as quickly as practical and freeze.

Breads

Sandy's Corn Chili Cornbread

By Alan

This recipe is the result of several stages of evolution from the original recipes that were in Mama Rombauer's and James Beard's cookbook. It's now a very good, low fat cornbread with corn kernels and chili bits mixed throughout.It's a quite simple recipe. Note that this is not an ordinary cornbread, it's not really a bread, it's more of a side dish. For example, it's great with North Lane Chili.

    1 cup Cornmeal
    1 and ½ teaspoons Salt
    1 tablespoon double-acting Baking Powder
    2 Eggs
    1 cup Yogurt
    ¾ cup Skim Milk
    1 and 1/2 cups frozen Corn
    1 small can (4-4,5 ounce) of chopped Green Chili Peppers

Beat the eggs, mix with all of the other ingredients, and pour into a buttered baking dish or pan--a 9 inch square dish is about right.Bake in a preheated 350°F oven for 1 hour.It should be light brown on top.NOTE: now that non-fat sour cream is widely available, you could substitute that for the yogurt.We prefer the sharper taste of yogurt, but I expect the sour cream version would also be good.

Sandy's Chile Relleno Substitute (Also Known As Chili Cornbread)

By Sandy and Alan

This recipe originated when Sandy tried various recipes for cornbread, including the one in James Beard's Beard on Bread cookbook which he attributed to Helen Evans Brown, and the one in Mama Rombauer's cookbook. It has gone through numerous evolutions as we tried to eat low fat, then became more carb conscious. The final version happened after we had some wonderful Chile Rellenos in Fresno, California. While this recipe does not attempt to duplicate the soufflé-like coating around the Poblano peppers in the Fresno dish, it does create a similar taste.

> 6 whole fresh Poblano Chili Peppers
> 6 ounces of good Cheddar Cheese
> ¾ cup of Flour
> 2 and ½ teaspoons Baking Powder
> ¾ teaspoon Salt
> 1 and ¼ cups Cornmeal
> 1 Egg
> 1 cup Milk

Roast and skin the Poblanos. Slit open one side, and remove all the seeds. Put about 1 ounce of cheese inside each pepper. Reserve the stuffed peppers. Mix the flour, baking powder, salt, and cornmeal. Add the unbeaten egg and the milk and immediately whisk until well mixed. Pour about 1/3 of the batter into a buttered baking dish or pan, place all of the stuffed Poblanos carefully on top of the batter in the dish, and add the rest of the batter making sure the Poblanos are covered. Bake in a preheated 425°F oven for 5 minutes, then turn the oven temperature down to 350°F and continue baking for about 25 minutes, or until brown on top. These are really good!

Note: you can use frozen Poblanos (after thawing) which were roasted and skinned before freezing

Bruléed Cornbread

This cornbread recipe is a modification of the cornbread recipe from the Zynodoa Restaurant in Staunton, VA. The crisp sweet crust and moist interior makes it a special treat. I used buttermilk instead of some of the milk and cut down on the original amount of sugar (1 Cup) and still find it plenty sweet.

2 heaping cups (9 ounces) all-purpose flour
2 ¼ cups (11 ounces) cornmeal
½ cup sugar, plus extra for brûléeing
2 ¼ teaspoons baking powder
¾ teaspoon salt
2 eggs
1 ½ cups buttermilk
1 ½ cup whole milk (approximately)
1 cup (2 sticks) butter, melted, divided

In a large bowl, whisk together the flour, cornmeal, 1/2 cup sugar, baking powder and salt.

In a separate bowl, whisk the eggs with the buttermilk. Slowly whisk the liquids in with the dry ingredients.

Continue adding more milk, slowly whisking it in, until the batter is thick but pour-able. You may not use all of the milk.

Whisk in ½ cup melted butter. This makes about 5 cups batter. Set the batter aside to rest for up to an hour. Meanwhile, heat the oven to 400 degrees.

Add 1 Tb butter to a 10-inch cast-iron skillet and heat it in the oven for 10 minutes.

Pour the batter into the heated skillet and bake until golden around the edges and a toothpick inserted in the center comes out clean, about 30 minutes.

Brush the reserved melted butter across the top of the cornbread and sprinkle over a light coating of sugar. Place the bread under the broiler or use a torch to brûlée the sugar until it caramelizes. Serve warm.

Freezes and reheats well, although never as crisp as when it was at first.

Alan's Rustic Italian Bread

By Alan

This rustic Italian bread recipe makes one large free-form loaf of very crusty bread, with a somewhat firmer crumb than typical French bread. This recipe is my modification of one printed in *Cook's Illustrated*, Jan 2003, page 9.

I recommend that anyone planning to follow this recipe read it all before starting. It's a fairly long drawn-out project, but the work is not nearly as much as the elapsed time would suggest. You begin the afternoon or evening of the day before the bread is to be baked, but only about 20 minutes is needed, including clean-up. The next day, you may begin as early as you wish, or as late as 3 p.m. or so, recognizing you will need about 7 hours of elapsed time before the bread is done baking. (That time can be shortened by at least an hour if necessary, but the longer time seems to produce better bread, so it's better to plan on the 7 hours.) The baker will spend no more than an hour of this time working on the bread, but must be available for most of it, with no more than 1 hour gaps.

A brief summary of the procedure is as follows: some of the flour, water, and yeast is mixed to make a BIGA—a very wet and sticky mixture. This is allowed to sit on the counter and ferment overnight. The next day more four, water, and yeast is mixed separately and allowed to rest 20 minutes. The two mixtures are combined with salt and enough more flour to make a dough of the proper consistency, then rolled into a ball and allowed to rest for 1 hour. The dough ball is then folded in two directions, reformed into a ball, and allowed to rise for an hour. The baking stone is put into the oven, and preheated. The last dough folding and rising step is repeated again. Then the dough is shaped into a loaf, placed on a large piece of parchment paper that is sitting on a baker's peel, and allowed to rise for about an hour. Just before baking, cut a slit in the top of the risen dough, spray with a water mister, then bake for about an hour.

Special Equipment
Kitchen Aid mixer with dough hook and preferably 2 bowls
Plastic dough scraper
Baker's peel
Water mister (I use a sprayer designed for oil)
Baking stone—preferably 18" x 12" (a 13" round can be used if the dough is shaped into a round.)
Parchment paper
Large metal bowl—about 12" in diameter x 5" high works well

Ingredients
A total of about 6 ½ cups of bread flour (I normally use Pillsbury or Gen. Mills)
2 teaspoons of salt
2 to 3 ounces of dried yeast
2 1/3 cups of water

Whenever you are not working on a flour and water mixture (dough), keep it covered with plastic wrap.

Clean the plastic dough scraper after every use. Dough dries rapidly in small amounts and is very hard to remove when dry. Similarly, at least fill bowls with water when done using them, and dunk dough hooks in water when done using them if you are not ready to clean them up immediately.

Cleaning dough covered equipment is best done with room temperature water and fingers! This is somewhat counter-intuitive, but is good advice. Using a sponge or pad works, but really messes up the sponge or pad. It is then harder to clean the sponge or pad then to clean the bowl! Hot water tends to set the dough, while cold water is mostly uncomfortable to the hands. I usually fill doughy bowls with water, then when I am ready to clean them, turn on the water and just scrape the dough off the bowl with my fingers. After cleaning the bowl, you will need to clean your fingernails, but that is easy!

The more you use the plastic dough scraper, the easier it will become to move sticky dough around.

Use lowest mixer speed unless otherwise directed.

Step 1

Making the Biga. The night before the day the bread is to be baked, make a Biga. (Italian bread starter) In a mixing bowl, add 2 cups flour, 1 rounded teaspoon of yeast, and 1 cup of warm water. Warm means not too hot to put on hand. Mix 3 minutes with bread hook. This sponge will be wet and sticky. Remove bowl and dough hook from mixer stand, scrape sponge off of hook into bowl with dough scraper, cover bowl with plastic wrap, and allow to ferment at room temperature overnight. Temperatures as low as 64 degrees seem to work fine, also as high as 80°F. Note: if you only have one mixer bowl, move the sponge to a different metal bowl for the overnight. You will need the mixer bowl when you take the next step.

Step 2

Wetting the flour. In a clean mixer bowl, add 3 cups flour, 1 rounded teaspoon of yeast, and 1 1/3 cups of warm water. Mix with dough hook for 3 minutes. Leaving the bowl and hook on the stand, cover with plastic wrap and let rest for 20 minutes.

Step 3

Making the dough. Uncover the mixer, unhook the dough hook (but leave in the bowl) and take bowl off of mixer stand. Add 1 cup of flour, all of the salt, and using the plastic dough scraper, add the biga which has fermented overnight. (Note: the biga should have risen overnight to 2x or more its original volume. It should smell yeasty and alcoholic. And it will still be sticky. As you move it, it will deflate. Put the bowl with hook and contents back on stand and mix for 3 minutes. If dough is not correct texture (see next paragraph for my attempt to describe the correct texture!), add flour or water, then mix 3 more minutes. Repeat this last step until correct texture is achieved. You must mix 3 minutes each time in order to be sure that the ingredients are sufficiently mixed that the texture is representative of what you have added. After correct texture is achieved, mix at 1 speed higher than the lowest speed for 1 more minute.

How To Tell When The Dough Is The Right Texture.

Since flour varies in moisture content with brand and season, I can not specify an exact amount. In my recent experience, the quantities given above will produce a dough which is a little bit too sticky. I will usually need to add about ½ cup more flour. HOWEVER, note that it is much easier to adjust a too sticky dough by adding more flour than to adjust a too dry dough by adding water. For some reason, the added water mixes poorly with the too dry dough—it will mix, but is slow and usually messy in that initially the water mixes with a little bit of the dough to make a goo, which then eventually mixes with the rest of the dough. The Kitchen Aid mixer with dough hook can handle a very sticky dough, so if you start there and add ¼ cup increments of flour until you achieve the desired result, it will be easier.

When the dough is "right", it will still be a little sticky, but not impossible to touch without a massive stickup. It will have a smooth, almost shiny, look to it and as it mixes, it will form a mass with arms that rotate around the bowl. Usually it looks like a schmoo with two arms whirling around. In my opinion, the best texture is when it sticks to your finger but not the dough scraper. Some bakers like it stickier, beginners will invariably like it not sticky at all. In fact, if you just barely add enough flour to get to the not-sticky state, it will still make good bread. Handling the "a little sticky" dough is more difficult, but not too hard with practice, and it is safer to stop at this texture than to try to achieve non-sticky without any dryness!

Step 3. –Continued

When the dough is the right texture, put it in the large bowl using the plastic dough scraper. As described in the special equipment, this bowl is about 3 x the size of the dough, which allows room for it to rise. Cover with plastic wrap and allow to rise at room temperature for an hour. I don't think either the time or the temperature for this is very critical. Clearly if it is much colder the dough will rise slower. Conversely if it's warmer. Sometimes if I am in a hurry, I might only let it rise a half hour. It might not be quite as good, but still seems acceptable.

Step 4: Rising and Turning the dough. After an hour rise, deflate the dough with your plastic dough scraper. Then with the dough scraper, fold 1/3 of it over the middle third, then fold the other side over the middle. Then, at right angles to the first fold, fold half of this dough over the rest. Re-position the dough in the middle of the bowl, and make a smooth mound. I often use my fingers for this.

Step 5: First, put the baking stone in a middle rack of the oven, and preheat at 500°F. Leave oven on until after baking. Then REPEAT STEP 4.

Step 6: Shaping the loaf. Prepare a counter top on which to shape the dough.Either stone or wood works. During the shaping you will dust the surface, your hands, and the dough with flour. USE AS LITTLE AS POSSIBLE, the only purpose of the dusting is to control the stickiness. Dust a little flour over an 18" x18" area. Using the dough scraper,

Baking the loaf. Remove the plastic wrap from the risen loaf carefully so as to not deflate it. Using a sterile one-edged razor blade, cut a slit in the top of the loaf ¼ inch deep across the loaf to about 1 inch of each end.Mist the whole loaf with water.

The next step is best done with 2 people, although one can do it. These directions are for using an old conventional electric oven. I have no experience with convection ovens, and gas ovens appear to be a little easier than my electric. With my oven, it is important to minimize the time the door is open so as to lose as little heat as possible. This is important because if the oven cools, the heating element on the oven ceiling will come on too much, and likely burn the top of the bread.

Begin by lowering the oven thermostat to 450°F. Then have a helper open the oven door and pull out the rack with the baking stone on it while you quickly put the end of the baker's peel on the stone, then pull the parchment paper with the risen loaf on to the stone. The helper then rapidly closes the oven door.

Bake for 10 minutes. Lower oven thermostat to 400°F. Get your mister pumped up, then rapidly open the oven door and mist the airspace in the oven. Avoid spraying all of the water on the loaf, but some mist on it will be fine. Quickly close oven door.

move the dough from its bowl onto the dusted surface. Dust a little flour on top of the dough. Wash and thoroughly dry your hands. Dust them with a little four. With your hands, stretch the dough as evenly as possible into an approximately 14" x 8" rectangle. Starting with the short side away from you, fold in the corners of the dough, then roll it into a log. Stretch the dough around each end, and pinch all of the seams together. Ideally, it will appear to be one smooth surface, but small raised seams or bumps will disappear during the next rising. It is important that all seams be closed and the log has no tendency to unroll.

Cut a piece of parchment paper that is a few inches larger than the baker's peel. Place it on the peel, then center the dough loaf on it. Dust the top of the loaf with flour, and cover lightly with plastic wrap. If the plastic is loose, it will hopefully not stick to the loaf.Light sticking will not be a problem.

Allow the covered loaf to rise for about an hour. It should double. Depending on temperature, it might take more or less time to approximately double. I have not found 80°F to cause a problem, but temperatures below 70°F will likely require longer rising times. Also, a slightly under-risen loaf will usually expand in the oven.

Step 7: Bake for 50 minutes more. If you are nervous about how it is doing, you can peek very briefly. If it is getting too dark on top, put a loose piece of aluminum foil over the top—but over as little of the sides as possible. After the 50 minutes have elapsed, turn off oven, remove baked bread using baker's peel, and place hot bread on wire rack Allow to cool before slicing (I sometimes yield to temptation and cut an end while it is slightly warm!)

Step 8: Storing the bread. Do not bag bread in plastic until the day after baking. It will be too wet, and it will get soggy. If you cut the bread the first day, cover just the cut surface with plastic wrap to prevent that end from drying out. The bread will be best the first day, and gradually get less wonderful. It should be put in a plastic bag after the first day to keep it from getting too dry. It can be frozen, but will not be as good afterwards.

Step 9: Finally, don't forget to take the baking stone out of the oven after it has cooled. Otherwise you will probably annoy yourself or other cooks who forget to look in the oven before preheating it for another cooking purpose.

Oatmeal Bread

By Alan

I got this recipe from James Beard's book "Beard on Bread". He says it is as good an oatmeal bread as he has ever tasted. I agree, and also it is pretty easy! The original recipe is for 2 loaves, this recipe is for 1 loaf.

1 cup oats, I usually use old fashioned rolled oats
1 and ½ cups boiling water
About 3 cups of unbleached flour
1 teaspoon yeast
1 and ½ teaspoons salt
4 teaspoons corn oil, or other vegetable oil
2 tablespoons molasses, I usually use Black-strap

The night before you will make the bread, in a metal pan used in the mixer, add the boiling water to the oats, briefly stir, and let cool. When the wet oats are just warm to the touch, add the yeast and ¾ cup of the flour. Let bubble overnight. In the morning, add the oil and molasses and mix. Separately, mix 1 and ¾ cups of the flour and the salt. Mix the dry ingredients with the wet ones. Add more flour in ¼ cup increments as needed to make a stiff, not too sticky dough. Turn out dough on a floured surface and knead. Beard says you cannot knead too much! I get tired after 5-10 minutes, and if the dough seems elastic and not too sticky, I quit! Oil a 9 x 5 x 3 inch bread pan with the same oil used in the recipe. Form the dough into a loaf, place in pan, and allow to rise until doubled, about an hour and a half. Bake in a preheated 350°F oven for 50 minutes, or until nicely browned. Cool on a rack before slicing.

Anadama Bread

By Alan

We also like this bread, which contains cornmeal. The recipe is adapted from Mama Rombauer's.

It really makes great toast. It is also good with meals when a sweeter, coarser crumbed bread would be appropriate. Just writing about it reminds me that we haven't made it very recently. Sandy: how about making some Anadama bread?

1 scant tablespoon Dry Yeast
1 and ¼ cups Water
1 teaspoon sugar
1/2 cup cornmeal
2 tablespoons brown sugar
2 and 1/2 teaspoons Salt
2 tablespoons Butter
4 cups Flour

Proof the yeast with ¼ cup of the water and the sugar. Boil the remaining water, stir in the cornmeal, and add the butter, sugar, and salt. Stir and let stand for several minutes or until just warm to the touch. Stir in the proofed yeast. Add about 3 cups of the flour and allow the mixer to knead until well mixed. Continue adding flour in about 1/2 cup increments until a good elastic dough is achieved. Be sure to pause between flour additions to be sure the dough has incorporated all of the flour, and you can see how it is. (That's a Julia Child saying, "you can see how it is"!) Turn out the dough on a hard surface and knead until it feels elastic and not too sticky. If it feels too sticky, add a little more flour, and knead again! Place dough in a buttered bowl, cover, and allow to rise until doubled in bulk. Punch down, and shape in a greased bread pan. Allow to rise again until doubled in bulk. Bake in a preheated oven at 375°F for about 40 minutes, or until brown and thunky.

Special Holiday Bread Rolls

By Alan

This is the recipe which Sandy uses to make rolls for Thanksgiving, Christmas, or other special occasions. They are very good, but a lot of work--that's why we only have them for holidays.

2 envelopes Dried Yeast
1/2 cup Water
1 teaspoon Sugar
1 cup Scalded Milk
5 tablespoons Butter
6 tablespoons Sugar
1 and 1/2 teaspoons Salt
5 to 6 cups Flour
1 Egg

Proof the yeast with the water and 1 teaspoon of sugar. Cool the milk to lukewarm, melt the butter, beat the egg, and mix all ingredients except flour together in a mixer bowl. Put a bread hook on the mixer and add flour while mixing until the dough is firm but not ridiculously sticky. Continue to knead the dough with the mixer for 15 minutes. Shape the dough into a ball, place in a greased bowl, cover with a damp towel, and allow to rise in a warm place until doubled in bulk. Punch down and rise again. Punch down again, and shape rolls on a greased baking sheet. Shaping is somewhat of an art, but can be approximated by taking a Ping-Pong sized lump of dough, flattening it, and folding each of three sides under the center. Cover the rolls with a damp towel, and allow to rise in a warm place. Bake at 342°F for 22 minutes, or until nicely browned on the top. These are best fresh and warm, but are also very good the next day if kept in a plastic bag.

I (John) will add a couple of optional shapes. One: the knot, this is made by rolling out the lump of dough into a finger diameter rod and then tying an over hand knot. Two: the potato patch roll, this yields a slightly larger roll. Start by buttering a regular size muffin tin. Take walnut sized lumps of dough and shape them into balls and place three dough balls in each muffin hole.

James Beards Bread (Christmas Stollen)

By John, Alan and Sandy

As the name implies, we got this recipe from James Beard's newspaper column many years ago. Although we have modified it to make it somewhat easier to make, it still looks and tastes like the original recipe. We like it so much, it has become a traditional part of our Christmas and John has begun to make it on his own. Its great fresh, also very good toasted, even good stale if toasted. Beard liked to butter it, but I see no need for that with such rich bread.

2/3 cup Seedless Raisins (golden are preferred)
2/3 cup Currants
1 cup mixed Candied Orange and Lemon Peel
1/3 cup thinly sliced Citron
1/2 cup thinly sliced Candied Pineapple
1/2 cup Cognac
2 packages dry Yeast
1/2 cup (141g) Water
1 teaspoon (7g) Sugar
1/4 cup (61g) Flour

1/2 cup (1 stick) Butter divided
1 cup (241g) Milk
1/2 cup (112g) Sugar
1 and 1/2 teaspoons (11g) Salt
1 tablespoon fresh grated Lemon Peel
1/2 teaspoon Vanilla extract
8 cups (950g) Flour
2 Eggs
2 tablespoons Sugar
Confectioner's Sugar for dusting

Put the raisins, currants, candied orange and lemon peel, citron, and candied pineapple in a bowl and pour the cognac over them. (NOTE: I am doubtful that VSOP Remy Martin is needed in this recipe with all of the other flavors.)

Mix the fruit thoroughly with the cognac and allow to soak for at least an hour, overnight is ok if you want get a head start. Drain the fruit, reserving the cognac. Sprinkle the dry fruits with the 1/4 cup of flour, mix well and reserve.

Dissolve the yeast in the 1/2 cup of lukewarm water with the teaspoon of sugar. Allow to stand several minutes to proof.

Melt 1/4 cup of butter and add to 1 cup of milk in the large bowl of a mixer that is suitable for bread making and is equipped with a bread hook.

Add 1/2 cup sugar and the salt and stir until dissolved. The liquid should be lukewarm (less than 110°F) at this point.

Add the reserved cognac, the lemon peel, the vanilla, the eggs, and about 5 cups of the flour. Gradually add the rest of the flour and knead with the dough hook until a shaggy ball is formed.

Allow to rest for 10-15 minutes for the flour to hydrate.

Continue kneading for about another 15 minutes or until the dough passes the window pane test. The dough should not get too stiff.

Flatten the dough and work in the fruit gradually until it is all added.

Butter a large bowl, form the dough into a ball and turn until it is coated with butter on all sides.

Cover and allow to rise until doubled in bulk. It must rise very well.

Punch the dough down and divide into two. Let rest a few minutes, then shape into ovals.

Fold over so one edge is a third of the way from the other edge, like a giant Parker House roll, and press down lightly.

Smooth it out with your hands and place on buttered baking sheets. Brush each stollen with melted butter and let rise in a warm place until doubled in bulk.

Bake in a preheated 375°F oven for 40 minutes until they are beautifully brown and crusty and sound hollow when rapped with your knuckles.

Cool on a rack.

Some notes by a frequent maker *(by John)***:** First I have found that once you reach the stage of adding the fruit, using a mixer is unsatisfactory and a very large steel bowl works the best. I do not wait for the fruit to finish soaking but start right in with the making of the dough by making a sponge with about 1/2 the total flour.

Note, however, that the chef will find that more flour is needed typically than stated in the recipe. Like in most breads the more kneading the better, at least 15 min. before putting in fruit and 15 after is what I do. When the fruit is added if your bowl is big enough you can simply add it all at once. You will know that you are done when the fruit no longer falls out of the dough when kneading and the dough is not sticky.

Cardamom Bread (Christmas bread)

By Alan

This is another Bemis family tradition. We eat this bread on Christmas morning while opening the presents. Some people like to butter it, or toast it, or both. We found the recipe in *Smorgasbord and Scandinavian Cookery* by Brobeck and Kjellberg where it is said to be a Finnish bread, and is called Coffee Ring from Viipuri. It's delicious.

1 heaping tablespoon Yeast
1 cup Skim Milk
4 cups Flour
6 tablespoons Sugar
1 teaspoon Salt
1 teaspoon crushed Cardamom Seeds
1/4 teaspoon ground Mace
1/4 cup Butter
2 Eggs

Preheat the oven to 400°F. Warm the milk to lukewarm—30 seconds in a microwave works. Mix the warmed milk with 3 tablespoons of the sugar and the yeast. Let rise. Put the proofed yeast mixture in a mixing bowl, add 2 cups of the flour, and mix with the dough hook. Let this soft dough mixture rise until about doubled. Separately, crush the cardamom seeds in a mortar and pestle, and add the crushed cardamom to a large bowl and add the salt, the mace, the remaining sugar, and the remaining flour. Mix these dry ingredients and reserve. Separately, melt the butter (about 30 seconds in a microwave), and mix the melted butter with the beaten eggs. Add this liquid mixture, and the reserved dry ingredients to the risen soft dough, and mix with the dough hook. Continue to knead in the mixer for 10 minutes. Remove the dough, form it into a ball, put in a buttered bowl, and let it rise in a warm place. When risen and light, knead it again, this time by hand. If the dough is too sticky, add more flour in ¼ cup increments until the dough is elastic and not too sticky.

Cut the dough in two parts. Shape each into a long roll about 2 inches thick. Twist each like a corkscrew and form a ring. Lay the rings on a buttered and lightly floured baking sheet and let the rings rise until doubled in a warm place. Bake at 400°F for 20 minutes or until the rings are golden brown. It would be wise to check the bread a few minutes early because 20 minutes in a convection oven at 400°F gave very brown rings!

French Bread

By Alan

The recipe we use for French bread for dinner parties is given in the original edition of The Gourmet Cookbook, volume I, published in 1957.However, we often make what we call Italian Bread, which is about the same as what Gourmet calls pain ordinaire.Both kinds of "French bread" are good.

1 scant tablespoon of Dry Yeast
1 and 1/2 cups Water
1/2 cup Milk
1 tablespoon Butter
1 tablespoon Sugar
1 and 1/2 teaspoons Salt
5 cups Bread Flour
Milk to brush loaf with

Dissolve yeast in 1/4 cup of lukewarm water.Scald the milk, add the butter, sugar, and the salt and let this mixture cool.When it is lukewarm, add the rest of the lukewarm water (1 and 1/4 cups more) and mix in the dissolved yeast in the bowl of a mixer equipped with a bread hook.With the mixer running, gradually add about 5 cups of flour.In this recipe, Sandy believes that bread flour works better than all-purpose flour.After adding 4 cups, be sure to allow the mixer to work in all of the flour before adding more.Continue adding in about 1/2 cup increments until the dough is smooth, elastic, and only slightly sticky.Place the dough in a buttered bowl, cover with a clean towel, and allow to rest until doubled in bulk which will take an hour or two.It really depends on the temperature--if you have a cool kitchen it will take longer.Some people say that the slower, cooler rising is better.If your room is very cool, you could warm the oven SLIGHTLY, turn it off, and do the rising in there.You would not want a very warm oven.Punch the dough down, and let it rise again--this time it should take less than an hour to double in bulk. Take the dough, knead it briefly on a floured board, and divide into two. Shape each loaf into a long cylindrical shape. Place the loaves on a buttered baking sheet, cover, and let them rise for about an hour or until doubled in bulk.Cut small diagonal slits about 1/4 inch deep every two inches when the loaves are half risen.If you like a browner loaf, brush the tops before baking with milk. Bake in a preheated 400°F oven for 50 minutes or until golden brown and crusty.For a very crusty loaf, place a large flat pan filled with boiling water in the bottom of the oven.An alternate idea which we often use, and the source of which I have been unable to find, is to brush the loaf several times during baking with water using a pastry brush.We also use a French bread pan--it has two perforated metal half cylinders to hold two loaves.This also helps to give a crustier bread.

Italian Bread or Pain Ordinaire

This is the usual way we make "French bread".It's the same as the above recipe, except the butter and sugar is omitted, and water is substituted for the milk.That's right, it has only yeast, water, and flour.We also like to make a stiffer dough, so Sandy will add more flour until the dough is not at all sticky.We always splash water on this while it's baking to get a very crusty bread.

Basic Brioche

I took this recipe for a soft rich dough from the cookbook <u>Flour</u> by Joanne Chang. It makes two loaves of brioche or two pans of buns. According to Joanne, you cannot make ½ of a batch because it will not mix properly in the mixer.

315 grams all purpose flour (~2¼ cups)
340 grams bread flour (~2¼ cups)
2 tsp yeast
82 grams sugar (~ 1/3 cup + 1 Tbs)
1 Tablespoon kosher salt
120 grams water (1½ cup)
5 eggs
2 ¾ sticks butter cut into 10-12 pieces

Required equipment

Stand Mixer with dough hook

In the mixer, combine the flours, sugar, yeast, salt, water and the eggs, mix on low until the ingredients are well combined, scrape the bowl a couple of times to make sure all the flour is incorporated, beat 3-4 minutes more on low.

Continue to mix on low, add the butter one piece at a time waiting between until each piece is completely mixed in. Mix for 10 minutes, scraping the bowl periodically   Keep mixing until the butter is completely incorporated into the dough.

Increase the mixer to medium and beat for 15 minutes until the dough becomes shiny, be patient. it will become silky and smooth.   Turn the speed to medium high and beat for 1 minute.   Test for completeness by pulling at the dough, it should stretch a bit and have a little give if it seems too wet, add flour a couple tablespoons at a time continuing to mix on medium.

Cover the dough and proof in the fridge overnight.

Here you have a choice, what to make?

Some options are

- Cinnamon Rolls (page 38)

- Sticky morning buns (page 39)

- Brioche loaves

- Brioche dinner rolls

Brioche loaves or rolls

The brioche dough can be shaped into two 9x5 loaves or a tray of dinner rolls.

For the loaves, using ½ a batch of dough, press into 9 inch square fold in thirds like a letter. Press the seams and place in 9x5 loaf pan with seam side down.

For the rolls, divide the dough into 18 roughly equal pieces. With each piece, fold several times in all directions and pinch together. Place seam side down in a 9 x 13 inch baking pan spacing the rolls evenly throughout.

Raise in a warm spot for 4-5 hours until nearly doubled. If making rolls, the rolls should now be touching and fill the entire pan.

Brush the top with beaten egg

Bake in 350 oven for 35 to 45 minutes until completely golden brown

Hoagie Rolls and Hamburger Buns

I developed this recipe because we don't like supermarket hamburger buns.

400 grams Bread Flour
10 grams Yeast (Instant is preferred)
8 grams Sugar
9 grams salt
5 grams Diastatic Malt Powder (err on the side of using less)
Milk and Water, 1 cup Milk + enough water to make 250 grams, slightly warm (100°F)
4 tablespoons Shortening (Butter is ok if you do not have shortening)
1 egg
Sesame seeds

Combine Yeast with Sugar in a small bowl with about 100g of the Milk/Water mixture.

In a mixing bowl, weigh Flour, Salt, and Malt Powder. While mixing with a dough hook, add the yeast mixture followed by the rest of the liquid.

Continue to mix and once the dough has come together in a rough ball, add the shortening 1 tablespoon at a time, mixing each in before adding the next.

Stop the mixer and allow to rest for 15 minutes

After resting, mix on medium speed for 5 minutes before starting to test the dough.

Test the dough by stretching a portion out flat between your finger. If the dough holds together long enough to see light through, it passes the window pane test and is done. Otherwise continue to mix, testing again every couple minutes.

Cover and allow to rise on the counter until doubled, or cover and place in the refrigerator overnight. If refrigerated allow the dough to rest on the counter for 30 minutes to warm somewhat before continuing.

Punch the dough down and divide into 6 (Hoagie rolls) or 8 (buns) equal portions

For Hoagie Rolls, stretch and roll a portion out into a rectangle about 8 by 6 inches. Roll the dough up, pinching and tucking in the ends

For Buns, form the dough into balls, stretching ans pinching to form a smooth ball.

Arrange on a parchment line sheet tray and loosely cover with oiled saran wrap

Allow to rise until about doubled

For Hoagie rolls, slash the rolls lengthwise with a lame or razor

Brush with a beaten egg and sprinkle with sesame seeds

Bake in a 400°F oven checking after 15 minutes

Quick and Easy Drop Biscuits

I remember fondly, weekend mornings with biscuits and cream dried beef, to this day one of the top comfort foods. Generally we used a pre-made mix to make drop biscuits, but this scratch recipe is almost as easy.

    4 ounces (1 stick) cold unsalted Butter, cut into 1/4-inch pieces and refrigerated
    1 1/2 cups All-purpose Flour (8 ounces)
    2 tablespoons Baking Powder
    1 teaspoon Kosher Salt
    3/4 cup Buttermilk

Preheat oven to 400°F and line a baking sheet with parchment paper; alternatively grease a baking sheet with butter.

In a large bowl, whisk together flour, baking powder, and salt.

Toss butter into the dry ingredients until coated with flour. Working quickly and using your fingers or a pastry blender, rub or cut butter into flour until it resembles coarse meal. Alternatively, add flour mixture and butter to food processor and pulse 2 to 3 times to form pea-sized pieces; transfer to a large bowl.

Add milk and stir with a fork until it just comes together into a slightly sticky, shaggy dough.

Using a spoon scoop and mound balls of dough onto the prepared baking sheet according to the size of biscuits you desire.

Bake biscuits until golden brown, about 15 minutes for small biscuits and 20 minutes for large ones. Let cool slightly, then transfer to wire rack to prevent.

Buttermilk Biscuits

This recipe is the closest I have come yet to the biscuits that Ridley describes from her childhood.

2 ½ cups flour
1 teaspoon sugar
2 tablespoons baking powder
1 teaspoon salt
8 Tablespoons butter, frozen then grated coarsely
1 cup cold buttermilk plus more as needed
1-2 Tb butter, melted

Preheat oven to 425 F

Cut butter into small cubes and put in freezer

Combine flour, baking powder, sugar, and salt in food processor, pulse to combine well.

The rest should be done as quickly as possible.

Add frozen butter to flour mixture and pulse several times until the largest lump is pea sized

Turn mixture out into a large shallow bowl, make a well in the center and pour in milk & egg. Mix together until dough just begins to stick together.

Turn out of bowl onto floured parchment

Pat dough into a rectangle about 1 inch thick

Fold rectangle in thirds, the first few times it may seem like it is not working, but then around the third of fourth set of folds, suddenly everything comes together and you can use a rolling pin.

Repeat 4 to 5 times

Pat out into rectangle about 1½ inches thick, chill in fridge for 20-30 minutes

Cut out biscuits with very sharp biscuit cutter or knife and arrange on a baking sheet

Brush biscuit tops with melted butter and bake for 15 minutes until golden brown

Sandy's Unnoticeably Healthy Sourdough Bread

By Alan

This recipe originated as a combination of recipes from Gourmet and James Beard. Sandy used to make two loaves twice a week, today we eat less bread, and when we do make it, I usually make Rustic Italian or Beard's Oatmeal. It's always good, but it's not always the same. Sometimes it rises higher and makes a huge tall loaf. Sometimes it gets an extra rising and tastes more sourdough. Also, Sandy doesn't look at the recipe when she makes it, so the exact quantities of ingredients may vary a little--and thus the bread may be a little different each time. Some days she thinks we need to be healthier, so she uses 2 cups of whole-wheat flour, and then less white flour. Some days we are in a hurry, so it gets less rising, and maybe a hotter oven. Also, if you use different brands of flour, the quantities needed will vary. All of these things affect the bread, but I have noticed that it always gets gobbled up! You may wish to experiment on your own when you have done this recipe a few times. I will warn you, it is a lot of work including keeping the starter going. This IS a sourdough bread, but not as sour as some. You will have to start by making the starter--instructions for that are given after this recipe.

2 cups Water
1 tablespoon Dry Yeast
1 tablespoon Sugar
1 and 1/2 cups Starter
1 cup Whole Wheat Flour
1 and 1/3 cups Rolled Oats (usually uncooked "quick oatmeal")
6 cups Unsifted Flour
1 scant tablespoon Salt

In a non-metal bowl, mix water yeast, and sugar and allow to proof.Stir in starter.Add whole wheat flour and oats.Add about 1 cup of the white flour--enough to make a goopy sponge.By goopy, I mean that it has some thickness to it, but is still a liquid, and can easily be stirred.Let rise in a warm place until it doubles in bulk--about an hour.This is not too critical, it can rise longer, but should be real bubbly looking.Now stir to reduce bulk, and move to a metal mixing bowl in a mixer equipped with a dough hook.Add salt and rest of flour.We find that the most effective way is to add about 4 cups more of the flour and turn on the mixer.Then add more flour in about 1/2 cup increments.You may need more or less than the total (additional 5 cups) specified.What you want is a non-sticky bread dough, but you have to let it knead in the machine for a while between additions or you may add too much.Let this rise until doubled in bulk.Punch it down, knead a few times by hand, divide into two, and put in buttered bread pans which are 4 x 10.If your bread pans are smaller than this, you may need to divide into three loaves.Let rise in pans until they about triple in bulk, coming above the sides of the pans.Bake at 375°F for 40-45 minutes or until brown and thunky.(Hit the top of the bread with your snapped forefinger, and listen and feel for the thunk!)Smaller loaves will take less time.Remove immediately from pans and cool on racks or on top of pans.See next page for starter recipe.NOTE: Flour--brand names seem slightly better than house kinds.All-purpose works as well as special bread flour in this recipe.

Starter for Sourdough Bread

By Alan

We originally bought the starter from The Nichols Seed Company. It was called French Sourdough Starter. We follow their directions for maintaining it. The instructions below assume you have bought the starter and followed their directions for getting it going.

You are going to make bread. Take the crock of starter (we use a 2 quart plastic bowl with a tight fitting cover) out of the refrigerator. Mix it thoroughly. Take out the 1 and 1/2 cups of starter you need for your bread. Add to crock 1 cup of lukewarm water and 1 and 1/2 cups of flour. Stir in thoroughly. Add more or less flour if it seems too thick or liquid. Allow to stand loosely covered for 8 to 12 hours, or even longer at room temperature. Starter should have lots of bubbles at this point. Refrigerate until next use. It should be used weekly, although we have gone more than two weeks without killing it. You should expect it will be slower to grow if you leave it a long time.

Sourdough Starter

Although you can buy sourdough starter, making your own starter is incredibly easy, and the starter is not difficult to maintain. But it is like a pet and does need some care and feeding and occasional exercise (use).

50 grams unbleached Flour
50 grams spring Water

Using a wooden or plastic spoon and a glass or plastic mixing bowl, mix the dry ingredients. Never use metal spoons or mixing bowl with sourdough starter. Acid and metal don't mix.

Gradually stir in water, and mix until it forms a thick paste. Don't worry about lumps. They'll disappear.

Cover bowl with a dishtowel, and let it sit in a warm place for 2 to 3 days, stirring the mixture a couple times a day. It's ready when it develops a pleasant sour smell and looks bubbly.

Store in the refrigerator. (I keep mine in a 1-quart glass Mason jar covered loosely with a plastic sandwich bag.)

The night before using starter in a recipe, remove about a cup of starter and mix it in a bowl with equal parts water and flour. (Some recipes, like my pancake recipe, specify how much starter and additional flour and water to use.)

Cover bowl with a towel and let mixture sit on counter overnight. The next day, return at least 1/2 cup starter to container in refrigerator and stir. Use the rest in the recipe.

You should use the starter at least once a month to maintain its potency.

Sandwiches

133

Italian Sub

Inspired by a sandwich made at our corner bakery (On the Rise) in Roanoke, this is our version.

Hoagie rolls, Split horizontally (page 127)
Sliced cold cuts, some combination of at least three kinds including Ham, salami, pepperoni, roast beef, soppressata, mortadella, etc.
Sliced Cheese, provolone is traditional
Lettuce, cut in strips
Tomato, sliced
White Onion, very thine slices
Pickle, Sliced
Hoagie spread (mixture of hot cherry peppers)
mayo
mustard
Vinegar & olive oil
Salt & Pepper

Scale the amounts for number of sandwiches being constructed.

Mix equal parts mayo and hoagie spread and spread on both sides of hoagie

In a small bowl, dress tomato & lettuce with vinegar, oil, salt and pepper

Layer each ingredient

While there is not required order, my usual sequence is a follows

Bottom of roll
Meat (ham)
mustard
pickle
Meat (mortadella)
onion
Meat (Salami)
cheese
Meat (soppressata)
Tomato
lettuce
Top of Roll

This step is critical, carefully wrap the sandwich in butcher paper or saran wrap as tightly as possible. Allow to sit at least 10 minutes.
Cut the sandwich in halve on a bias (diagonally)
Enjoy / Serve

Italian Beef

This is a personal favorite of mine, a specialty of Chicago. This sandwich is very messy to eat, when done properly it is dripping in juice. Scale the amounts to the number of sandwiches constructed.

Thin sliced roast beef
Au Jus from roast beef
Provolone cheese
Bell pepper sliced
Hoagie Rolls, split horizontally ()
Mayo if desired
Giardiniera, about 2 Tb per sandwich

Shred beef and add to hot Au Jus, simmer while prepping the rest of the sandwich

Saute the bell peppers in olive oil or butter until soft, seasoning with salt and pepper

Spread mayo on both side of the split roll is desired, toast until light brown

The next steps take place at serving time

Add a generous portion of beef using tongs and only draining a bit.

Add peppers and Giardiniera

Top with Provolone and broil to melt.

Serve with Au Jus or dip the sandwich in Au Jus as serving

Supply extra napkins

French Dip

It is important to keep the beef as rare as possible and sliced as thin as possible. As other sandwich recipes scale the ingredients to the number of sandwiches and your preferences.

    French baguette, a hoagie roll will work
    Beef, sliced as thinly as possible
    Mayonnaise
    Au Jus from roast beef
    provolone
    Onions, sliced
    butter

Saute onions in butter until lightly browned

Cut a 5-6 inch section of a french baguette and split it horizontally so that it folds open. If you would less bred, you can optionally, scoop some of the insides from either side of the bread.

Folding the bread open, Lightly toast the inside

Spread a light coat of mayo on both sides

Pile meat generously on one side of the roll and add onions on top

Add a couple slices of provolone

Put under a broiler for a minute or two to melt the cheese, but not cook the meat at all.

Serve with hot Au Jus

Leftovers

One of the best things you can do the day after a special meal is to make a sandwich.

Steak/ Roast Beef

Bread, sliced I prefer whole grain for this, but a leftover dinner rolls is good too

    Sliced steak or roast
    mayo
    horseradish
    lettuce
    tomato
    Salt and Pepper

Toast bread, spread each sides with mayo

Layer each of the ingredients, adding the horseradish on top of the beef along with salt and pepper.

Other ingredients to taste including: pickle, onion, etc.

Thanksgiving

    2 slices Bread, I like hearty white for this but anything will be fine
    Sliced turkey
    stuffing
    Gravy (optional)
    Cranberry sauce
    lettuce
    tomato
    mayo

Toasting is optional, I generally prefer to help the bread stand up to the moisture.

Mayo on both sides and layer according to the following sequence

Bottom slice of bread, Lettuce, tomato, turkey, cranberry, stuffing, gravy, top bread

I generally would advise stopping here as there is already a lot going on already.

137

Quesadillas

One of our favorite quick meal options is quesadilla, these are quick, easy, low mess and can be adjusted to use anything on hand.

Tortillas
Cheese, grated
spinach
Mushrooms, sliced
Pickled jalapenos
Meat (chicken, shrimp, beef fajitas, etc.)
Onions, sliced

Saute the vegetables, either separately or together, reserve

Place a tortilla in a dry skillet on medium heat, start by covering the entire tortilla in a layer of grated cheese.

Layer on all your other ingredients, be somewhat sparing

Once the cheese begins to melt, fold the tortilla in half

Brown on both sides until the filling is hot and melty

Cut into wedges and serve with Salsa, Guacamole, or Pico de Gallo (page 49), sour cream, etc.

Pizza

I have added this section because among all comfort foods, pizza is my personal weakness. Growing up in a suburb of Chicago exposed me to great deep dish pizza my personal favorites being Gino's East and Pizzeria Uno, the original location only, the chain is not even close.

Basic Pizza Dough

This is an updated recipe, I have gotten more sophisticated with my dough making and have come to appreciate the advantages of weighing ingredients for bread and pizza This pizza dough is based on percent hydration for the flour and 65% seems to be pretty good.

  350 grams bread flour
  8-10 grams yeast (instant)
  11 gram salt
  13 grams sugar
  31 grams olive oil
  5 grams Diastatic Malt Powder (optional)
  207 grams water

I weigh everything into the same bowl and then mix with a stand mixed and dough hook for 5-10 minutes until a nice stretchy dough forms and cleans the bowl. The dough will be somewhat sticky, but not so much it coats the bowl.

For better flavor one can now rise the dough slowly in the refrigerator overnight. If refrigerated, allow the dough to come to room temp. Roll and stretch the dough to fit the pizza pan and allow to rise for 45 minutes.

When baking pizza, the temperature depends on the thickness. The thinner the pizza, the hotter the oven should be. So Thin: hot and quick, thick: cooler and slower. I typically bake a thin crust at 500°F

Greek Pizza

By John

1 recipe basic pizza dough

4-5 bell peppers, sliced, assorted colors is pretty, but not necessary
3 cloves garlic smashed and chopped

¼ - ½ pound feta cheese
¼ - ½ cup very good extra virgin olive oil
10-15 cloves garlic, crushed
¼ tsp oregano
¼ tsp basil
Salt and fresh ground black pepper to taste

Stretch dough on to a cookie sheet.

While dough rises, sauté bell peppers and garlic in a small amount of olive oil until soft and then allow to cool. When the peppers are cool, mix olive oil and crushed garlic and spread evenly on dough and then peppers. Sprinkle cheese and seasoning over the top. Brush exposed peppers with olive oil to prevent burning.

Bake in a hot oven (>450°F) for 20 minutes, until cheese is lightly browned and crust crisp.

Seafood pizza

This was inspired by a pizza that Ridley and I had when we were just getting to know each other on Union Island in the Grenadines. We were on a sailing trip and had stopped to re-provision the boat and happened into a little restaurant called The Bougainvillea. We decided to have soup and share the seafood pizza, the soup was unremarkable, but the pizza was fabulous. This is the best of our attempts so far to recreate the recipe.

1 recipe basic pizza dough

1 ½ cup Béchamel sauce
3-4 cloves garlic, crushed

1 pound shrimp
1 pound red snapper

2 cups Bell pepper, sliced thin, a multi colored assortment is prettiest
1 cup mushrooms, slices thin

1 cup mozzarella cheese

First stretch the dough on a pizza wheel or cookie sheet and allow to rise for 30-45 minutes.

Par cook the snapper by grilling or broiling until it is just short of being cooked through.

Sauté the pepper and mushrooms until just softened.

Spread the béchamel and garlic on the pizza dough spread half the peppers around then arrange randomly all of the fish and shrimp and then sprinkle ½ the cheese then the rest of the peppers and finally the rest of the cheese. Bake at 450°F for about 20 minutes until the cheese is nicely browned and the crust is crisp.

Thin Crust Pizza

This is a simple recipe for a thin crust pizza for an easy treat. The key is to bake the pizza at the hottest temp as possible to get a nice crunchy crust. I like to bake directly on a pizza stone for an especially crunchy crust, I sometimes wish I had a wood or coal fired oven to really cook these pies

    1 recipe basic pizza dough

    3-4 cloves garlic, crushed
    2 Tb olive oil
    1 bell pepper sliced thin
    1 cup mushrooms, sliced thin

    ½ - 1 pound Italian sausage

    1-2 cups good melting cheese, i.e. mozzarella

Preheat your oven to the hottest setting 550+° F if possible.

Stretch the dough onto the desired pan. If you are feeling lucky this is even better when stretched on a pizza peel and baked directly on a pizza stone.

The peppers and mushrooms should be sautéed in a little olive oil just until they soften.

The pizza is assembled by mixing the crushed garlic and olive oil and spreading o the dough. The ingredients are then spread around not to thick, leaving some cheese to the end to sprinkle over everything.

Bake until browned and crisp.

John's Original Deep Dish Pizza

1½ recipe basic pizza dough

2 lb hamburger
2 lb bulk Italian sausage

1 bell pepper, sliced thin

2 cans crushed tomatoes
1 teaspoon Oregano
1 tablespoon Basil
2 Bay leaves
2 cloves Garlic, crushed
Salt and fresh cracked black pepper

1 pound Mozzarella cheese
1 pound Swiss cheese

Stretch pizza dough in a deep baking dish or deep dish pizza pan. Allow to rise 1 hr.

While dough is rising, sauté hamburger and Italian sausage separately then drain off the fat.

In one pan, sauté ¾ of the bell pepper until soft.

Cook tomatoes with seasoning until reduced almost to a paste.

Allow all the above to cool until near room temp.

Layer all the ingredients reserving the raw bell pepper. A

Arrange the bell pepper decoratively on top.

Bake at 375-400°F until filling is bubbling hot. It may be necessary to place some tin foil over the top to prevent burning the top.

Alan- We first had Deep Dish Pizza and Greek Pizza (p97) when John made them for us. Both are truly wonderful, although while the Greek pizza can be used as a great appetizer, the Deep Dish pizza is a meal by itself!"

Chicago Style Pizza

This is my best take on duplicating the pizza from Gino's East in Chicago. A big craving of mine from time to time. The thing about this recipe that was the hardest to accept was the fact that you do not precook the sausage, the thought of this giant disc of raw sausage was a little unsettling … but it works and somehow with a good quality Italian sausage it is not even greasy… or at least not any greasier than a good pizza should be.

Dough
½ pound All-purpose Flour (about 1¾ cups)
½ Bread Flour (about 1¾ cups)
3 tablespoons corn flour
1 teaspoon salt
1 teaspoon cream of tartar
1 cup water, warm but not hot
1 tablespoon yeast
1/4 cup corn oil
3 tablespoons Butter, melted
1 tablespoon Extra-Virgin Olive Oil
1 tablespoon sugar

Wisk together Cream of Tartar, Flours and salt and set aside.

Measure water, yeast, oils, and sugar and mix together until yeast and sugar are dissolved. Add flour slowly and knead until dough forms a flexible ball. Seal the dough ball in a container with extra space and refrigerate overnight. The next day remove the dough from the fridge about 1 hour before you need to use it.

Tomato Sauce
½ tablespoon olive oil
1 medium onion, chopped
½ bell pepper, chopped
1 large (28 ounce) can Whole tomatoes
1 tablespoon   Basil
2 Bay leaves
1 teaspoon Salt
1 teaspoon Black Pepper

Sauté the onion and bell pepper in the olive oil until the onions start to brown. Add spices and the liquid from the can of tomatoes. With an immersion blender or potato masher crush up tomatoes in can and then add to sauce. Simmer for 30 minutes and allow to cool. Can be done the day before and refrigerated.

Other Ingredient Preparation

Press the raw Italian sausage between two layers of parchment or plastic wrap to form a disc the size of the pizza pan. If including mushrooms, green peppers, or Spinach precook these by sautéing those separately in a little olive oil until they are soft and have lost a lot of their water.

Assembly

Layers
Crust
Sliced Cheese
Hot Italian Sausage
Tomato Sauce
Optional
Mushrooms and Green Peppers
Spinach

Pre heat oven to 375°F.

Butter a deep dish pizza or spring form pan making sure to cover every inch of it. Line the bottom and sides of the pan with the dough. Line the dough with sliced provolone or mozzarella cheese covering the whole bottom and as much of the sides as possible. Add just enough tomato sauce to cover the bottom. Add par cooked sliced mushrooms and green peppers here. Now add the disc of sausage making sure the press it around to reach all sides. If you are including spinach, add a thin layer of tomatoes followed by the spinach and then another thin layer of tomatoes. If not including spinach just add a thick layer of tomato sauce. Top with a sprinkling of shredded mozzarella and slice mushrooms and green pepper for decoration.

Bake for at least 1 hour

Beef

For recipes on smoking and grilling see the barbecue section on page 235

Christmas Roast Prime Rib

Alan- Although we like a standing rib of beef very much, we only have it once a year because of the cost involved. It's very expensive by the pound, and there is a fair amount of waste in bones and fat. Also, it's great the first day, but not as wonderful the next (it's still good, so the leftovers do get eaten!). So let's say there will be 5 of us for dinner. We would order a six rib roast, which would weigh about 12 pounds before cooking. I don't have to say that I wouldn't bother with anything except the best quality--we order our from the meat market. For Christmas we try to go with prime beef, but choice will work in a pinch. Select grade beef is not worth the trouble except for pot roast or brisket.

Alan & Sandy's Traditional Method

The cooking procedure we use comes from Rene` Verdon--read his chapter on roasting beef if you want to get the full story. But the key is to roast it a high temperature, Rene` says if you can't hear it cooking, it isn't right. Assuming the roast has been properly cut by the butcher, no pre-treatment is needed.

Put it into a large enough roasting pan to hold the roast, the juice which will form, and a lot of potatoes and parsnips and then put into a preheated oven (are you listening Sandy?) at 450°F and roast for 15 to 20 minutes until nicely brown.

Then turn down the oven to 325°F. Don't abandon your roast at this point! Come back in 10 minutes and listen to it! If it isn't crackling, turn the heat up. Continue to look at it every 15 minutes or so until it is done.

We usually figure 15 minutes per pound, or 3 hours in this case of a 12 pound roast. We also use a meat thermometer to be sure it doesn't get over cooked; it should read 130°F in a center spot. This will produce a roast which is well done on each end, is medium for the next rib in, and is rare for the middle ribs. If your family is like ours, you will need the various degrees of doneness, as we have all kinds of eaters from the savages to those who don't really like red meat! It is also important to let the roast rest for an hour after cooking. It will cook a little more during this period, and also become much easier to carve. It also allows time to bake the rolls, cook the green veggies, and toss the salad and especially for the cook to enjoy cocktail hour and have a little pâté.

We also cook the potatoes and the parsnips with the prime rib. The potatoes are prepared by peeling russets, and slicing them about 90% through, but leaving them in one piece. A good trick to do this is to lay two wooden spoons with the handles of the spoons along both in front and in back of the potato and then make slices with the spoons preventing the knife from going all the way through. Make the slices as thin as you are able. This can be done ahead of time and the potatoes stored under water until time to cook. The potatoes are put in about 1 hour before the roast is done, and basted with the fat in the bottom of the pan. The parsnips are put in about 1/2 hour before the roast is done, and also basted. The basting should be done every 15 minutes or so. After the roast is done, remove it from the pan, and put the pan with the potatoes and the parsnips back in the oven for 10 minutes along with the rolls at this point so that they will get brown. The oven temperature is increased to 425°F for the rolls also at this point. The cooking of the rest of the menu is described elsewhere, or is obvious! In recent years we have not had desert after this dinner--everyone is rather full! However, we will have Christmas cookies, homemade fruitcake, mincemeat tarts, and brandy after midnight church if anyone is able to stay awake.

John's preferred method: reverse sear

This is a technique that I adopted after much research and thought on how to make the preparation of holiday meals less chaotic. The reverse sear method has two main advantages, first, it results in a much more even cook of the meat and the ability to more easily hit a temperature target; second, it allows a flexible window between when the roast is cooked and the entire meal brought to the table.

Start a day or two prior to cooking with a dry brine.

    2 tablespoons coarse Salt
    1 tablespoon fresh ground coarse black pepper
    1 tablespoon rosemary leaves

Mix the rub ingredients together and rub all over the roast

Allow the roast to sit in the fridge until ready to cook

Pre-heat the oven to 180 degrees, or as low as your oven will go

Place roast in a roasting pan, on a rack if possible.

Ideally you will insert a remote thermometer into the center of the roast at this time.

Roast the beef until your target temp is reached, there will be very little carry over temperature rise, 2-3 degree in my experience. I go to 115 degrees which results in very rare meat, if you prefer more medium rare to medium you want to go a bit further maybe 120-125 degrees. I wont on principal talk about cooking a roast to well done, why bother?

Once the beef hits your target, remove from oven and tent with foil. The roast can rest in this state for a minimum of 30 minutes and a max of about 2 hours.

Once you have finished all your other preparations and are about 10 minutes from bringing the roast to the table. Place roast on a sheet tray and put under a broiler on high. Cook until desired crust is formed, 5 to 10 minutes

Your can carve immediately because the roast is pre-rested at this point.

Beef and Greens

*Alan & Sandy- A*dapted by Sandy Bemis from "Flank and Greens" from *A Fork in the Road* by Paul Prudhomme. His recipe was modified to not need bread, rice, or other carbs. However, it still goes extremely well over rice, or potatoes, or with bread!

Seasoning Mix
1 tablespoon sweet Paprika
2 teaspoon Dry Mustard
1 ½ teaspoon Onion powder
1 teaspoon Garlic powder
1 teaspoon Dried Thyme Leaves
1 teaspoon ground Ginger
1 ½ teaspoons ground black pepper
1 heaping teaspoon Whole Cumin, then ground
1/4 teaspoon Cayenne

Olive Oil
3 pounds Beef(chuck, flank, etc.) chopped into 1 inch cubes
3 cups chopped Onion
2 cups Stock, salted

About 12 cups mixed greens washed and rough chopped
(5 cups mustard greens, coarsely cut into pieces, about 1-2 inches square
5 cups turnip greens, coarsely cut into pieces, about 1-2 inches square
1 pound spinach, chopped. Frozen is fine.)

Combine seasoning mix in a small bowl. Dust beef with 2 Tb of the seasoning mix and rub in well.

Preheat a heavy 5 quart stock pot (big enough for about 12 cups of greens), over high heat for four minutes. Add a small amount of olive oil, Add seasoned meat and brown it on all sides, about 2-3 minutes.Remove the meat from pan, take care to retain any juices released by the meat. Note: pan may need deglazing between meat and onions.

Add onions, the remaining seasoning mix and 1/2 cup of each type of greens.

Add a small amount of olive oil if needed. Cook with stirring and scraping up brown bits until onions are soft.

Return meat to the pot add 2 cups stock. Add water to cover meat/onions. Bake at 325°F until meat is tender, about 1-2 hours.

Taste for salt and add if needed. Add rest of greens. Cook until greens are tender, about 15 minutes. Serve in bowls without rice as if it were a hearty soup.

Note: If you are using a non-lean cut then you may refrigerate after the oven step to allow the fat to rise to the surface and congeal at which time you may easily remove it.

Alternatives

For those eating carbs, serve separately starch of your choice such as rice, potato, or bread. Cornbread is especially good. Another idea for lo-carbists is Karen's recipe for a cauliflower-based substitute for mashed potatoes.

For those who want more gravy

6 cups Beef Stock
5 tablespoons Flour
2 tablespoon Butter

Combine the butter with the flour and cook until brown. Slowly add about two cups of the stock to the roux whisking constantly. Add the roux stock mixture to the soup along with the remainder of the stock. Simmer until slight thickened, about 5 minute.

Beef Curry

1 ½ to 2 lb chuck roast
¾ cup yogurt
2 Tb Garam Masala
1 tsp Salt
1 medium onion
3 jalapenos
1 Tb olive oil
2 cups beef stock (Chicken will do)
1 can coconut milk
1-2 Tb Thai red curry paste

The night before, cut beef into ~2 inch cubes, Mix salt, Garam Masala and yogurt together and add to beef in a zip lock bag. Massage well to make sure all surfaces of the beef is coated in yogurt mixture.

Cover a sheet tray in tin foil, Spread beef in an even layer on the tray, separating the cubes as much as possible,

Broil on high until beef is well seared, flip cubes and repeat for the other side.

Meanwhile, saute onions and peppers in olive oil until onion gains some color.

Add beef cubes to onions, using stock to deglaze the sheet tray. Add coconut milk and curry paste.

Bring to a bare Simmer and cook until beef is tender.

Ginger, Lemon Grass, and Beef Stir Fry

1-2 pound Skirt Steak
1 stick Lemon Grass
4 Tb fresh Ginger Root sliced as thinly as possible
½ cup Bourbon or Rum

4 Tb combination of Canola and Olive oils
3 cloves Garlic, finely chopped
1 medium to large Onion, julienne
1lb Mushrooms, quartered
2 med Jalapeños seeded and sliced into rounds
1 medium to large Napa Cabbage, sliced in ½ inch strips
Salt and fresh ground Pepper

2 Tb Hosin Sauce
3 Tb Soy Sauce

Cut the skirt steak into 4 inch squares and then slice each square into ¼ inch strips across the grain. Put meat into a 1 gallon zip-lock bag. Cut the lemon grass into 2inch lengths and pound flat with a mallet, add to meat. Add thinly sliced ginger as well. Pour in bourbon or rum. Seal bag and massage thoroughly and allow to rest 1 hour at room temp or overnight in the fridge.

Heat wok on high heat until very hot. Add 2 Tb canola oil and 2 Tb olive oil and add meat in amounts small enough that the wok does not cool off too much. Add the jalapeños immediately. Sauté until meat is mostly browned. Add garlic and cook for a couple minutes. Add onions and stir-fry until onions begin to brown. Add mushrooms and cook for a couple minutes. Add stem ends of cabbage and cook for one minute then add the rest of the cabbage and toss on high heat until wilted. Add Soy and Hosin and toss until coated.

Introduction to Braised Beef

Alan- This introduction is important because there is much confusion about what a pot roast is and what a pot roast is not.What many people call pot roast is, according to Rene' Verdon, actually braised beef.Both of these dishes are beef which is cooked in a covered pot along with flavoring ingredients and vegetables.The distinction between them is the amount of liquid added or present. In fact, in cooking beef there is really a continuum between boiling beef, and dry roasting beef, with pot-roasting and braising being somewhere in the middle.

Pot Roast.In a "true" pot roast, little or no liquid is added.Browning the meat and vegetables creates some liquid, and more is made as the pot roast cooks.But there is never very much liquid in the pot--maybe a half-inch at most.Pot roasts are delicious if well done, but are (I think) much more difficult to cook, and perhaps not as good as braised beef.I include a recipe for Garlic Beef, which can be made either as a pot roast, or braised beef, or as we usually do, something in between!

Braised Beef.Rene' Verdon says "Braised beef is the greatest triumph of French cooking"!He further says "The sheer flavor that saturates this meat astounds the taste.Its succulence is unequaled in all of cooking.Its tenderness and texture are inexplicable.It is at once firm without resistance, juicy without moistness. It is like carving, chewing, and swallowing a rich brown sauce.It bathes the throat in a savory glory.It is a mystery.And it takes some careful cooking."Although I am not French, nor am I a trained Chef,must agree with him, because braised beef is my favorite food. As Sandy can tell you, I can eat braised beef day after day, and never complain--it's so wonderful.In order to understand what braised beef is, you need to read and use the recipes that follow, but in summary, braised beef is a piece of beef cooked in a covered pot with vegetables and herbs and spices, and enough liquid to (just) cover the meat. Interestingly, beef stew can be viewed as braised beef, where the piece of beef has been cut into smaller chunks.In fact, a good beef stew is just as good as a good braised beef dish. I love Beef Bourguignonne.

Grand French Recipes.I suggest you read Rene' Verdon's book in order to appreciate the degree to which braised beef can be raised.The ultimate dish is "Braised Beef in the Grand Manner" which would probably take a week to make, including the stocks and sauces required!I will be very honest with you: Sandy and I made this dish once, and we would never try to do it again.IT WAS WONDERFUL, but IT TOOK AN INCREDIBLE EFFORT!Rene' offers two simpler recipes—for Braised Beef Home Style and for Beef Bourguignonne, which I will hereafter call Beef B. These two recipes do not differ significantly except that one is a large piece of beef, the other is a stew. Rene' Verdon says that these two taste every bit as good as the Grand recipe, but are much easier to make if less elegant. I include here the recipe for Beef B. which we usually make for Christmas. I call your attention to my statement that we usually start this recipe THREE days before it is to be eaten!

Italian, German, Indian, Mexican, and American Recipes. There are good versions of braised beef and pot roast in many cuisines. The recipes which I include here are ones which we have used, modified, and liked.The second recipe (Sandy's Everyday Braised Beef) is our standard—it's very good, perhaps not quite as wonderful as Rene's recipes, BUT much faster and easier to make--and it's not THAT much less wonderful!

Garlic Beef (a pot roast or braised beef?)

This is an excellent recipe whose origin I haven't discovered.If you love garlic, as I do, you will absolutely go bananas over this dish.If you don't like garlic, forget it!(I also feel you are missing a great treat.)This is basically a pot roast, with perhaps a touch more liquid--but its best made without too much liquid.If you can't keep a close watch on it, by all means add more liquid--it's not good burnt: garlic does not burn well!For some reason this dish is best with beef brisket, but rump roast or bottom round can also be used. Brisket is however, much more expensive than the others. Sandy says chuck is too mild. When you buy the beef, try to get one piece rather than several small pieces tied together.

    4 pounds of beef
    6 or more cloves of garlic
    ·   salt--probably about 1/2 teaspoon
    ·   water
    1 or 2 heels of good black rye bread

Skin and clean the garlic, then crush some of it.Sprinkle salt on the beef and rub garlic into it.Tuck pieces of garlic into any folds or holes in meat.If necessary, make slits with a knife.Put into a large metal roasting pan with a tight fitting lid.Brown to a golden brown.In this case, you don't want to try to brown as much as we do the chuck roasts because the garlic would burn and not taste good.You can brown under the broiler, but because of the concern about over browning, Sandy often browns on the stove top, using a little lard in the roasting pan.

After its browned, add water to the pan until the liquid is about 1/2 inch high from the bottom, and add the rye bread.Cook at 325°F for 3 to 4 hours in the oven, tightly covered.

Check it every 20 minutes or so to be sure the liquid level has not gone down greatly--adding more water if necessary.Baste the beef with the liquid in the pot,if this is difficult, turn the 2 or 3 times.

As I said in the beginning, if you are not going to watch it, add more liquid.It will still be good, but the sauce will not be quite as strongly flavored.

Sandy's Everyday Braised Beef(We used to call it pot roast!)

Alan and Sandy- BRAISED BEEF IS MY FAVORITE FOOD. I know, I know I already said that in the introduction.But just in case you skipped the introduction against advice, I say it again!And I bet it will be yours also after you learn how to make it!!!The origin of this recipe is lost in time. At least in modern time.Sandy has made so many different pot roasts from so many different recipes and cookbooks that I can't remember which was which.However, this recipe certainly has elements in it from Mama Rombauer and Rene Verdon.Sandy says it's mostly a method' that she remembers her mother making.Anyway you taste it, it's a great dish, and is even better as leftovers.The longer it cooks the better, as long as it is braising! The secret, as usual, is to BROWN the beef thoroughly.One of the important things about this recipe is that while it makes a great dish, it's really fairly easy.It does take about 4 or more hours from start to finish, but only about an hour of this is actual hands-on time in the kitchen.Once it's in the oven, you won't have to spend much time with it, just a look at it once in a while to be sure the liquid level is right and it's cooking properly.This is just the first version of several,tuned.

  4 pound beef chuck roast, either arm bone or round bone (more likely boneless)
  1 large (28 ounce) can tomatoes, whole or diced
  3 or more medium onions(I like more)
  8 carrots
  2-3 Bay Leaves
  1 teaspoon dried thyme(2 good sprigs fresh)
  Pepper to taste (wait to add salt until you taste it just before adding carrots)
  Water to cover

There are a lot of ways you can make this dish.It can all be done on top of the stove, but the easiest way is to use the electric oven and broiler.You need a large metal pot with a tight fitting cover. Put the chuck roast in the uncovered pan and put it close to the broiler, and until the top side is very brown.Turn the roast, and broil the other side until it too is also very brown.

The chuck roast should be so brown that you are very worried about it turning black and burning! in, however, Don't skip it because this is the step where most of the flavor comes from.If you start with a frozen chuck roast, I microwave it on high for 10 minutes and then put it under the broiler, with the door open.It takes about 20 minutes to brown the first side, and 10 minutes for the second.If your roast is not frozen, it will take about 10 minutes per side.

When the meat is really browned well, put the stewed tomatoes on top of it, and alongside of it, along with the bay leaves and thyme.Clean and quarter the onions, and add these now also.

One critical parameter is the amount of liquid.You need enough to cover the meat while it is braising, but ideally you want as little as needed so as to have a more concentrated sauce when the cooking is complete.Also, some liquid is produced during the cooking process, so that the level of liquid rises during the first hour or so.You should start with the liquid coming up about 75% to the top of the meat.Add water (or good beef stock if you have it) if necessary.

Cover the pot with its lid and cook at 300°F.Check the meat after a half hour to see if the liquid level is right.Usually the liquid level stabilizes after about an hour; if it is not covering the meat at this point, add more liquid. This is important: the meat will dry out and get tough if cooked dry for the length of time given here. Total braising time is about to 4 hours or until the meat falls apart. Scrape the carrots, and cut into 4 inch lengths. We usually add the carrots about an hour before we plan to finish the cooking. OH. YES, check the salt. I don't like to add salt if I am using canned veggies, since they are so over salted. But, you may need to add a little salt........possibly, doubtfully......at least I seldom need to. Now you are ready for the feast: some potatoes, some fresh homemade bread, a little salad, and the pot roast--I mean the braised beef! And a bottle of good red wine. Now THAT'S living.

Braised Beef Flemish Style

Alan- Sandy created this recipe one day when she wanted to see what Rene' Verdon's recipe for "Carbonades of Beef A La Flamande" would be like. But Rene's recipe is for a stew! Instead of following his recipe, she used similar ingredients with a chuck roast and braised it. We thought it was good, but only if you use Guinness or a similar dark beer.

4 pound beef chuck roast
1 tablespoon lard
1/4 teaspoon black pepper
2 pounds onions
2 cups brown stock. If salt free stock, add ½ teaspoon of salt
6 cloves garlic
2 tablespoons red wine vinegar
2 tablespoons brown sugar
4 tablespoons parsley, chopped
2 bay leaves
1 teaspoon thyme
2 bottles of good dark beer such as Guinness

Cooking is similar to Sandy's Everyday Braised Beef recipe. The chuck roast is browned in its braising pan under the broiler until well browned. The onions are thickly sliced, and lightly browned in the lard in a separate frying pan on top of the stove. The garlic is chopped or crushed and added to the onions for 30 seconds just before the onions are removed from the fry pan. Remove the onions and garlic and add to the chuck roast. Add everything remaining in the fry pan to the chuck roast, along with all of the other ingredients. Check the liquid level carefully— DON"T LET IT BURN! Use a good dark beer—Guinness works! Braise with the lid on tight for 3 hours at 300°F. Serve with the same beer you used for braising, and potatoes, or noodles.

Braised Beef German Style

Alan- Sandy believes this version also originated with her mother, although Mama Rombauer has a similar recipe.It's GOOD!

3-4 pound beef chuck roast
1 large (28 ounce) can tomatoes diced or whole
4 medium onions
6 whole cloves of garlic
10 whole allspice
1 bay leaf
1 inch piece of stick cinnamon
15 whole black peppercorns
4 carrots, medium sized

This version is also cooked the same as Sandy's Everyday Braised Beef.Add all of the spices when you add the onions and tomatoes.Add the carrots and potatoes about 1 hour before the braising is to be completed.The way we make this dish, the whole peppercorns, cloves, and allspice end up in the sauce.This can be slightly annoying, but you could either put them in a little cloth sack or you could strain the sauce.Since it doesn't seem to hurt the flavor of the dish to leave them in, we do it the easy way, and kind of look out for them when we eat! We often serve this dish with boiled potatoes.

Pot Roast with Chili Sauce

Alan- This is probably closer to an authentic "pot roast" according to Rene' Verdon's definition. However, it is quite different than any other recipes I have seen. Sandy invented it years ago when she started making homemade chili sauce. It's a wonderful dish, but it's more of a trick to cook.Preparation is easy, but it's also easy to burn and ruin the pot roast.YOU CAN'T LEAVE THIS ONE ALONE FOR HOURS!

   4 pound Beef Chuck Roast
   1 teaspoon Salt
   1 cup homemade Chili Sauce
   1/2 cup Water or as needed

As in the braised beef recipes, you need a large metal roasting pan with a tight fitting lid.

Brown the chuck roast in the pan, uncovered, under the broiler. Make sure it's really well browned on both sides.

Add the salt and cover the roast with the chili sauce.

Add ½ cup of water to the bottom of the pan.

Cover and roast at 325°F.Now, DON'T FORGET TO CHECK THE POT EVERY 20 MINUTES! You may need to add a little water each time--the idea is to keep a small amount of water in the bottom, but not too much. If you let it all dry out, it will get tough and black, and won't be as good. The amount of liquid is a judgment call and has been known to lead to a spirited discussion.

It may take about 2 hours to cook, although it can cook longer if you keep watching it.

Also, I don't advise using commercial chili sauces--which are usually too much like ketchup; too sweet. Go ahead; make your own chili sauce: it's a great thing to have for other purposes.

Beef a la Bourguignonne

Alan and Sandy- (a Ragout or French stew) In recent years we have made Beef Bourguignonne (hereafter called Beef B.) for Christmas Eve dinner for two reasons. (1) While Sandy and John prefer Prime Rib of Beef, the cost of buying that cut has become incredible (prime is two or three quality levels above the usual grade in the supermarket, and prime rib is naturally a cut with lots of fat and bones, thus the cost per pound of actual meat is very high) and (2) As some of us (Alan) have begun their 7th decade, it's gotten harder to eat a big meal with lots of wine and stay awake to attend midnight mass. So we have been attending the early Christmas Eve evening service (usually starting at 5 p.m.) and having our Christmas feast afterwards. This makes timing the roasting of a prime rib quite difficult,(see recipe this section) because it must be cooked so it has both rare and medium rare meat, and according to Rene Verdon, must be cooked in a hot oven. Beef B., made the day before, can be easily heated in a slow oven during church, and tastes every bit as delicious (some say better) than the day it was cooked!

Beef Bourguignonne and its taste equivalent, the French Braised Beef Home-Style, are my favorite meat dishes. (Alan). However making Beef B. is a fairly large amount of work, taking at least two days (three is better) and must be done rather carefully. This recipe is adapted from Rene Verdon's "French Cooking for the American Table" who says "every ingredient and step are necessary and important to get the wonderful quality. He also says braised beef is the glory of French cooking. One small anecdote: a few years ago Sandy made Beef B. and I complained that it didn't taste as wonderful as I expected. We both thought perhaps the quality of the beef had declined (it has), but we discovered that she had omitted the marinating. Since marinating— including drying each beef cube—is a lot of work, I volunteered to do this "unnecessary step". Well, we both thought the result was much better. Today we make it together as there is more than enough work for two people, and we start 3 days early! The extra day allows us to chill the cooked stew overnight and remove the solid fat.

4 pounds choice Chuck, cut in 2 inch cubes. We buy chuck roasts and trim and cut them ourselves. Rene says rump or round can also be used, but not a loin cut. Rene says "expensive meat will spoil the stew"
1 tsp salt
¼ tsp pepper
1 bottle Pinot Noir red wine (quality should be one you would drink, but not the most expensive)
1 carrot, thinly sliced
1 Onion, thinly sliced
3 sprigs Parsley (Italian or plain leaf)
1 Bay Leaf, crumbled
Thyme, 1 pinch
3 cloves Garlic, crushed
½ pound Slab Bacon, fresh Pork Fat, or Salt Pork—all with rind
1 tablespoon Lard
½ teaspoon Sugar
3 tablespoons Flour
3 tablespoons Tomato Puree
3-4 cups Brown Stock. This is one place we deviate from Rene. We use commercial beef stock which is made from beef and vegetables, not bouillon. Some powdered beef stock such as "Better than Bouillon" is also acceptable.

166

For Serving:
24 small White Onions
1 pound Mushrooms, halved or quartered
4 tablespoons Clarified Butter
3 tablespoons Parsley, chopped
Cooking Equipment: heavy skillet and heavy casserole with tight fitting lid

Purchase a 4 ½ pound choice chuck roast. Cut into 2 inch cubes, discarding bone, excessive fat, and gristle. Season it with salt and pepper. Marinate it overnight in the wine with the carrot, onion, bay leaf, thyme, and garlic.

Cut the rind from the bacon, fresh pork fat, or salt pork and save the rind. Cut the fat into lardons, little sticks of fat that are ¼ inch thick and 1 ½ inches long.

If using bacon or salt pork, simmer the lardons in water to remove the cured or salt taste, then drain and dry them. Lightly sauté the lardons in lard. Remove from pan

Remove the meat and vegetables from the marinade. Thoroughly dry each piece of beef and brown it in very hot lard in a heavy skillet.

Be careful! Even if you have dried the beef well, it may splatter hot fat and burn you. It is important to brown the meat rapidly, it should not steam. Do not add too many pieces of beef to the skillet at once. Turn each piece with tongs until browned well on all sides. Remove each piece when done and add new ones until all are browned. Lower the heat and dry the vegetables from the marinade. Brown them in the skillet, sprinkling with sugar to help them brown.

Place the browned meat in the casserole and sprinkle with flour. Mix the meat until the flour is well distributed, then put the casserole in a 450°F oven, without lid, for about 10 minutes, stirring once or twice, to brown the flour.

Remove the casserole from the oven, put the pork rind on the bottom under the beef, and add the sautéed lardons and browned vegetables. Deglaze the skillet with some marinade and pour into casserole. Add remainder of marinade with parsley, bay leaf, and garlic. Add the tomato puree' and enough brown stock to just cover the meat.

Bring to a boil, cover tightly, and bake in oven at 325°F for about 4 hours. Be sure the meat is covered by liquid, add more if necessary. As the time nears the end, check the meat with a knife. It should pierce the meat with no resistance when it's done.

Rene' advises not to overcook the meat, and warns it will become dry and stringy. We have not observed this.

Separately brown the white onions in clarified butter and simmer them in stock or red wine until tender. Also sauté the mushrooms in butter.

We normally chill the stew in its casserole overnight and remove the solidified fat layer on top. We then warm the casserole in a slow oven, and serve it in its casserole.

The white onions and mushrooms are served separately. A green vegetable, salad, bottle of pinot noir, and a loaf of homemade bread are appropriate accompaniments.

Leftover stew, if any, freezes well.

Crock-pot Short Rib Bourguignon

Adapted by John Bemis from https://www.halfbakedharvest.com/short-rib-bourguignon/ while at Anna & Gus's house.

Note: This is best as a two day recipe, if you really have to do it in one day, start the beef marinating in the wine as soon as possible.

Day 1:
1 bottle (750ml) dry red wine, such as Pinot Noir
5 pounds bone-in beef short ribs
2 dried bay leaves
1 tablespoons chopped fresh thyme
Day 2:
Part 1
1 tsp Salt
3 shallots, thinly sliced
2-3 carrots, chopped into ½ inch pieces
8 garlic cloves, smashed
2 cups beef broth (Homemade is preferred)
Part 2
 2
1/2 cup cognac *(Bourbon is a decent substitute)*
2 tablespoons tomato paste
Part 3
3 tablespoons salted butter
2 cups sliced cremini mushrooms
2 Tablespoons all purpose flour
1 tablespoon finely chopped fresh sage
1 tablespoons finely chopped fresh thyme

Day 1:

Place short ribs in a large bowl with the bay leaves and 1 Tb of thyme. Pour red wine over the meat covering as much as possible. Cover and refrigerate overnight or up to 2 days.

Day 2:

Preheat the oven to 325° F.

Part 1

Saving the wine, remove the meat into a colander to drain (collecting any juices and adding to the wine mixture) Sprinkle the meat with about 1 tsp salt.

Place a Dutch oven over medium-high heat on stove-top. Once hot, add 2 Table olive oil. Working in batches brown all sides of each piece of short rib. Make sure to avoid crowding the pan. Sear until you get some brown crust (what you would expect on a good burger) on most of the sides.

Once all the meat is browned, return all the meat to the pot and add the wine mixture along with 3 shallots, 2-3 carrots, the beef broth and the smashed garlic.

Cover and place into a 325-degree oven for 1½ to 2 hours until the beef is starting to get tender.

Part 2

Add the rest of the carrots and shallots, the onions, tomato paste, the cognac. 5-6 grinds of black pepper. Cover and place back in the oven for 1-2 hours or until falling of the bone tender.

Part 3

While the meat cooks, sauté the mushrooms in butter until well browned, seasoning with salt and pepper. Once the mushrooms are done, add the flour and continue to cook, stirring until flour is lightly browned. Take off the heat and allow to rest while the beef finishes cooking.

When the beef is tender, remove the pot from the oven and carefully remove all the meat to a bowl. While the beef cools slightly, skim the fat off with a ladle or use a fat separator, there will be quite a bit. Add the mushrooms and flour to the Dutch oven along with the fresh sage and thyme.

Working carefully, clean vinyl or rubber gloves help with the heat here, remove the bones and any remaining sinew or cartilage, shredding the meat into the Dutch oven. Stir everything together and return to the oven for 20 minutes.

Serve over mashed potatoes or egg noodles or just with a good crusty bread.

Options:

If you are making ahead, you can stop at the point where you remove the meat to separate the bones. Allow everything to cool and put it in the refrigerator overnight. Then you can remove the solidified fat, separate and shred the meat when it is cold. Then you can combine it all and put in oven for 30 minutes to an hour to heat up, stirring occasionally.

Chili

North Lane Chili(lunch or supper entree')

Alan- This recipe is one of my favorite ways to make "chili".Sandy developed it based on many other recipes of chili that we had tried, and on her intuition about how it ought to be made.In her own words, "the following recipe was very good, but does produce a certain flatulence.It is actually quite elegant with a nice corn bread and green salad. I wouldn't hesitate to feed it to company"

2 pounds Stew Meat
2 large Onions
2 tablespoons Olive Oil
3 or more large cloves Garlic
6-8 Anaheim Chili Peppers
2 large (28 ounce) cans of Whole Tomatoes, preferably plum
1 can Beef broth
1 teaspoon powdered Cumin
1 teaspoon powdered Oregano
1 pound dried Pinto Beans (Optional but see note)

If using pinto beans, put them in a saucepan with water to cover by 2 inches, boil for about 2 minutes, take off the stove and allow to stand covered for at least 1 hour.The chili peppers must be roasted and peeled (see general instructions) before using.If you have a supply of roasted and peeled Anaheim peppers, they will work fine after defrosting.You can also use other kinds of chili peppers, but we prefer these. Remove seeds and chop the chili peppers and reserve them.Brown the stew meat under the broiler (see general instructions) until well browned on all sides. Separately chop onions and sauté in the oil.When onions are lightly browned, crush garlic and add to onions for 2 minutes--don't brown the garlic.Drain the beans and put in a large casserole or oven safe pot.Add the onions, and all of the rest of the ingredients.Mix briefly.Bake in an oven at 300-325°F for at least 2 hours; the meat and beans should be very tender.

Note: This dish can be made without the pinto beans, but will then need a starch to accompany it.Any kind of pasta works--people often serve Cincinnati chili on spaghetti.

This recipe is one of my favorite ways to make "chili". Sandy developed it based on many other recipes for chili that we tried, and on her intuitions about how it ought to be made. In he own words "It is actually quite elegant with a nice cornbread and green salad. I wouldn't hesitate to feed it to company!"

John's Spicy Brisket Chili

1 tablespoon Olive Oil
1 ½ pounds Beef Chuck meat, cut into 1 inch cubes

1 large Onion, chopped
1 large Green Pepper, chopped
4 Jalapeños, chopped
1 tablespoon Salt
1 tablespoon Black Pepper
1 teaspoon Paprika
1 teaspoon Cumin
1 teaspoon Cinnamon
½ teaspoon Nutmeg
4 tablespoons Chili powder
1 tablespoon Garlic powder
1 tablespoon dried ground Mustard

½ small (6-8 ounces) can of Adobo Peppers with sauce, chop the peppers fine

1 pound smoked Brisket, chopped roughly
3 small can diced Tomatoes
1 small can Tomato Paste
12 ounce good Beer

3 cans Mixed Beans

In a large stock pot, heat olive oil over high heat, add the Chuck in bathes and brown on all sides. Add the spice mixture along with the onions and peppers. Cook until onions start to caramelize and peppers are translucent.

Add adobo peppers and sauce and stir in and allow to cook ~ 1 min

Add the tomatoes, beer and brisket. Bring to a simmer and allow to cook for about 1 hour. Drain about half of the liquid from the beans and add them to the chili. Simmer for an additional 30 minutes.

Serve with shredded cheese on top (optional)don't think most people will want extra hot sauce.

Sloppy Joe

This is a somewhat healthier version than usual

1 lb Hamburger
3 Carrots, finely diced
2 cups mushrooms finely chopped
1 small green pepper diced
1 large onion, diced
28 ox crushed tomatoes
2-3 cups of chicken stock
1 Tb Worcestershire sauce
1 Tb brown sugar or maple syrup
2 Tb cider vinegar
2 tsp thyme
1 tsp garlic powder
1 tsp allspice
1 tsp fresh ground black pepper
1 tsp salt

Separately brown the onions, peppers, carrots, ground beef, and mushrooms and add them to a medium stock pot as they are ready.. Mean while measure all the other ingredients into the pot, reserving a cup or so of the stock to deglaze the skillet.   You can begin to bring the contents to a simmer even before all the browned ingredients are added.

Simmer for 15-30 minutes and serve

Pork

Crown Roast of Pork with Cranberry Stuffing

Alan- Sandy first made this dish over 50 years ago.Recently, we were wanting to have it and started looking for the recipe.We thought it was in the Gourmet Cookbook--but the recipe didn't seem right to her.Then she realized that we were looking in the NEW Gourmet Cookbook, and back when we first made the crown roast we would have been using the OLD Gourmet Cookbook, that is the first edition published in 1957!As we have found on other occasions, the second edition has sometimes different recipes than the first edition.Sure enough, we found the right recipe in Volume 1 of the first edition.(It's either a compliment to the editors or a criticism of the book binders to admit that we bought a new set of Gourmet Cookbooks some years ago because our copies were wearing out)

An 8 pound Crown Roast of Pork(about 16 pork chops)
Salt, Pepper, and Flour

For the stuffing:
1 and 1/2 cups fresh Cranberries
3 tablespoons Sugar
1/3 cup Butter, melted
4 cups dry Bread Crumbs
1/2 teaspoon sweet Marjoram
1 teaspoon Salt
1/8 teaspoon each Ground Black Pepper, powdered mace, thyme, and dill
2 tablespoons grated Onion
1 garlic Clove, mashed

Prepare the stuffing. Roughly chop the cranberries in a food processor.Mix them in a saucepan with the other ingredients.Mix well, and cook on medium heat for 10 minutes with constant stirring.Cool the stuffing before putting it into the pork.

Have your butcher prepare the crown roast of pork ready for stuffing.If white paper caps are on each of the bones, they must be removed before roasting.(If you like, the paper caps can be put on the cooked roast before serving.)Cover the end of each bone with a small piece of aluminum foil to prevent burning it.Alternatively, put a piece of salt pork or raw potato on the end of the bone. As an option, wrap strips of bacon around the lowest part of the roast.Rub the meat well with mixed salt, pepper, and flour.

Fill the center of the crown with the cranberry stuffing, and roast in a moderate oven (350°F) for about 25 minutes per pound.Remove the aluminum foil or salt pork or potatoes from the rib bones before serving.

The crown roast of pork is traditionally served with glazed apples and potatoes duchesse.

Braised Pork Loin

Alan- This recipe can be expanded to fit the size of the roast. We suggest a Hard Cider like angry orchard that has some ginger, because it seems to fit this recipe. It may not be a good choice for other recipes where a hard cider is specified.

> 3-4 pound pork loin
> 1 tablespoon sugar
> 1 teaspoon salt
> 1 teaspoon ground ginger
> 12 ounce bottle of hard cider.

Mix spices and rub outside of pork loin. Place in oven safe pan with lid. With lid off, brown under broiler until golden on all sides. Pour cider over and cover. Bake at 300°F until 155-160°F on a meat thermometer.

Braised Pork Chops

By Sandy and Alan

For this recipe, we prefer center cut pork chops with a bone because they get the most tender. However, you can use boneless.

6-8 pork chops
1 large onion, sliced
Milk, skim or whole, or half and half cream
Salt and pepper to taste
Butter or oil for browning

Generously salt and pepper one side of pork chops. Place oil or butter in a frying pan over medium heat and place pork chops in pan, seasoned side down. Salt and pepper the top side. Brown both sides to a deep caramel color. Remove pork chops to an oven safe pot with a lid.

Put sliced onions in frying pan, add a little water, and scrape brown bits from browning pork chops loose from the pan. Sauté until water is evaporated, and onions are golden brown. Add onions to the pork chops. Cover with milk or cream. The sauce will be richer and thicker if you use cream, and skim milk may separate. The taste will be fine for all, however. Bake slowly at 275-300°F until the pork chops are very tender. Alan likes them falling off the bone!

Jerked Ham

We started making this for Easter as a way of dressing up an average ham, however, the better the ham you start with the better this will be. The jerk will be quite spicy, but the interior of the ham will just have a beautiful hint of the jerk flavor without being overwhelmingly hot.

1 smoked cured ham (not a country ham)
This works fine for a whole ham or a half, either butt or shank.

For the jerk seasoning:

3 cloves of garlic
3 red shallots
3 fresh Scotch bonnet chilies, stems removed
½ a bunch (15g) fresh thyme
3 fresh bay leaves
½ a bunch (15g) fresh chives
1 tbsp runny honey
1 tbsp each ground allspice, ground nutmeg, ground cloves grind them fresh if possible
100ml golden rum
100ml malt vinegar

For the glaze:

1 orange
150ml golden rum
3 tbsp quality bitter orange marmalade

Warning !!!!! Use Gloves when handling the uncooked jerk rub !!!!!!!

Combine all the jerk ingredients in a food processor or blender and pulse to a smooth paste.

Slice a pattern of cross hatched scoring about 1 inch apart and 1/8 inch deep or just through the fat layer all over the ham. Spread the jerk seasoning as evenly as possible all over the Ham.

Bake for about 10 minutes per pound at 350 degrees

Combine the juice from the orange and rum and marmalade

Remove from oven and pour half the glaze over the ham. Return to the oven and bake for another 30 minutes basting with the remaining glaze every 10 minutes.

Remove from oven and allow to rest for 15 minutes

Brush off any loose jerk before transferring the Ham to a platter.

Slice and serve. It is great hot, room temp or cold.

Poultry

Sandy's Roast Turkey

Alan and John- We prepare and cook the turkey as described in most cookbooks. We usually get a fresh turkey from the meat market. Although our meat market always gives us a bird in perfect condition, we will inspect it for pin feathers, remove the giblets and neck, and wash it thoroughly in cool water. It should then be dried with an impeccably clean towel.

Before stuffing, separate the skin from the meat as much as possible, open up the pockets behind each leg. Both cavities are stuffed (we like real stuffing, not the kind cooked separately and there is never enough room to satisfy our appetites). Make sure to get stuffing down into all the pockets, even stretching the skin so you can get more in. Close up the openings with metal pins and twine as best you can, typically they don't give you much to work with any more.

Place the turkey in a roasting pan large enough to hold it without touching the sides, breasts sides up. Butter the top and sides. Put about a cup of stock into the pan.

The bird is roasted at 325°F for 4 and 3/4 hours for a 21 pound turkey (that's a total time of about 15 minutes per pound).

However, we also use a meat thermometer to make sure the bird is done. You can also tell if it is done by wiggling the legs and wings, which should be almost ready to fall off.

During the roasting, the bird should be frequently basted with the liquid in the bottom of the pan, and if the top gets too dark, a clean cloth should be placed over it and kept damp.

The turkey should rest about a half hour after roasting before carving so that the carver does not burn his (usually mine) thumb, but can rest much longer if need be. In my experience, even two hours later the bird was still quite hot inside.

Gravy

Alan and John- We also always make turkey gravy, using the neck and all of the giblets except the liver and heart. Once upon a time, those two organs were the exclusive property of Little Dickens, better known to all of us as CAT. She would spend all of Thanksgiving Day talking to us about the turkey!

The rest of the giblets and neck are simmered in water until a good broth is obtained, and this is combined with the drippings in the roasting pan, and thickened with a roux to make the gravy. I (John) will add a word about making good gravy here. This is an art as much as science because the character and concentration of the juices is highly variable.

First the pan juices must be strained and de-fatted, usually by skimming or with a separator. I start by melting two tablespoons butter in a 2-4 quart saucepan over medium heat. Then I add ¼ cup of all-purpose flour and whisk continuously until the flour turns a medium brown. I then turn off the heat and allow the roux to cool a bit, still stirring at first to prevent hold over heat from burning the flour. This allows the addition of the liquids without generating scalding steam. Once the roux has cooled I turn the heat back to medium and start very slowly adding de-fatted juice and stock about 4-5 cups while whisking. Bring the gravy to a simmer and cook until thickened.

The Stuffing

Alan- The recipe below hardly talks about the turkey. And to some extent that parallels the reality of our typical Thanksgiving dinner. IT'S THE STUFFING THAT GETS MOST OF THE ATTENTION! Everyone in the family eats lots of turkey, which is delicious, and all of the usual other dishes (sweet potatoes, cranberries, Brussels sprouts, sometimes mashed potatoes, salad-- often an apple/grapefruit/lettuce combination--and cranberry chutney) get eaten enough that their serving dishes are quite depleted, but everybody wants STUFFING!

For 21 Pound Fresh Turkey

3 cups Onion
2 and 1/2 cups Celery
2 and 1/2 sticks Butter
16 cups Bread toast
1 pound bulk Pork Sausage
3 heaping tablespoons fresh Sage Leaves
2-3 teaspoons of fresh Thyme.
1/2 cup Chicken or Turkey Stock
2 Eggs, beaten
1 tablespoon Salt
fresh ground Pepper to taste--we use only a few grinds

Chop the onions and celery into small pieces.

If you have a helper available--which is traditional on Thanksgiving Day--have her or him (in our house it was usually John) begin toasting the bread. You can use stale bread or fresh, homemade or store-bought, but its better if it's not bunny-bread. It should be toasted to a medium brown, but no burned parts should be used. Break the toast into small pieces and measure.

Meanwhile, sweat the onions and celery in some of the butter until they are soft. Reserve them.

Fry the sausage until cooked and light brown, breaking it into small pieces during the cooking. Drain off the grease, and dry the sausage with paper towels.

In a very large bowl or pot, mix the toast pieces, the onions, the celery, the sausage, the eggs, and all of the other ingredients.

Another of our Thanksgiving traditions is that I go outside and pick the sage and thyme from our herb garden. John resorts to buying them from a store but fresh herbs are a requirement, dried herbs won't cut it. Before using the sage and thyme, the leaves should be removed from the stems and the stems discarded.

Mix thoroughly, but do not compress--the texture of the stuffing before cooking should not be heavy or wet, although it will not be dry either!

Cornbread Stuffing

I first made this for a roast chicken but it would work for a turkey just fine. I could not find a recipe that I particularly liked so this is a combination of a bunch of ideas/

1.5 cups Onion
2 cups Celery
6 Tablespoons Butter
4 cups toasted cornbread
3 heaping tablespoons fresh Sage Leaves
2-3 teaspoons of fresh Thyme.
1 cup pecans
1 cup dried cranberries
2 teaspoons Salt
fresh ground Pepper to taste--we use only a few grinds
1/2 cup Chicken or Turkey Stock

Make cornbread or muffins ahead of time, slice and toast before breaking into small pieces.

Toast and chop pecans

Chop the onions and celery into small pieces saute in butter until onions begin to get a small amount of color

Chop the sage and thyme finely

Mix all ingredients in a large bowl, adding the chicken stock last using only enough to moisten the mixture.

Coq-Au-Vin

This is a dish I started to cook after we returned from Germany in 2013. This is great on its own, but can be served over egg noodles for a great winter comfort meal.

2 pieces of Bacon
6 Chicken Thighs (1.5 – 2 lbs.)
Extra Virgin Olive Oil
One medium Onion chopped
One Green Pepper chopped
3-4 cloves Garlic finely chopped
1 Bay Leaf
1 tsp dried Thyme
1 ½ teaspoon Salt
½ teaspoon Black Pepper, freshly ground
1 small can Tomato Paste
1 lb. small Button Mushrooms
1 lb. Pearl Onions
5-6 Carrots peeled and chopped into 1 inch pieces
3 cups Dry Red Wine (Cabernet, Pinot Noir, Cote de Rhone, etc)
Chicken Stock

2 Tablespoons Butter
4 Tablespoons Flour

Pat the chicken dry. Add 1-2 Tbsp. of olive oil to a wide skillet, heat over medium heat until oil is hot. Add the chicken; cook on medium, turning occasionally until chicken is browned on all sides.

If time allows marinate the chicken thighs in the red wine to cover, Refrigerate overnight up to 2 days. If this step is eliminated, the dish is still good, but not as good.

If marinating, drain the chicken, reserving the wine.

Chop bacon into small "lardon" like strips. Add, along with 1 Tbsp. olive oil to a large casserole (5 quart Dutch oven). Cook on medium until bacon is fully rendered and lightly browned. Reserve the bacon, leaving the fat in the pan.

Add chopped onion and green pepper and garlic; continue to cook until the onion begins to brown. Add the butter and flour and cook until flour is browned, stirring constantly.

Add chicken with marinade (or add wine at this point if not marinating) Add bay leaf, thyme, salt, black pepper, and tomato paste. Cook, stirring constantly, until thickened. Add chicken stock to thin the sauce to desired consistency.

Add carrots and simmer for 5 minutes, stirring occasionally. Now add the pearl onions and mushrooms. Simmer for 30-45 minutes until chicken and carrots are tender, adding chicken stock to maintain desired thickness of the sauce.

Caraway Chicken

1 Lemon sliced thin keeping as much juice as possible
2 cloves Garlic sliced thin
2 lb. skinless Chicken Thighs (boneless is nice too, but optional)
Salt
Olive Oil
1 medium Onion roughly chopped (larger than a dice)
4 Carrots roughly chopped (larger than a dice)
4 sticks Celery roughly chopped (larger than a dice)
½ cup White Wine
½ cup Chicken Stock
½ tsp Caraway seeds
2 Tb Parsley, finely chopped
1 head Broccoli roughly chopped (optional peel and chop stems separately)

Marinade the chicken with the lemon slices and garlic, overnight if possible.

Sauté chicken in a small amount of olive oil salting to taste until well browned; remove chicken from the pan. Add a little more olive oil if necessary and sauté onion, carrots, and celery until browned. Remove the pan from the heat and deglaze the pan with wine and chicken stock. Arrange chicken in the pan on top vegetables and sprinkle caraway seeds and parsley over the top. If you have peeled and chopped the broccoli stems sprinkle them on top now.

Bake in 350°F oven for 45 minutes

Add chopped broccoli on top and bake for an additional 15 minutes until broccoli is tender.

Arroz con Pollo

This is a recipe I first had at my Uncle Steve's (Mom's Brother) house in Minnesota. He showed me how he made it and gave me the recipe.

1 small Chicken cut into pieces
2 cloves Garlic, minced
1 tsp. dried Oregano
4 1/2 tsp. Salt
2 tsp. freshly ground Black Pepper
2 Tb Olive Oil
The juice of 1 Lime
1 oz. Salt Pork, cut in 1/4-inch cubes
1/2 lb. Ham Steak, cut in 1/2 inch cubes
1 Onion, Diced
10 Green Olives
1 Tb. Capers
1/4 cup Tomato Sauce
3 cups White Rice
4 cups Chicken Stock

Place chicken, garlic, oregano, lime juice salt, pepper and olive oil in a large zip-lock bag. Massage bag to mix all ingredients and coat chicken well. Place in the refrigerator for at least two hours to marinate.

In a large, heavy bottomed pot, sauté salt pork until crispy and brown; add ham and rapidly brown. Reduce heat to medium. Add chicken and cook for 5 minutes until golden brown on all sides. Add onion. Sauté for 10 minutes, stirring occasionally.

Add olives, capers, tomato sauce, and rice. Mix over medium heat for 2 minutes. Add chicken stock and mix well, cooking uncovered over moderate heat until rice has absorbed all the liquid. With a fork, turn rice from bottom to top. Cover and cook over low heat (as low as possible) for 55 minutes, turning rice again after 20 minutes.

Serve immediately. If desired, garnish with heated pimientos and a few extra capers.

Moroccan Chicken with Preserved Meyer Lemons and Green Olives

This recipe is just one of the countless ways to use preserved lemons.

5-6 Chicken Thighs, preferable boneless and skinless
2 tablespoons Olive Oil
2 medium Onions, sliced inch thick
2 Garlic cloves, thinly sliced
1/2 teaspoon Turmeric
1/2 teaspoon freshly ground Black Pepper
8 pieces Preserved Meyer Lemon
1/2 cup Chicken Broth
1/4 cup dry White Wine
16 pitted Green Olives, halved
2 tablespoons coarsely chopped fresh Cilantro

Pat chicken dry, then season with salt and pepper. Heat 1 tablespoon oil in a 12-inch nonstick skillet over moderately high heat until hot but not smoking, then sauté chicken until golden brown, about 3 minutes on each side. Transfer chicken to a plate and keep warm, covered.

Add remaining tablespoon oil to skillet and reduce heat to moderate. Cook onions and garlic, stirring frequently, until softened but not browned, 8 to 10 minutes. Add turmeric and pepper and cook, stirring, 1 minute.

Scrape pulp from preserved lemon, reserving for another use. Cut rind into thin strips and add to onions with broth, wine, and olives.

Return chicken, with any juices accumulated on plate, to skillet. Braise, covered, until chicken is cooked through, about 12 minutes. Serve sprinkled with cilantro.
Serves 3-4.

By Alan

Preserved Meyer Lemons and Moroccan Chicken are two more foods which were introduced to us by John. He has 2 Meyer lemon trees in his yard in Houston, and makes and shares with us preserved Meyer lemons and Meyer lemon marmalade. The latter is really wonderful, and Sandy has learned to make the delicious Moroccan Chicken with the preserved Meyer lemons.

Jerk Chicken

6-8 chicken thighs

Marinade
    4 habenaro peppers
    4 cloves garlic
    2 Tb ginger
    1 tsp nutmeg
    1 Tb Allspice
    1 tsp cloves
    ½ tsp cinnamon
    1 tsp salt
    2 tsp thyme
    3 Tb olive oil
    2 Tb brown sugar

Glaze
  1 Tb soy sauce
  1 Tb Maple syrup
  1 Tb Hosin sauce

Sauce
mushrooms
sherry
thyme
salt
pepper
Chicken stock/beer
Heavy cream

Combine all marinade ingredients in a food processor and process to a paste. Transfer the marinade paste to a zip-lock bag with chicken and massage to make sure all the chicken is thoroughly coated. Refrigerate for 1-2 days.

Saving the excess marinade, grill the chicken over a hot fire, basting both sides once with glaze half way through.

The sauce is made by sauteing the mushrooms in a small amount of olive oil, deglaze with sherry. Using the chicken stock to assist, transfer the excess marinade to the pan. Add the rest of the ingredients except the cream. Cook for a few minutes until the mushrooms are tender, add cream and cook to desired consistency.

Chicken Tinga

This is a favorite of Ridley's from a small Mexican place near our home in Houston called Romero's. She thinks this is pretty close.

4 Chicken Thighs (you could use breasts if you want, sometimes I go with just 2 thighs)
2 medium tomatillos
1 medium tomato
1 large shallot or medium onion
1 large or 2 small jalapenos
1 teaspoon cumin powder
2 tablespoons oil (avocado or other high smoke point oil preferred)
2 tsp Oregano
2 bay leaves
3 cloves Garlic, crushed
2 cups chicken stock (homemade is highly preferred)
½ cup white wine
1 tablespoon chopped chipotle plus 1 tablespoon chipotle sauce
2 tablespoons Apple Cider Vinegar
2 tablespoons tomato paste
1 teaspoon Annatto powder
1 tablespoon Cilantro,chopped plus some for garnish
1 tablespoon Lime juice (~½ of a lime)
Salt and fresh ground black pepper

Gather chicken, tomatillos, tomato, onion, and jalapeno in a bowl and drizzle with oil, make sure everything is coated well. Sprinkle the chicken with cumin and salt.

Grill everything on a hot grill until the vegetables are charred on all sides and chicken is browned well. This can also be done under a broiler if a grill is not available.

Return the the kitchen and chop the vegetables roughly, removing the seeds from the jalapeno and add to a large skillet with the chicken.

Add the rest of the ingredients to the pan, bring to a simmer and cook until chicken is very tender.

Remove the chicken to a bowl and using two forks, shred into small pieces.

Meanwhile, remove the bay leaves and discard. Using an immersion blender, blend sauce until mostly smooth. It may work best to move the sauce to a bowl or even use a blender for this as an immersion blender is challenging to use in a skillet.

Bring the sauce back to a simmer and reduce to desired consistency. Add the shredded chicken and bring back to a simmer

Serve on flour or corn tortilla's with extra lime wedges and cilantro

Seafood

John's Spicy Chipotle Shrimp

1 lb Jumbo shrimp 16-20
5-4 jalapeños seeded and quartered length wise
4-5 slices Bacon halved once width wise and once lengthwise
Toothpicks

Lay bacon on a jelly roll pan and par-bake for 15 minutes at 400 degrees

Wrap one shrimp and jalapeño quarter with a bacon strip and secure with a toothpick.

Grill on low heat BBQ until shrimp are cooked and bacon is crisp.

Chipotle sauce

½ small (6-8 ounces) can of Chipotle Peppers in adobo sauce
½ large Onion finely diced
3-4 cloves Garlic
2 Tb Butter
2 Tb Olive Oil
½ cup Bourbon
1 Tb Worcestershire Sauce
The juice of one Lime
Salt and Pepper to taste

Add onions and olive oil for sauté pan and sauté on medium heat until onions are translucent, add butter and continue to cook until onions are slightly brown. Remove from heat and add chipotle peppers and adobo sauce. Pour mixture into a food processor and pulse until smooth. Return the mixture to sauté pan on medium heat. Add bourbon, Worcestershire, lime juice, salt and pepper. Cook until mixture is well melded.

Pour over shrimp or use as a dipping sauce.

Shrimp and Grits a la Bemis

I made this for Ridley first on a lazy Sunday summer morning

This recipe makes two servings. This makes a great brunch for Sunday mornings.

2/3 cup Quick Grits (2 servings)
2 2/3 cups Hot Water
1/2 tsp Salt
1 Tb Butter
1/4 cup Mozzarella

2 Tb Extra Virgin Olive Oil
1/4 cup Onion, chopped
2 small Jalapeño Peppers
2 cloves Garlic, sliced thin
4 cups fresh Spinach
Salt and Pepper to taste

Juice of one Lime
2 cloves Garlic, crushed
2 Tb Olive Oil
8 jumbo Shrimp, shelled

Marinate Shrimp in the lime juice, crushed garlic and 2 Tb olive oil for a few minutes while preparing other parts of this dish.

Bring Water to a boil and add quick grits and salt bring to a boil then turn down to a simmer for 6 minutes.Add butter and mozzarella and simmer on low for 10 minutes while preparing spinach.

Sauté onion, pepper and garlic in olive oil until slightly brown. Add spinach and toss until completely wilted.

Remove the spinach from the sauté pan and add the shrimp, sauté for a couple of minutes until the shrimp are done.

Plate by starting with a good sized dollop of grits on a plate, mound some spinach on top and them place four shrimp on top.

Curry Shrimp and Grits

Grits
2/3 cup quick grits (Anson Mills)
1-2 cups chicken stock
1 Tb butter
1 cup milk
½ cup cheese, shredded (Gruyere, Monterrey jack, mozzarella, etc.)
½ tsp salt
Shrimp
1 lb shrimp
1 tsp salt
½ tsp baking soda
¼ tsp corn starch
½ cup smoked sausage, sliced thin
½ green pepper, diced
1 small onion, diced
1 medium carrot, sliced thin
4 cloves garlic, minced
1 Tablespoon green curry paste
1 teaspoon sriracha chili paste
½ cup coconut milk

Juice from ½ lime
¼ cup cilantro, chopped

Toss the shrimp in the salt, baking soda and corn starch.

Combine grits, butter, salt, stock and milk in a sauce pan and heat on medium until simmering. Reduce to low, add cheese. Cook on low, adding water as needed to keep desired consistency until the grits are creamy, about 30 minutes.

Saute sausage until browned and reserve on a paper towel to drain. Drain all grease from pan.

Saute the onions, pepper and carrots in a bit of olive oil, reserve. Saute garlic in a bit of olive oil until it starts to color, add curry and chili pastes and cook for 30 seconds.

Add the shrimp, vegetables, sausage, lime juice, coconut milk and cook until shrimp are cooked.

Add lime and cilantro. Serve immediately over grits

Creamy garlic shrimp and grits

Grits
2/3 cup quick grits
1-2 cups chicken stock
1 Tb butter
1 cup milk
½ cup cheese, shredded (Monterrey jack, mozzarella, etc.)
½ tsp salt

Shrimp
2 Tb salted butter
6 cloves garlic, crushed
1 pound shrimp or prawns, tails on or off
1 small yellow onion, finely diced
1-2 stalks celery, finely diced
1 jalapeno pepper, finely diced
½ cup white wine
½ cup dried tomatoes chopped (can use ½ Tomatoes and ½ tomatillos)
½ cup heavy cream
½ cup half & half or milk
1 pinch salt to taste
1 pinch pepper to taste
3 cups baby spinach leaves washed
½ cup Parmesan cheese shredded
1 tsp dried parsley or 1 Tb fresh
½ tsp dried oregano
1 tsp dried basil
½ tsp dried thyme

Combine grits, butter, salt, stock and milk in a sauce pan and heat on medium until simmering. Reduce to low, add cheese. Cook on low, adding water as needed to keep desired consistency until the grits are creamy, about 30 minutes.

Heat a large skillet over medium-high heat. Melt the butter and add in the garlic and fry until fragrant (about one minute). Add in the shrimp and fry two minutes on each side, until just cooked through and pink. Transfer to a bowl; set aside.

Saute the onion, celery and pepper in the butter remaining in the skillet until they begin to color. Add the roasted tomatoes and fry for 1-2 minutes to release their flavors. Deglaze with the white wine , and allow to reduce to half, while scraping any bits off of the bottom of the pan. Add in the spinach leaves and allow to wilt.

Reduce heat to low-medium heat, add the cream and bring to a gentle simmer, while stirring occasionally. Season with salt and pepper to your taste. Add in the Parmesan cheese and herbs.

Allow sauce to simmer for a further minute until cheese melts and the sauce thickens.

Add the shrimp back into the pan and stir through.

202

BBQ Shrimp New Orleans Style

1/2 cup Quick Grits (2 servings)
1 cup milk
2 cups Hot Water
1/2 tsp Salt
1 Tb Butter
1/4 cup Mozzarella

1lb Shrimp Jumbo 10/15
2 Tb Extra Virgin Olive Oil
½ lemon

3 Tb butter
½ cup onion minced
½ cup bell pepper minced
6 cloves garlic, crushed
1 Tb Tabasco Hot Sauce
1 tsp thyme
¼ cup lime juice
Salt and Pepper to taste

¼ cup chopped green onions
¼ cup chopped parsley

Marinate Shrimp in the lemon juice & olive oil for 5-10 minuets

Melt butter

Gulf Style Shrimp Boil

A great casual way to cook shrimp that does not take much effort, we do this a lot on summer weekday dinners, quick and easy and perfect for when you can get fresh corn on the cob.

1-2 pounds Shrimp, wild gulf unpeeled, heads off
2-4 ears Corn, broken in half
1 pound Smoked Sausage, cut into 1 ½ inch chunks
1 small package, or ½ cup Shrimp Boil seasoning
1 Tablespoon Salt
Optional
       1-2 pounds small Potatoes

In a large, 8-10 quart pot bring at least a gallon of water to a boil. Add salt and seasoning. Add the sausage and potatoes and simmer for 10 minutes. Add the corn and shrimp and turn the heat off. Cover and allow to stand 3-4 minutes. Serve with cocktail sauce and butter.

Costa Rican Tilapia

3 tablespoons fresh Lime Juice
3 tablespoons Olive oil, divided
4 tablespoons finely chopped fresh Cilantro or Parsley, divided
4 teaspoons minced Garlic, divided
1 1/2 teaspoons Kosher Salt, divided
1/4 teaspoon Sugar
6 (5 ounce) Tilapia Fillets
3/4 cup Long-Grain Rice
1 cup chopped Onions
2 Oranges, peeled, seeded, coarsely chopped
1 (28 ounce) can diced Tomatoes, un-drained
1 (15 ounce) can Black Beans or Pinto Beans, drained, rinsed
1 teaspoon dried Oregano Leaves
1/2 teaspoon fresh Ground Black Pepper
1/4 teaspoon Cayenne Pepper

For the tilapia marinade, combine lime juice, 1 tablespoon olive oil, 2 tablespoons cilantro, 1 teaspoon garlic, 1/2 teaspoon salt, and sugar in a shallow dish.

Add tilapia and marinate 15 minutes, turning once.

To prepare the bean and rice mixture, cook the rice according to package and keep warm while the tilapia is marinating.

Preheat oven to 400°F. In a large, skillet or saucepan, heat 2 tablespoons olive oil on medium heat. Add remaining garlic and onions; sauté until translucent, about 5 minutes, stirring. Add 2 tablespoons

Cilantro, oranges, tomatoes, beans, oregano, 1 teaspoon salt, pepper, and cayenne.

Cook, uncovered, until hot, 7 to 8 minutes, stirring occasionally.

Transfer hot rice to a 9 by 13 inch baking dish. Spoon the bean mixture on top of rice and gently blend. Slightly overlap tilapia fillets on top and scrape marinade over fillets.

Bake 16 to 20 minutes.

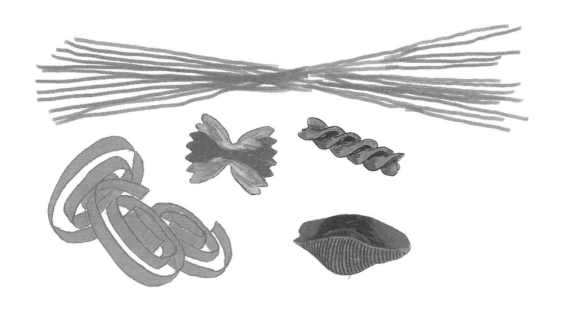

Pasta

Pesto Carbonara

1 lb Linguine or similar pasta

6 slices bacon
 1 small onion, diced
1 clove garlic minced
¾ cup mushrooms, chopped

¾ cup green peas

¼ cup heavy cream
1 tsp fresh ground black pepper
2 egg yolks

3 cloves garlic
3 Tbs grated Parmesan
2 cups fresh basil leaves
½ tsp salt
 3 Tbs pecans or pine nuts
3-5 Tbs good extra virgin olive oil

Cook pasta in a minimum of water with some, but at most 1 Tbs salt until just past al dente

In a food processor, blend together the 3 cloves garlic, Parmesan, basil, salt, nuts and olive oil.

Cook bacon until crispy, drain the grease leaving a film on the pan.   Cook the onions and mushrooms until lightly colored, adding the 1 clove garlic at the end.

Blanch or microwave the peas until just hot.

In a large bowl, whisk together the egg yolks, cream and pepper.   When the past is done. Using tongs scoop a small portion of the pasta without allowing it to drain, add it to the egg mixture and quickly stir it until the egg mixture thickens. Continue adding tong fulls of pasta and stirring until it is all added.   Add more pasta water as needed to add to the sauce.   Toss the pasta with the bacon and vegetables. Stir the pesto mixture into the pasta and serve with thin sliced green scallions as garnish.

Spaghetti Sauce

Alan- This is my recipe for spaghetti sauce.If you would rather, it can be called pasta sauce.I certainly use it on any of the long narrow kinds of pasta such as linguine, spaghettini, fettuccine, etc.I actually "invented" this recipe one day when I was looking for a good recipe for good old fashioned meaty/tomatoey spaghetti sauce.I found an old recipe of my Dad's which sounded good (see list of ingredients below) and I read several recipes in Italian cookbooks for Sauce Bolognese, none of which I particularly liked, and some of which sounded real weird!Anyway, I ended up making something rather different than any of these, as given below:

> 2 pounds Ground Chuck, low fat
> 1 tablespoon Olive Oil
> 4 cups chopped Onions
> 4 cloves Garlic
> 2 cups sliced Carrots
> 1 green Bell Pepper
> ½ cup Flat Leafed Parsley
> 2 large (28 ounce) cans Whole Tomatoes
> Salt (but be careful)

In a large steel pot (6+ quarts) brown the ground chuck on medium high heat.If you can buy very low fat ground chuck, you will have some trouble with sticking and burning, and may want to use a tiny amount of olive oil.Your reward for using very low fat meat is no visible fat in the browned ground chuck.If you have to use a higher fat content ground beef, you should pour off the oil that forms during the browning.The meat should be thoroughly browned until no pink parts remain, and some of the bits are quite brown.But not black!If you start with frozen ground beef, it will be much easier to work with it if it is thawed completely before browning.I use a microwave to thaw it, and in this case you can even do it on high since if some of the outside meat cooks, it won't hurt anything.After the ground chuck is thoroughly browned, remove it from the pot. If necessary clean the bottom of the pot, add a little olive oil and sauté the onions which were chopped roughly while the meat was browning.The onions should be cooked until transparent, and some are beginning to brown.Be careful not to burn.Mince the garlic and add it to the onions for just a minute at the end of the sautéing.Remove the onions and garlic from the pot, clean the bottom if necessary(it should not be necessary if you haven't burned anything), add a little olive oil, and add the carrots which you have cleaned and sliced thinly.Sauté the carrots until they are softened and slightly browned.Remove the carrots, add a small amount of olive oil, and add the pepper which has been chopped into small pieces.Sauté the pepper until it is soft and beginning to brown.Remove the pot from the burner.If the bottom of the pot has burned or stuck material, remove the pepper and clean the pot.Add all of the browned meat and vegetables back to the pot. Drain the canned tomatoes and add them to the pot.Roughly chop the parsley and add it to the pot.Put the pot on the burner and simmer until the sauce is thick enough to stick to spaghetti, and all of the vegetables and meat have combined into a single substance.You won't likely find the onions!The simmering will take at least an hour, maybe several.You can hurry it by not putting a lid on the pot, and by squeezing the tomatoes to remove all of their juice before adding them to the pot.I would rather add the tomatoes fairly wet and let it simmer longer. SALT: Be Careful. Most canned tomatoes have enough salt in them for this sauce.TASTE the sauce before adding more salt!Since the salt can be added towards the end of the simmering, this is no problem, and can help you decide if you want to simmer longer, or even add any other ingredients.

GOOD OPTION: Add fresh basil in place of parsley.

Dads Spaghetti Sauce

Dad's list of ingredients (cooking directions essentially the same)

1 pound Ground Chuck
1 small Onion
1 tablespoon Olive Oil
2 stalks Celery
1/4 green Bell Pepper
3- small (3 ounce) cans of Tomato Paste
Some Water to make the sauce blend together
Small pinch of Oregano

Marinara Sauce

This is out go-to sauce for meatballs, chicken parm, and other things for dipping.

2 cans whole peeled tomatoes
1 medium onion, chopped
2 cloves garlic, chopped fine
½ medium green pepper, chopped
1 tablespoon olive oil
1 tablespoon dried basil
1 tablespoon dried oregano
2-3 bay leaves
1 teaspoon red pepper flakes
2 teaspoons salt
1 teaspoon fresh ground black pepper

Drain tomatoes, reserving liquid

Smash tomatoes by hand, allowing the liquid to drain into the reserved juice.

Saute onions, garlic and green pepper until the onions have some color

Added spices and ½ of tomatoes solids and cooks until the tomatoes have some color

Put all ingredients except reserved liquid into a food processor with chopping blade

Process in short pulses until it is not quite smooth

Put liquid into a sauce pan and reduce over medium heat until reduced by at least 255

Add the mixture from the processor and bring to a simmer. Do not cook further .

If you have it, Add some finely chopped fresh basil or parsley immediately before serving.

Johns Garlicky and Basily Pasta Sauce

This is my recipe for pasta sauce. As you can see, it is quite different than Dad's or Grandpa's. Nevertheless it is quite good, particularly with a bottle of Big House Red from Ca' del Solo.

    1 pound Ground Beef
    2 large Onions
    2 green Peppers
    1 teaspoon dried Oregano
    1 handful frozen Basil
    2 Bay Leaves
    8 Garlic Cloves (more is better)
    1 28 ounce can Tomatoes (crushed is preferred)
    1 12 ounce can Tomato Paste
    water

Heat a good saucepan on high (best to use an all metal pot with copper bottom or equivalent) until it is good and hot. Put ground beef (low fat ground chuck is what we use) in the pan and turn down to medium high.Brown meat until moisture is gone and meat is not red anywhere. You can use frozen ground beef, but the browning process is more difficult. You may need to turn up the burner from time to time if the meat is steaming rather than browning. The meat should make a good sizzling noise while it is browning. Chop onions coarsely and add to the pot when the meat is all browned. Crush the garlic by pushing on it with the flat blade of a chef's knife, discarding the skin, and put it in the pot. Chop the green pepper coarsely and put it in the pot. Add the bay leaf, oregano, and basil. Cook all of this until the onion is translucent. John says this is important: the SECRET to the recipe. Actually, as in my recipe, I would go further and say it is very important to brown the meat and veggies--even beyond the translucent onion stage. According to John, if you are in no hurry (this seldom happens) you should cook the meat and veggies for 30 minutes more at this stage, but if you are hungry (as usual) it's no tragedy if you proceed. Add the tomatoes, both crushed and paste, and about an equal amount of water to the paste. Stir until well mixed, reduce burner temperature until it is just simmering--say about medium low-- and simmer for an hour. If you are very hungry, John says you can eat it even earlier.

This recipe will serve 4 big eaters, and should be served with a short and curly type of pasta. John is willing to eat it with just short such as mostaccioli. A green salad and a loaf of fresh home-made French or Italian bread and a bottle of Big House Red makes a great dinner.

Chicken Alfredo Sauce

This is warm creamy comfort food. If you use low fat milk, it need not be too un-healthy. It's a great way to use up leftover rotisserie chicken or turkey from thanksgiving.

   3 tablespoons butter
   ½ pound Mushrooms, roughly chopped
   1 medium Onion, diced
   2 tablespoons All-purpose Flour
   2 cups Milk (low fat)
   ½ cup shredded Jack Cheese
   ½ cup grated Parmesan Cheese
   2 cups Cooked Chicken, ½ inch cubes
   Salt
   Fresh ground Black Pepper

Sauté mushrooms and onions in the butter until they begin to brown slightly. Sprinkle with the flour and cook until flour begins to brown. Slowly add milk while stirring constantly to avoid lumps. When smooth, add cheese slowly also stirring constantly, allow to simmer for a few minutes and then stir in chicken and season to taste with salt and pepper.

Hurricane Pasta

The basics of this dish developed out of what we had on hand during hurricane Ike. We were triaging the fridge deciding what we needed to cook now and what could wait.

1 pound large Shrimp, shelled and tail fins removed
3 cloves Garlic, crushed
Juice of ½ Lemon

1 pound small curly Pasta
1-2 pound Spinach, chopped
3 tablespoon Olive Oil
3-4 cloves Garlic, diced finely
½ large Onion, diced
½ pound Mushrooms, sliced
~15 Cherry Tomatoes, halved
Salt and fresh ground Black Pepper to taste

Marinate shrimp in garlic olive oil and lemon juice for 20-30 minutes.

Cook the pasta in simmering heavily salted water until just barely done, drain and reserve.

Sauté garlic, onion in 1 Tb olive oil when the onions are translucent, add mushrooms and sauté until they start to soften. Add the remaining olive oil and then the spinach. Toss over medium heat until the spinach is completely wilted, add the cherry tomatoes and mix until tomatoes are hot. Add to pasta season with salt and pepper and reserve.

Grill or sauté shrimp until just cooked

Fold shrimp into pasta mixture and serve with fresh Parmesan cheese

Lamb Ragu

2 lb ground lambs
1 large can whole peeled tomatoes
1 medium can crushed tomatoes
6 medium carrots
1 large onion
2 stalks celery
4 cloves garlic, chopped fine
1 tablespoon olive oil
1 tablespoon dried oregano
2 teaspoons ground fennel seed
2 teaspoons salt
1 teaspoon fresh ground black pepper

Quantity chopped fresh basil
Paparadelle pasta

Brown onions and reserve
Brown lamb drain and reserve
Using 1 Tb fat from lamb saute carrots and celery

One Pot Tortellini and Asparagus Alfredo

This recipe came about from a recipe I saw in an old gourmet magazine,

10 oz Tortellini
1 lb Asparagus
½ cup Chicken Stock
2 cloves Garlic, crushed
½ cup Heavy Cream
½ cup Shredded Cheese
1/3 tsp Black Pepper, fresh ground

Bring 3 quarts of water with 2 Tbs salt to a rolling boil

Cook tortellini for 4 minutes, remove from water and reserve

Bring water back to a boil and cook asparagus for 4 minutes, remove asparagus and allow to cool

Discard water and add stock, cream, garlic and cheese to pot, bring to a simmer.

Chop asparagus in 2 inch pieces

Add asparagus bottom sections to sauce ans simmer for a minute

Add the remaining asparagus and tortellini and simmer while stirring until desired consistency is reached.

218

Other Entrées

Chili Rellenos My Way

I invented this recipe because I love the taste of Poblano chili peppers, but I am always disappointed in the ones you find in restaurants. I don't like the coating and frying part most of all, it always seems to end up soggy by the time it makes it to the table.

4-6 Large Poblano chili peppers
2 cups of shredded meat, can be anything, I prefer chicken or shrimp chopped in 1 inch pieces.
1-2 cups diced vegetables (mushrooms, carrots, bell pepper, etc)
1 Onion, diced
3-4 cloves garlic crushed
3-4 Jalapeño peppers, diced
1 small can diced tomatoes
Salt and fresh ground Black Pepper to taste
1 cup shredded cheese, Monetary Jack or Mozzarella plus additional for topping
¾ cup toasted pecans, chopped (optional)

First char the Poblanos all over and place in an airtight container or bag to soften the skin.

Sauté the onion and garlic in a little olive oil until translucent, add diced vegetables and jalapeños and cook until softened. Stir in meat, and nuts and season with salt and pepper. Allow to cool

Rinse the skins off the Poblano peppers under running water. Slice off the stem ends reserving the top to replace later. Remove the seeds and membrane leaving the pepper as intact as possible. The more membrane you leave behind the hotter the final result. This step can be done in advance and the peppers stored in the freezer

When the meat mixture is cooled enough to work with, stir in the cheese.

Stuff the Poblanos with this mixture as much as possible and arrange them in a baking dish sized to fit them all.

Pour the remaining mixture and diced tomatoes over the top and sprinkle with cheese.

Bake at 375°F for 30 minutes or until bubbling and the peppers are fork tender.

Jambalaya

This is a Cajun dish that lends it self well to a variety of meats, depending on what you have. This is especially good with shrimp if you have a crowd and are not planning on leftovers.

1 pound of meat (Chicken, shrimp, etc.)
1 pound andouille sausage
2 cups onions, diced
1 cup bell pepper, diced
1 cup celery, diced
3 cloves garlic, crushed
2-3 bay leaves
2 cups diced tomatoes, substitute 1 cup of hot tomatoes for a more spicy dish.
1 ½ cups rice
3 cups chicken stock
Olive oil
Salt and pepper
Spice mix
1 tablespoon paprika
1 tablespoon onion powder
2 teaspoons garlic powder
2 teaspoons black pepper
1 teaspoon dry mustard
1 teaspoon dried thyme
½ teaspoon ground cumin
½ teaspoon ground cayenne pepper

Whisk all the spice mixture ingredients together and divide into 1/3 and 2/3 amounts

If using a meat other than shrimp cut into small pieces 1-1 ½ inches

Add 2/3 of the spice mixture to the meat and toss to coat all surfaces. Reserve

In a small amount of olive oil, saute the vegetables and the sausage separately setting them aside.

If using a type of meat other than seafood, brown the meat Once the meat is browned on all sides, add the rice and remaining spice mixture and bay leaves.

Saute the rice and meat until the rice is toasted and spices are aromatic, about 5 minutes on medium heat be careful not to allow to burn.

Add the tomatoes and chicken stock. Deglaze the pan then add the rest of the ingredients.

Cook on low until rice is tender, adding water as necessary if the rice absorbs all the liquid. If using seafood, at it at this time. Folding into the rice and cook until the seafood is just cooked.

Serve as a main course or a side.

Lamb Keema

This is a recipe designed to reproduce the Keema Fries at the Red Lion Pub in Houston. This relies on the warm flavors of the Indian spice mixture Garam masala generally consisting of a combination of turmeric, black pepper, cloves, cinnamon, cumin, and black and green cardamom. Other similar spices may be included as the exact recipe varies by cook.

1 pound ground Lamb
1/2 pound ground Beef
1 teaspoon Cumin
1 teaspoon Coriander
1 teaspoon Salt
1 teaspoon fresh ground Pepper
1 teaspoon Turmeric
2 tablespoons Garam Masala

½ tablespoon Olive Oil
1 large Onion, chopped 1/4 inch
4-5 Jalapenos, chopped 1/4 inch
5 cloves Garlic, crushed
1 2 inch piece of Ginger chopped fine
½ cup Chicken stock

1/4 cup chopped Parsley
1 14 ounce can diced Tomatoes
1 14 ounce can crushed Tomatoes
1 6 ounce can Tomato Paste
Chicken Stock

1 ½ cups fresh or frozen peas

Sauté ground meat on medium high heat, until the meat begins to caramelize. Add spices and cook for a couple minutes.

Meanwhile, sauté the onions and Jalapenos in the olive oil until they begin to brown. Crush the ginger and garlic together and add to onions and continue to sauté for a minute. With the chicken stock, deglaze the onion mixture into the meat. Add the parsley and tomatoes and simmer for 30 minutes adding chicken stock as necessary to maintain enough liquid. Add peas and simmer for a couple minutes more.

May be served over fries or with naan or noodles.

223

Vindaloo

Alan- I adapted this recipe from one I found in a lovely cookbook titled *Curries Without Worries* (Sudha Koul, Cashmir, 1989)which is just as much fun to cook from as the title implies. Vindaloo is a delightful spicy, peppery curry which has a very well balanced taste--not just hot red pepper. In fact it can be made just as mild or hot as you like--I like it so you can taste the chili peppers, but not so my tongue is burnt!I will warn you that you should be very careful during the frying of the spices and meat stages which are done at medium high heat.The oil tends to spatter, which may cause burning and even more likely staining due to the bright orange-yellow color!The final dish is well worth the trouble.

2 and 1/2 pounds of boneless Pork cut in 1 to 2 inch cubes ("pork stew meat")
6 tablespoons White Cider Vinegar
2 large Yellow Onions
2 tablespoons chopped fresh Ginger
6 garlic Cloves
4 Ancho Peppers (dried chili peppers)
1 tablespoon whole Cumin Seeds
1 stick of Cinnamon
6 tablespoons of Corn or Peanut Oil
1 tablespoon ground Turmeric
1 teaspoon ground Black Pepper
3 Anaheim Peppers (fresh chili peppers)
1/2 teaspoon Salt
1 teaspoon Sugar
1/2 teaspoon ground Cloves
2 cups Water

Marinate the meat in 2 tablespoons of the vinegar for 4 hours in the refrigerator.Prepare the Anaheim peppers by removing the stem and the seeds, and roughly chopping them.Reserve the Anaheim peppers for later in the recipe.Slice the onions, chop the ginger and rough chop the garlic.Remove the stems and seeds from the Ancho peppers.Coarsely crush the cinnamon.Blend the onions, ginger, garlic, Ancho peppers, cinnamon and cumin with the remaining vinegar in a food processor to make a paste.If it seems too dry, add one or two tablespoons of water. Heat the oil in a large saucepan on medium high heat.Add the paste and fry briskly (!) for a couple of minutes.Add the turmeric, black pepper, pork, and the marinade.Fry for 10 more minutes, stirring constantly to prevent burning.Add the Anaheim medium, and simmer for about 45 minutes, or until the sauce thickens and the meat is well cooked.Serve hot on freshly cooked rice.(Our favorite rice for curry is Basmati rice.) Note: you can substitute other chili peppers for the ones specified.However, if you use Jalapenos or other very hot peppers, the dish will be much hotter. As given in the recipe above, it has a very definite hotness, but ones tongue and lips recover fairly rapidly!

Sandy's Swedish Meatballs

Alan- This recipe, which is one of my all-time favorites, was created by Sandy as an attempt to duplicate the dish which her mother and her paternal aunts made, a traditional Swedish dish. Sandy read several Swedish cookbooks, but finally made her own choices. There are really two variations of Swedish meatballs: an appetizer and a dinner entree'. The ingredients and cooking directions are the same for the meatballs in each case, but Sandy makes the meatballs smaller if they are to be appetizers, and omits the gravy. I like them best as a dinner entree'--one a cold night after a long day out hiking, or just after a frustrating day shopping--the Swedish meatballs make a person feel human again. Of course the quality of the meat is important, and extra lean make little or no fat during cooking, which is best particularly for those of us who don't need any extra calories, but the critical ingredient is the black pepper. It should be freshly ground, and if you like black pepper, you might wish to use twice as much as the minimum given below.

1 tablespoon Butter (you may substitute olive oil)
1 medium-large Onion
1 large Egg
½ cup Rolled Oats, or 3/4 cup homemade Bread Crumbs
At least 1½ teaspoon freshly ground Black Pepper
1 teaspoon Salt
2 pounds of lean Ground Meat. (Beef or a mixture of Beef, Pork, and Veal sold as meatloaf mix.)
For the gravy: 1-2 tablespoons Flour and 1 cup Milk

Finely chop the onion and sauté' in a skillet on top of the stove. Do not brown, just cook until transparent. While the onion is frying, mix the egg, bread crumbs, pepper, salt, and meat together using your hands.

Remove the onion from the stove, allow to cool until it will not burn you, and mix it also into the meat mixture.

Form the meat into balls, again with your impeccably clean hands. If this is for dinner, make the meatballs about 1 1/2 inches in diameter, if it's for an appetizer, make them about 1 inch in diameter.Actually the size isn't critical for taste, but smaller balls are more convenient for people to eat while standing around, and larger balls are a little faster to make and a little easier to cook.

Sauté' the meatballs in the same skillet you used for the onions until they are nicely browned on most sides.This is important for taste.

At this point you can finish the cooking in the skillet or put them in an oven safe dish and bake them until done.

They should be well-done, not rare.If the dish is for dinner, Sandy makes gravy to go with it, and serves the meatballs over baked or boiled potatoes. (no other sauce on the potatoes, but most people will probably want to put a little salt on them.) She makes a simple milk gravy.

You can remove the meatballs from the skillet if you wish before making the gravy, but it is not necessary. If you used a grade of meat with a high fat content, you should pour off most of the fat from the skillet before beginning.

Leave no more than i tablespoon. If you used extra lean, there will be little or no visible fat.

Add 1 or 2 tablespoons of flour to the skillet and stir it around with the bits of meat and any fat until the flour is cooked and slightly colored (longer is better, but can be tricky because the flour will burn easily as it gets brown).

Add the milk and mix thoroughly. If you are finishing the cooking on top of the stove, add the meatballs back into the skillet (if you took them out) and allow to simmer gently for 30 minutes or so.

If you are going to bake the dish, add the gravy to the meatballs in the oven safe dish, cover, and bake at 300°F for at least 45 minutes. The advantage of the oven is you do not have to watch it carefully.

You will be surprised at how much of this dish that 4 hungry hikers will eat!!

Best Italian American Meatballs

1 pound ground beef
1 pound ground pork
1 pound ground chicken or turkey
1/2 cup homemade chicken stock
3 ounces fresh white bread, cut into 1/2-inch cubes (about 2 unpacked cups)
1/2 cup buttermilk, plus more as needed
1 medium yellow onion, minced
2 strips bacon, finely minced
2 ounces (55g) Parmigiano-Reggiano, grated, plus more for serving
8 medium cloves garlic, crushed
1/2 cup loosely packed fresh parsley leaves, minced
4 large egg yolks
1 teaspoon dried oregano
1 teaspoon ground fennel seed
½ tablespoon salt
Freshly ground black pepper
½ cup panko bread crumbs (if necessary)

In the bowl of a stand mixer, combine bread with buttermilk & chicken stock, tossing to coat. Let stand, tossing occasionally, until bread is completely moist, about 10 minutes. Squeeze bread between your fingers or mash with a spoon to make sure there are no dry spots; if there are dry spots that refuse to moisten, add more buttermilk, 1 tablespoon at a time, until bread is moist throughout.

Add onion, bacon, Parmigiano-Reggiano, garlic, parsley, egg yolks, oregano, fennel, salt, and pepper to bread/buttermilk mixture

Starting at low speed and gradually increasing to medium-high speed, beat bread mixture until thoroughly blended, stopping to scrape down sides as necessary. Add 1/3 each of the chicken, beef and pork and beat at medium-high speed until thoroughly blended with bread mixture.

Remove bowl from stand mixer and add remaining beef and pork. Gently fold meatball mixture, separating the ground meat just until the ground meat is thoroughly mixed in and no pockets of unincorporated meat remain; avoid mixing any more than is necessary for even distribution.

At this point make a test meatball and if the mixture is too wet and loose to keep that ball shape, stir the panko in and give it a couple minutes to absorb some of the liquid.

Form meatballs into walnut sized balls and arrange on a parchment or foil lined sheet pan. Bake in oven at 400 degrees for 20 minutes and then broil on both sides or until well browned.

These meatballs freeze well so they are a great make ahead option.

Greek Style Meatballs

I came up with this recipe for a potluck supper

1 pound ground Turkey
1 pound ground Lamb
1 pound ground Beef Chuck
1 cup Breadcrumbs
2 eggs

2 tablespoons Fresh Rosemary, chopped fine
3 tablespoons Fresh mint, chopped fine
1 tablespoons dried Oregano
1 teaspoon ground Coriander
2 teaspoon ground Cumin
1 tablespoons ground Black pepper
1 teaspoon Szechwan Peppercorns
1 tablespoons Salt
2 tablespoons dried Parsley
1 tablespoons Garlic Powder

1 medium/large Onion chopped
4 Jalapeno Peppers seeded and chopped

Sauté the onion and jalapeno peppers in a little bit of olive oil until light brown and soft. Allow to cool somewhat

Preheat the oven to 375°F

Combine all ingredients in a large bowl and mix gently until uniformly combined.

Make small (1-1.5 inch) balls and place in a parchment lined sheet pan.

Bake until browned (~20 minutes) turn and bake for another 20 minutes until browned on the second side.

Serve with tomato sauce as a main, or with toothpicks as an appetizer. When used as an appetizer tzatziki sauce is a good accompaniment.

Cabbage Rolls

This recipe was inspired by some leftover Hong Kong duck we brought home from a Chinese restaurant. You probably could use just about any leftover meat, although a relatively robust tasting variety would be preferred, for example Duck, smoked turkey, lamb, brisket, etc.

We started with ~1 lbs. of crispy duck w/ bones, ½ lb. rotisserie chicken, off the bone, 3 cups leftover brown rice. I made some duck stock after removing the meat while reserving the bones and skin from the duck and simmering the bones in 3 cups of water with 2 bay leaves and ½ cup fresh parsley. Simmered for about an hour and then strained and the solids discarded.

    6-8 large Cabbage Leaves, carefully separated from the head
    4-5 medium Cabbage leaves
    1 lb. of cooked Meat, chopped
    3 cup chicken or Duck Stock
    3 cups cooked Brown Rice
    1 medium Onion, diced
    2 medium (14 ounce) cans diced Tomatoes
    6-8 medium Mushrooms, 2 dices, the rest thinly sliced

    Nutmeg
    Salt
    Fresh ground Black Pepper

Steam Cabbage leaves until soft

Drain the juice from one can of dice tomatoes, reserving the tomato solids.

Sauté onions in a small amount of olive oil until they start to brown. Reserve 1/3 of the onions. To the remaining onions add the sliced mushrooms and continue to cook. Once the mushrooms are soft, add the rest of the stock, the tomato juice and the second can of dice tomatoes. Season with ½ tsp salt and ½ tsp black pepper. Cook until reduced by at least half and somewhat thickened.

Combine meat, brown rice, diced mushrooms, season with ½ tsp salt and ½ tsp pepper, add ½ cup stock, reserved onions, and tomato solids. Stir meat/rice mixture until thoroughly combined.

Line the bottom of a 9 by 12 casserole dish with the medium cabbage leaves.

Roll about ½ to ¾ cup of the meat/rice mixture into each large cabbage leaf and place seam down into the casserole, packing them together. After rolling all the leaves, sprinkle with salt and pepper and grate a little nutmeg.

Pour the tomato sauce over the top. Cover with tin foil or lid and bake in a 350°F oven for 90 minutes. Remove the lid, sprinkle with grated cheese and broil for a few minutes until the cheese is bubbly and almost browning.

Remove from the oven and allow to rest for 20-30 minutes.

Eggplant Parmesan

This is a rather healthier, somewhat simplified version which we prefer. I generally just use my standard marinara (page 212), which we usually have in the freezer, for the sauce .

1 large Eggplant
Salt
2 Chicken breasts (optional)
Olive Oil (Extra Virgin not needed)

Coating
1 cup Panko Breadcrumbs
½ cup Corn Flour
½ tsp Black Pepper
1 tsp Salt
1 tsp Garlic powder
3 Eggs
½ cup Milk

Sauce
2 medium (14 ounce) cans diced Tomatoes
1 small (~6 ounce) can Tomato Paste
½ tablespoon. Oregano
1 tablespoon Basil
2 tablespoons fresh Parsley, chopped
1 tablespoon Olive Oil
1 medium Onion, chopped medium/fine
4 cloves Garlic, minced
½ Bell Pepper, chopped fine

Peel and slice the eggplant into ¼ inch thick slices.\

Layer in a sheet pan on top of paper towels, sprinkling each side of the eggplant slices with salt, top with additional paper towel and put another sheet pan on top with something to weight it down.

Allow to sit and drain for at least 1 hour.

Meanwhile prepare sauce by sautéing onion, garlic, and bell pepper in a tablespoon of olive oil until onion begins to brown.

Add the rest of the sauce ingredients and simmer for at least 30 minutes.

Rinse eggplant with cold water to remove salt and pat dry with paper towels.

If you are including chicken, cut each breast into two pieces and gently pound flat between parchment until ¼ inch thick.

In a wide shallow dish mix breadcrumbs, corn flour, black pepper, salt and garlic powder to create dry mixture. In a separate shallow bowl whisk eggs and milk together.

Well coat eggplant (and chicken) with egg mixture and dredge in the dry mixture until well coated, set on a wire rack to rest.

Put another wire rack in a 300°F oven.

Add oil to a deep dish frying pan to a ¼ inch depth. Heat over medium high heat until breadcrumbs dropped in create bubbles.

Cook the eggplant (and chicken) in batches until well browned on both side and drain on the wire rack in the oven.

If desired, place a slice of cheese on top of the eggplant (and chicken) to melt in the oven.

Serve immediately with the tomato sauce and Parmesan cheese.

Zucchini Lasagna

I don't often make this because of the amount of work it is to put together. The result is quite good and the most important element is to get rid of all the liquid you can from the fresh ingredients (zucchini, mushrooms, spinach) as the dryer it starts out the better it will be.

Layers:
Zucchini, 4 medium or about 3 pounds, sliced 1/8 inch thick
Tomato sauce
Cheese (½ pounds mozzarella, grated)
Béchamel sauce
Optional
1 pound Spinach
2 pounds Mushrooms, sliced thin
1 pound Italian Sausage
Poblano Peppers, roasted and sliced

Tomato Sauce
1 large Onion chopped
4-6 Garlic cloves crushed
1 large (28 ounce) can crushed Tomatoes
½ teaspoon Thyme
½ teaspoon Oregano
1 Bay Leaf
Salt and fresh ground Black Pepper to taste

Béchamel Sauce
3 Tb Butter
¼ cup Flour
1 cup Milk
2 large Eggs
1¾ cup Ricotta, low fat is ok
½ cup Parmesan
½ teaspoon fresh grated Nutmeg
Salt and fresh ground Black Pepper to taste

½ cup Parmesan

Layer the zucchini between paper towels putting a liberal amount of salt on each layer. If possible put a medium weight on top.

Allow to sit for two hours, change the paper towels which will now be soaked, flipping the slices

and adding more salt. When you are ready to use the zucchini, make sure to rinse them thoroughly in cold water to remove the salt and then drain.

An alternative method to remove water from the zucchini is to freeze it first. This is also a good way to save extra zucchini in the summer is to pre-slice and freeze. Then thaw and drain.

While the zucchini drains, make the sauce. Sauté the onions in a small amount of olive oil until golden. Add the garlic, tomato, thyme, and bay leaf.

Simmer for 30 minutes. Season with salt and fresh ground black pepper to taste.

Optional Ingredients

If you are using mushrooms and/or spinach it is a good idea to sauté these until you remove excess liquid. Brown the Italian sausage and drain on a paper towel.

Melt the butter, add flour cook to a medium roux. Remove from heat and add milk slowly whisking constantly.

Bring to a simmer and cook two minutes. Remove from heat and allow to cool somewhat. Add the eggs beating well between each. Stir in the cheeses. Add nutmeg, salt and pepper to taste.

Layer the ingredients in at least thirds, starting with the béchamel filling and topping with Parmesan.

You can mix and match layers with some of the optional ingredients, but it is important that each layer group contain zucchini, tomato sauce, béchamel and cheese.

Bake at 375°F for 2 hours or until bubbling in the middle. Allow to cool at least 30 minutes before serving.

BBQ, Smoking, and Grilling

Introduction to BBQ

As a child growing up in the Chicago area, any outdoor cooking over fire was BBQ. After I moved to Texas, my BBQ horizons expanded and I discovered that what we had been doing was grilling and there is complete other side of BBQ which is smoking. BBQ /grilling used to be more of a regional thing. In the Midwest it was grilling, think burgers, brats and steaks, Texas has brisket and sausage, Kansas City and Memphis are about ribs, but not the same. The Carolinas is all pulled pork and whole hog BBQ. In many regions many people think of BBQ as meat with a sweet tomato-based sauce. More useful terms for outdoor cooking are smoking and grilling.

Smoking is what traditionally in the south is called BBQ. The term refers to the coking or preservation of meat by using smoke a relatively low temperature over a long period of time.

There are two types of smoking, cold and hot

Cold smoking is the preservation of meat/fish by infusing it with smoke, think bacon, ham, smoked salmon, etc.

Hot smoking is the use of smoke at a temperature between 150 and 300°F to cook meat, think brisket, pulled pork, smoked sausage, etc. This is the type of smoking we will address here.

Smoking can produce the most flavorful meat when done at lower temperatures (200°F to 300°F) for long (5-18 hours) times, using oak or hickory wood. Traditionally real Texas BBQ is smoked beef brisket, but many other meats can be smoked.

Grilling is what happens at higher temperatures and is the most common method of cooking meat outdoors in the US, and can be done two basic ways:

Direct grilling, where the cooking is done directly over the heat source. This is commonly for things like burgers, steak, sausage, etc

Indirect grilling, where the food is not directly over the heat source. Things that need to cook a bit slower, like spareribs use this technique

Alan- In most cases, sauce should not be used during grilling, or only at the very end, because it will burn. If the meat is to be basted, a non-tomato, non-sugary liquid such as wine, wine vinegar, or lemon juice—with appropriate seasonings—should be used. If the meat is marinated, the marinade is an excellent basting choice. If sauce is to be served with the meat, personal preference will indicate its composition. \

Well smoked or grilled meat usually does not need sauce, but a good complimentary sauce is sometimes desired, and often expected. Many, but not all, sauces are tomato-based. Mustard sauces, without tomato, are popular in the American Southeast, and there are even other sauces to be considered. We enjoy cranberry chutney with smoked pork! But we do use a traditional tomato sauce (peppery and not too sweet) with BBQ ribs.

Smoking

In this section we will stick to the hot smoking techniques. The best smoker is one with a separate firebox and smoking chamber, each with a controlled air flow. A common example is the New Braunfels Smoker, but many other smokers are available. A thermometer to measure air temperature in the smoking chamber is essential, and a way to humidify the air is desirable. The typical smoker has a pan of water that the smoke passes over before contacting the meat. Hickory, Pecan or oak wood are the most common types of wood used, however fruit-woods like apple and cherry are not uncommon.

A typical smoking process includes

Starting the fire- 15 minutes- Kicking off the fire in the fire box can be done in many ways: like a campfire with kindling and paper, skip the paper and use a torch to start the kindling, use a charcoal and a chimney or electric starter like getting a grill going. The use of accelerants such as lighter fluid are strongly discouraged, the lingering odor and taste of the fluid often can last longer than you think and contaminate the food.

Transition to pure hardwood- 30 minutes- Once the initial fire is going well, start adding only hard wood and begin to pace your additions to bring the fire into a steady more manageable state. Many people believe that the wood should be de-barked to provide the cleanest smoke. Begin adjusting the intake and outflow vents to provide the desired temperature, this will vary according to what you are smoking but 250°F is common. Ideally this should be controlled by the intake adjustment as much as possible.

Steady state- 1-16 hours- by this time you should have settled down to a regular addition of fuel, in most smoker, this should be no shorter than an hour between additions. All your cooking should be done in this stage. A remote thermometer is highly recommended here to monitor the internal temperature of your food.

Shutting down- 1 hour- Generally a smoker is shut down similar to most charcoal grills, that is by shutting off the supply of oxygen to the fire. Usually smokers have both a adjustable intake and and adjustable outflow, shot these both as tightly as possibly and the fire should extinguish relatively quickly.

Clean up- 15 minutes- Don't forget, it is a lot easier to get your smoker ready for next time now than wait and have to deal with everything later. Always clean up any water bath, probably contaminated with grease and drippings. Always give the grates a good brushing to remove any debris. Also clean the fire box of as much ash as possible, making sure that the fire is out and cold. Leaving ash in the firebox can result in early corrosion and rust-out.

Real Texas BBQ

When Texans use the term BBQ they mean beef brisket and they mean low temperatures and long cooking times. I have been able after extensive testing to come up with a technique which I like for making BBQ.

  12-15 pound whole packer cut brisket
  ~10-15 pieces BBQ Wood, (I have done an entire smoke using gathered pecan branches)
  ~5-10 pounds Hardwood Lump Charcoal

The first step is choosing the meat, selecting a brisket can be intimidating as for BBQ you want a whole (packer cut) brisket weighing in around 12 to 15 lb. of meat. You should always get one still sealed in the original vacuum sealed package from the meat packer.

A brisket is made of two parts, the flat and the point. The flat is the longer thinner section with more lean meat and the point is the end that is thicket and ends in well, a point. You want to look for a brisket with the largest flat to point ratio and a nice wide strip of lean muscle in the flat. Also you want the brisket to be floppy when lifted from the center. More flexibility indicates a brisket which already has a more tender muscle.

The next step will freak some people out, but I have been doing it for some time now and I believe that there is reasonable science and safety behind it. Remove the brisket from the vacuum package and rub with a liberal mixture of salt garlic powder, paprika, black pepper and cayenne. Put the brisket in a large sealed container and …here it comes …leave it out on the counter overnight.

Early the next morning, start up your smoker.

The Smoker. There are many kinds of smokers on the market. I do not have any experience with the pellet burning or electric type, but they seem more suited to cold smoking. For hot smoking like brisket, a wood burning smoker with a separate firebox is the trick. My experience does not show significant difference for brisket between vertical and horizontal smoke chambers.

The Wood. I will use Pecan wood when I can, but have used oak, hickory, and mesquite with good results. I will also use some good quality hardwood lump charcoal as in my opinion with a relatively small fire box, it helps stabilize the fire. But make sure there is some real wood on the fire at all times to keep the smoke coming.

Put a water pan in the bottom to help keep the environment moist and add thermal mass. Bring the temp to between 225 and 275°F

 Cook the brisket turning every couple hours and cook at least 9 hours and the internal temp reaches 175-180°F. It will hit a temperature plateau at about 165 and may stick there or hours while the collagen renders out. You will be rewarded for your patience, the time is important, If you stop while still in the stall, your brisket will be tough as nails.

Remove the brisket and allow to rest for 30 min to an hour.

Separate the point from the flat by identifying where the grain of the meat changes direction and slide a sharp carving knife between the two.

The Kansas City school of Q says put the point back in the smoker for another 6 hrs. If I have the time I will do this. I usually chop the point and freeze one pound portions for use in making my brisket chili.

Slice the flat across the grain and serve with a good BBQ sauce, sliced onions, and dill pickles. Traditionally in Texas BBQ is served with a couple slices of soft while bread, I usually skip this. If anything, I like some good whole grain bread.

I don't do briskets as often, first because it results in too much meat for anything less than a crowd. Also, outside of Texas, brisket is harder to find and/or more expensive. Supermarkets in the north rarely have whole briskets; some butchers may order them for you.

Pulled Pork

I do not make this very often because it make a huge amount and you need a crowd or your freezer if full of pork for awhile.

1 pork butt (shoulder) about 6-8 lb
Yellow mustard
Rub
¼ cup Salt
¼ cup pepper
1 Tb paprika
1 Tb Onion powder
1 Tb Garlic powder
Mop
Apple cider vinegar
Carolina BBQ sauce

Trim off any fat or bits that are hanging off

Rub mustard over the whole surface of the butt

Sprinkle rub mixture all over and pat in until you have a god coating all over

Smoke at about 275

Spritz with apple cider vinegar or apple juice every hour or so

When the fat cap begins to split it time to wrap,

Give the butt one last spritz and wrap tightly in aluminum foil

Return to smoker

After a total of eight hours, peel back the foil enough to give the bone a twist. If it pulls free of the meat easily, it is done. Otherwise re-wrap and continue checking every hour

Rest in foil for 30-40 minutes so that it will retain moisture

Once rested, put the butt on a large tray or pan and shred using a for and tongs

The meat should be moist and easily shred into small pieces

If desired, add about ½ cup of Carolina BBQ sauce () and mix into the shredded meat,

Serve with Cole Slaw (or)and buns and extra sauce

Carolina Barbecue Sauce

Also known as Carolina Gold, this mustard based sauce is quite a bit different from most other tomato based sauces.

    ¾ cup yellow mustard
    ½ cup honey
    ¼ cup brown sugar
    ½ cup apple cider vinegar
    2 tablespoons ketchup
    2 teaspoons Worcestershire sauce
    1 teaspoon garlic powder
    Pinch or more of cayenne
    ½ teaspoon salt
    Dash of hot sauce

Whisk all of the ingredients together in a large bowl.

Add to a small pot and simmer for 10 minutes. Cool.

Pour into a jar and cover. Refrigerate at least one day to let the flavors mingle.

All Purpose Barbecue Sauce

I found this recipe for barbecue sauce and it is fine, honestly, I would not bother to make something when I can get Sweet Baby Rays at the store.

    1¼ cups ketchup
    1 cup dark brown sugar
    ¼ cup molasses
    ¼ cup apple cider vinegar
    ¼ cup water
    1 tablespoon Worcestershire sauce
    3 teaspoons ground mustard
    2 teaspoons smoked paprika
    ¾ teaspoon garlic powder
    ½ teaspoon cayenne pepper
    1½ teaspoons   salt
    1 teaspoon black pepper

Combine all ingredients

Bring to a boil, stirring occasionally and cook for about 5 minutes.

If you want a thicker barbecue sauce, add 1 tablespoon corn starch mixed with 2 tablespoons cold water and stir and cook until the sauce starts to thicken.

Smoke Roasted Prime Rib

I have only done this a couple of times, but it came out great. The recipe lends it self well to the reverse sear method (page 154) of cooking a rib roast.

6-8 lb Standing Rib Roast - prime or choice
salt
Black pepper
Oil or mustard

If possible a day or two before cooking, rub the roast with oil or mustard, your choice.

Sprinkle generous amounts of salt and ground pepper all over and pat to make a crust

Set up your smoker to cook at 200 to 225 for reverse sear and 350-375 for a traditional roast

Smoke the roast until target temperature is reached, if you are using the traditional method, it will be much quicker as you would expect.

Remove from the smoker

Rest the roast for 30 minutes, if you are doing the reverse sear method you can rest longer if needed.

For the reverse sear method you now sear the roast under a broiler for 5-10 minutes

Carve and serve

Grilling

There are a lot of different ways and tools to grill, most can produce great results when used appropriately, some of the more common include

Charcoal grills- The most common type of grill is the covered kettle grill (think Weber) with adjustable draft holes in the cover and in the base. Ashes can be removed through the draft holes in the base.(It's a standard Weber kettle, but there are similar competitive grills available.)There are two grates inside, a smaller lower one which holds the charcoal, and a larger upper one where the food is held. A Charcoal grill is preferred for steaks and other foods where more smokey flavor is desired and often can reach higher temperatures than gas for searing.

Anyhow, now you are ready to cook something. We grill in several ways:

a.) plain direct grilling with no marinade or sauce. This is used for hamburgers, sausage (Polish, Italian, bratwurst, etc.), sirloin steak, fish, and pork chops. We have also done zucchini this way.

b.) Plain direct grilling with basting, usually used for various chicken dishes and meats that require marinating before grilling and basting with the marinade during grilling. Some chicken, chuck steaks, and round steak are done this way.

c.) marinating before grilling, basting with the marinade during grilling, and then basting with a separate sauce at the very end of the grilling. The last sauce has tomato and sugar in it, and would burn if used except at the end. We do pork steaks this way. Pork ribs are also done this way, except they are cooked slower, and thus must be done over an indirect fire. This variation is described in the pork ribs recipe.

Alan- I cook over a charcoal fire. We usually call this barbecuing, but it's really grilling. Mostly, I cook directly over the charcoal and do not apply a barbecue sauce. I always use a kettle and cook with the lid on. Sometimes we marinate the meat before cooking it, and then I may use the leftover marinade to baste the meat with.

Here is a typical description of starting a charcoal fire. Open the draft holes on the cover all the way. Remove the cover. Clean the upper grate so it is ready for food. Remove the upper grate. Stir the old charcoal around the lower grate until most of the ash has fallen through the grate. Open the lower draft holes all of the way, and remove the ash.

Fuels- Possible fuel options include charcoal briquettes, hardwood lump, raw wood

The fuel you choose to use has an impact on flavor, expense and effort.\

Charcoal briquettes are probably the most common and they are what I use. After experimenting with various fuels, I have come to the conclusion that good quality (e.g. Kingsforsd) briquettes work about as good as anything and are easier to handle and less expensive. I will add a small piece of hardwood if I am looking for extra smoky flavor.

Hardwood lump charcoal works very well, gives great flavor and may be preferred for application where you need as hot of a fire as possible. Something like fajita's might benefit, some people even cook them direct on the hardwood coals, not something I would recommend with briquettes

244

Plain wood is probably the least common fuel outside of camping trips. T takes more work and more time to build a bed of coals and is more unpredictable.

Starting options for lighting a charcoal fire include Chimney, Electric and Lighter fluid

Chimney- A charcoal chimney typically is a cylinder about 8 inches across and 16 inches tall, with with a grate 4-5" above the inside bottom and a handle on the side. More expensive models have a trigger on the outside to release the grate, and allow the charcoal to fall down. The top of the cylinder is filled with charcoal, and wadded paper is stuffed under the grate. The cylinder is set on the lower grate in the kettle, and paper is lit. Typically the chimney will hold enough for n average grilling session. Because of the chimney effect, it will light fairly quickly, usually in about 20 minutes. The advantage of the chimney is that nearly all the coals are fully lit when you dump it and so you can begin grilling immediately.

Electric starter- Typically an exposed oval heating element with a handle and cord. I put the oval element over about one layer of used charcoal, and then mound the rest of the charcoal, including enough new to make the right sized mound, over it. The cord is plugged into a regular outlet if you are attached to an extension cord, which is plugged into a regular outlet if you are lucky enough to have a convenient outdoor outlet, or use an extension cord. Generally an electric starter takes about 10 minutes to get the charcoal lit, and then must be removed before the fire gets too hot, follow the instructions which came with it. I have accidentally left it on nearly 20 minutes without ruining it, although it may be shortening its life.I usually get it out in 11 minutes. The mound will tumble when the starter is removed, so I rebuild it with a pair of charcoal tongs.It takes about 35 minutes from the time the starter is plugged in until all of the charcoal is evenly lit and gray.Even when I am in a hurry, I wait for this stage since it makes a much better grilling fire.

Lighter Fluid- Not recommended except as a lat resort, you need to be careful to use as little as possible and let the fire burn a bit longer before cooking to insure the chemical residue is all burned off. Starting with a mound of used and new charcoal, I would pour on just enough starter to wet the center of the mound. Wait one minute for the liquid to be absorbed into the charcoal, and then light it with a match. Generally takes about the same lighting time as the electric starter method.

Cooking- Once your coals are fully lit, spread the lit charcoal evenly over the lower grate, and place the upper grate back in position.I wait 3 to 5 minutes for the upper grate to get hot. It is a good practice to give the grate a quick brushing at this point and then let heat for a couple more minutes before putting the food on it.

It is generally best to cook with the lid on. It's much easier to grill on a kettle because you don't get the flames and burning of the food that usually happened when I tried to grill directly over charcoal without a closed grill.In the recipes, Taking the lid off or putting it back on is not generally stated in the recipes, assume that once the food is on the grill, the lid is always on unless you are turning the food or basting it.

When done cooking, remove the food and close both the upper and lower vents.The fire dies down very rapidly, and the leftover charcoal can be used next time.

You may need to adjust the amount of charcoal or even add charcoal during the cook as unusual recipes require.

Gas Grills- Propane gas grill come in all shapes and sizes, one of the better ones is a Fuego

Element, which looks very much like a charcoal kettle grill. Gas grills have the advantage of producing little waste, there is no ash, they light at the push of a button and heat up rapidly. Also they turn off instantly and cool down rapidly. Gas grilling is preferred for applications that don't depend on smoky flavor as much like chicken wings, stuffed pork chops, fish, etc. Gas is also a quick and easy way to grill on a work day where there is an advantage to speed and low clean up. For starting, temperature adjustment and shut down follow your grill's instructions.

Grilling accessories- There are a number of grilling accessories which can be very useful

Cleaning brushes- What type of brush to use is up to you, I use a wire bristle brush, however some like to use alternatives. What is not optional is cleaning the cooking grate before you begin.

Long tongs- Tongs and in particular, long tongs are essential to be able to manipulate the food you are grilling without burning yourself.

Baskets- For small or delicate things like shrimp, fish or vegetables as basket can greatly simplify the operation of turning the food on the grill and will prevent sticking to the grill itself.

Griddles- For some application you may want to cook something outside but not on a grate. A griddle will let you do things like smash burgers and onion burgers

Anyhow, now you are ready to Grill!

Steak

My dad an I both love steak, however we have different favorites and different techniques. I would say my dad's approach is the more traditional method and mine is more specialize to produce a specific outcome. Ridley and I like our steak very rare, so this may not be suitable for everyone.

Most steak needs no seasoning other than salt and pepper and the salt and pepper crust contrast nicely with the juicy rare center. The dog loves getting the bone, but only gets a turn after I have gnawed on it a bit.

n my opinion most steaks will benefit from some pre-seasoning. I usually try to salt them on both side with coarse salt the day before grilling ans let them rest in the fridge. Fillets can forgo this treatment and be salted immediately before cooking.

One of the trickiest parts of cooking a steak is how to judge if it is done and how to target the desired final doneness. I use the steakhouse scale of doneness where there are essentially four level definitions: Rare is a cool red center; Medium rare is a warm red center; Medium is some pink left in the center;Well Done is no pink at all and in my opinion is a waste of steak.

There are a variety o good choices when it comes to steaks

Chuck Steaks are not generally thought of as grill worthy cuts, however if you marinate them and sear them fast, they can be a tasty meal.

Skirt and flank steaks are not really a steaks in the classically meaning, see fajitas () for a good recipe for these.

Sirloin Steaks are the flavor kings. They have the most beefy flavor, but are not as tender as some other cuts. They do grill very well and make a great choice for those liking medium rare.

Alan- I use the direct grilling method without any marinade or sauce. This is one of our favorite grilled meats. I think that sirloin has the best flavor of any steaks done without marinating, but buying a good sirloin steak in Chicago is difficult. For example, we definitely like it better than T-bone or porterhouse steak, and much better than filet mignon--which although the tenderest of meats, has much less taste. Of course if you don't care for the taste of grilled aged beef, --but I can't imagine such a thing! If you can find an independent meat market with a real butcher, you may find a good bone-in sirloin. But the supermarkets, even those with "butchers" only sell boneless. Whatever steak you can find, get it cut at least 2 inches thick. Typically, a 2 inch boneless sirloin will take about 15 minutes (7 minutes on the first side, then turned) to produce a 125°F center temperature. Be sure to use a meat thermometer to avoid overcooking. A 125°F center temperature on the grill should produce a rare center, medium rare outside after resting with a plastic wrap cover. Reasonable alternatives to sirloin are bone-in T-bone and porterhouse steaks. One other thing--early in my learning how to grill before I had a kettle,sometimes over seared the steak (BURNED the first side!), and if you do this you can put a pat or two of butter on the seared side to soften the meat.Otherwise, I never put anything on a steak on the grill or at the table.Why ruin good sirloin?Don't worry about burning the steak if you use a kettle, it's hard to burn! Keep your menu simple when having sirloin.The sirloin should be the star, and you have certainly paid enough for it.A baked potato, a cooked veggie such as broccoli or beans, and a nice salad are perfect. If you want absolute luxury, you can put some Maytag blue cheese in your simple tossed salad and some fresh parsley on your baked potato.

Strip steak, sometimes referred to as a New York strip is a good choice, a bit more tender than the sirloin, but still packing good flavor.

Rib-eye steaks both boneless and bone in are more tender and the most marbled of the common steak cuts. This yields tender meat and when cooked properly the rendered fat brings the flavor . This is a steak that can forgive a little over cooking so a good choice medium lovers.

For best results, you want to choose a steak that is well marbled, choice or prime and is reasonable thick, about 2 inches. The choice of bone in or not often comes down to availability, I find bone-in produces a better result, but not enough to pay for the extra bone in a cowboy cut unless you are grilling for a special occasion.

The first step is removing the steak from the fridge a couple of hours before cooking, at room temp the meat will cook much better as the center will rise in temp fast enough to begin cooking before the outside is burnt. If you did not salt it yet, do so now.

Make sure your grill is as hot as you can get it, to insure a good seared crust. Place the steak directly on the hottest spot on the grill and depending on thickness, seared for 5-7 minutes and then turned and seared for an additional 7-10 minutes. With the thinnest steaks we have tried (~1½ inches thick) the time is more like 2 minutes per side. When the steak is turned if there is a heavy crust, I like to put a pat or two of butter to soften the crust as my father notes above. After cooking the steak is left to rest for 5 minutes.

T-Bone Steaks & Porterhouse are basically two variations on the same cut These steaks consist of two sides, one is filet and the other is strip, the only difference between the T-bone and porterhouse is that the Porterhouse has a larger filet section and so commands a premium price. As you would expect they can give you a two types of steak in one is you have guest who have different preferences. It does take some care to cook them properly since the filet side will cook more rapidly than the strip side. I generally use the same technique as the rib-eye.

Filet Mignon is the priciest, most tender and lean steak. Prized for it's tenderness, because of the lean character, it must be cooked more rare to avoid drying the steak out. If you don't like steak on the rare end of the spectrum, you probably want to choose something else.

Being as lean as they are, I typically just sear a filet on both sides really well until the center breaks 100°F and then pull the steak off and let it rest. This results in true steakhouse rare steak.

Hamburgers

*Alan and John- U*se the direct grilling method, and no marinade or sauce on the grill.

The key factors in grilling hamburgers are to buy good meat, to cook the hamburgers just done, and to use no sauce on the grill. If you have a local butcher purchase ground round, which is 5% fat from your local butcher. Most supermarkets carry a decent burger blend. Two pounds of ground beef will make 8 hamburgers.Sometimes I do use frozen, but fresh never frozen is best--it holds its juice better and makes a moister hamburger.

Sandy has found that salting the ground round and then mixing it with a little cold water makes a better hamburger, Jim Beard used cracked ice.

Form the hamburger into patties, sort of flattened balls, but still not very flat. If you want your burger more flat, flatten the balls and use your thumb to dimple each patty in the center, this will compensate for the swelling during cooking.

I cook them for about 3 minutes on the first side, then 5 minutes on the second side.Its best to only turn them once--they have a tendency to fall apart.

Also, the first side may stick to the grill. This can be minimized if you clean the cooking grate well and oil it slightly before heating it.

Since cooking times may vary, until you are familiar with your grill and how fast it cooks, you should look a hamburger to be sure it's not burning after maybe 2 minutes. It should be very brown and crusty looking, almost black in places.

The second side should also get quite brown. We like our hamburgers cooked to between medium rare and medium well done--just a little pink in the center, but retaining all of the juice.

Hamburgers cooked this way have an excellent smoky taste and do not require any sauce. However, those who want something, I suggest Sandy's homemade chili sauce () and/or a garlic dill pickle or some artichoke pickle ().

Smash burgers

These are best done on an outdoor griddle due to the amount of smoke produced, if you have a really good hood over your stove in the kitchen may be an option, not for me. They are going to be well done by their nature, so if you want a medium rare burger stick to the normal technique.

Start with a burger as above and form into smallish balls.

Heat your flattop to sizzling hot, just at the smoke point. Place the burgers on the griddle and using a stout spatula with addition pressure from above flatten the burgers as thin as you can.

Cook for maybe a minute until a good crust has formed, they should almost be cooked through.

Flip, add American cheese to the top and cook maybe 30 seconds.

Assemble and eat immediately for best results.

Onion burger variation

Before cooking the burger, put a small pile of very thinly sliced onion on the flattop and allow to cook somewhat, before the onion is fully softened put the burger patty on and smash into the onion really well. Continue as above.

Sausage

Alan- Use the direct grilling method.

By sausage, I mean some kind of meat in a casing which requires cooking.Examples are polish sausage, Italian sausage, and bratwurst.You can also use the following method to grill similar sausages including hot dogs, but you will have to be careful of the cooking times since hot dogs are much smaller.

Key factors in grilling sausage are buying good quality meat and cooking it properly so that it gets browned and loses a lot of the fat inside--but not all of its juice.

We buy sausages from our butcher who makes them.They are much lower in fat than some available at the grocery stores. There are also lots of variations, including some with cheese that I find very difficult to grill since the cheese melts and drips out of the sausage and makes quite a mess.

Cooking is quite simple.In contrast to hamburgers, I often turn the sausages 3 times.That is not critical.An example would be polish sausages that were about 1.5" in diameter and 8" long.I would cook the first side for 2 minutes, then turn and cook on the opposite side for another 2 minutes.If possible, I would turn to a third side and cook about 3 minutes, and finally a fourth side for another 3 minutes.The total cooking time will depend on how hot your fire is, how big the sausages are, and how much fat drips out and adds to the flames.We think that sausages should be cooked done--until the inside is not pink.They should also be well browned on the outside, and most of the fat should have dripped out through cracks in the skin.

A good sausage doesn't need any sauce, but many people like to eat them with good quality mustard such as Grey Poupon.I usually use mustard with brats, but I don't think a spicy Italian sausage needs it.

Bratwurst

There are a couple different way to cook bratwurst that I have enjoyed over the years. Most of the time we just grill them directly with no par-cooking but this makes for nice warm dish on a chilly October evening.

    1 tablespoon Butter
    6-8 whole Allspice
    2 Bay Leaves
    1 medium Onion sliced thin
    2 Apples peeled and sliced
    ½ Teaspoon Salt
    ¼ Teaspoon Black pepper

    1 Beer (Oktoberfest style preferred)

    5 Bratwurst

Sauté Onions, Apples, Butter and spices in a sauté pan until onions begin to brown slightly. Add beer and bratwurst, spoon onion/apple mixture on top of the brats and cover. Cook on low for 20 minutes.

Remove brats to a pan

Remove the allspice and bay leaves and discard. Turn heat up to medium high and reduce until most of the liquid is gone. Serve as a side with the brats.

Meanwhile grill brats on a pre-heated hot grill just until outsides are browned and crisped up as they are already fully cooked.

Serve with mustard, sauerkraut, pickles, artichoke pickle (page 317) etc.

Grilled Pork Chops

Alan- Use direct grilling method but on a relatively low fire. John has grilled thick-cut pork chops successfully. He got the idea from IOWA where grilled pork chops are common and good. The chops should be of good quality and at least 1" thick. The timing will vary depending on grilling conditions and exact thickness so use a thermometer and pull at 145°F, but they should be turned once and cooked until just barely well done--no pink left inside. If you go over very much you will get a dry tough chop. The outside should be well browned. No marinade or sauce is used for this, in contrast to the way we cook pork steaks as described later. These pork chops are smoky tasting and very good.

Spinach and Blue Cheese Stuffed Pork Chops

A recipe inspired by a meal at a local restaurant, this has become a grilling favorite of ours. When requesting or choosing the chops as for the rib type chops as they are better for stuffing.

2 large, thick cut Pork Chops
2 cups cleaned Spinach
4 tablespoons Blue Cheese cut into 8 chunks
Coarse Salt
Fresh coarse ground Black Pepper

Prepare the cops by carefully cutting a pocket into the chop, keeping the opening to the pocket as small as possible. Do this by inserting the knife in one spot and pivoting the knife to the blade side and then removing and reinserting the knife in the opposite direction and pivoting again. Stuff ½ of the spinach and cheese into each chop alternating bits of cheese with spinach. Finally sprinkle each side with coarse salt and pepper and pat in to make sure it stays on as much as possible. Grill over a medium-low fire turning every five-ten minutes until center registers over 150°F. Allow to rest for at least 5 minutes before serving.

Mushroom Marsala sauce

1 tablespoon Butter
½ pound Mushrooms, sliced
1 medium Onion, finely chopped
½ teaspoon Thyme
1 Tablespoon All-purpose Flour
½ cup Marsala Wine
1 cup Chicken Stock
Salt
Pepper

Prepare the sauce by sautéing the onions in the butter. Once they start to brown add the mushrooms and sauté until mushrooms begin to brown as well. Add the thyme and flour and cook until the flour is lightly toasted. Deglaze with the Marsala and then add the chicken stock. Salt and pepper to taste and simmer until slightly thickened, adding more stock to desired consistency.

Barbecued Spareribs(Pork Ribs)

Alan and John- Ribs can be grilled two different ways: direct and indirect.

Using the direct method, the goal on the grill is not to cook the ribs through, but to infuse them with smoky charred flavor.

Starting with ribs that have been rubbed with your favorite pork rub and allowed to sit at least overnight in the fridge. I usually buy in bulk and vacuum seal and freeze pre-rubbed racks

On a medium hot grill, cook the ribs, turning every 3-5 minutes until they are well browned. Remove from the grill.

Brush the ribs all over with your favorite barbecue sauce, we like Sweet Baby Rays

Wrap in aluminum foil and seal as tight as you can. Bake them in a low oven 250 to 300°F until they are as tender as you desire.

Serve with extra sauce

The indirect method is much slower, but some of us think produces better ribs. It uses ribs that have been marinated for several hours using the marinade given in the pork steak recipe. Depending on how many racks you are barbecuing, you may need more marinade.If we are doing 8 racks, Sandy will make twice as much marinade, and put them all in a big metal bowl, and turn them frequently.Marinated for several hours in the fridge.

Use a rib rack if you have one--this is a metal gadget which sits on the upper grate and holds the slabs of ribs in a vertical position.It will hold up to 8 slabs with the bones pointing up.The fire is made in the usual way, but after the charcoal is well lit, put a cheap aluminum foil pan(drip pan) in the center of the firebox and arrange the lit charcoal around the outside of it. Arrange the upper grill over the firebox so the holes in the handles are over the lit charcoal in order to be able to add charcoal.

During the grilling, the fire will tend to die out, so I add 3 or 4 lumps (2 inch square) to each side of the drip pan in order to maintain the fire, but not create too hot of a fire. Do not wait to add charcoal until the fire is low, that will be too late.

Place a rib rack over the drip pan on the upper grate, and place the ribs on that vertically. Keep the air vents on the grill open wide, and grill the ribs for 45 to 60 minutes, moving ones that brown first to cooler locations, and basting all the ribs every 5 minutes with the marinade.

Use a meat thermometer to determine when the ribs are done—a temperature of 170°F is good. When the ribs are done, brush both sides with the BBQ sauce described below. Leave on the grill only 1 minute to avoid burning the sauce.

These ribs are a lot of work, but they are really good and very popular.It's unusual to see any leftovers unless you made more than a rack per person (a rack is a lot of bones, a lot of sauce, but not really sooo much meat!)

Sparerib / Pork Steak Barbecue Sauce

This should be used only during the last few minutes of grilling and at the table.It is delicious, but will easily burn on the grill.

2 large Onions, chopped
1 teaspoon of Olive Oil
1 cup Tomato Paste
1 tablespoon Prepared Mustard
1 teaspoon dried Thyme
1 teaspoon Cumin Seed
2 tablespoons Worcestershire Sauce
2 tablespoons Sugar
2 tablespoons Chili Powder
1 cup Vinegar

Sauté' onions in the olive oil until they are transparent and just beginning to turn color.Add tomato paste, prepared mustard, dried thyme, cumin seed, Worcestershire sauce, sugar, chili powder, and vinegar.Mix well and simmer for 15 minutes.It is important to cook the sauce long enough for the flavors to meld together and taste like a sauce since it will be used at the table as well as on the grill.Don't let the sauce get too thick, it should not be runny, but it should be thin enough to apply with a brush.Add a little water if it gets too thick.

I (John) have a variation on the direct method that I like. I like to rub the ribs with a dry rub if possible the night before. Try to let the ribs warm to room temperature before grilling. I then grill the ribs on a low fire (lowest setting for gas) for approximately 10-15 minutes per side until they develop a nice brown crust. Then I remove the ribs and place them in a baking dish which is then sealed with a tight lid or tin foil. The ribs then go into a 275-300°F oven for 2-3 hours until the meat is falling off the bone tender.

Menu suggestions.Serve the ribs with the barbecue sauce; many people like to put more on at the table.The classic side dishes would be potato salad and corn on the cob, especially if this is the fourth of July.

Hot Wings

This is another of those recipes that lends itself to the freezer bag.

~10 Chicken Wings

Marinade (optional)
2 tablespoons Sriracha Hot Sauce
2 tablespoons Olive Oil
Juice from 1 Lemon or Lime
1 teaspoon Garlic powder or 2 cloves Garlic crushed
Salt
Pepper

Sauce
3 tablespoons Butter
4 tablespoons Franks Hot Sauce
2 tablespoons BBQ Sauce (sweet tomato based variety page 242)
Juice of one lime or lemon
1 clove Garlic crushed
Salt
Pepper

Cut wings into sections and reserve the wing tips for stock making. If you are going to marinade, combine marinade with wings and seal in vacuum bag allow to sit overnight or pop in the freezer for the future.

Remove the wings from marinade, drying as much as possible and put the wings on the grill on medium heat. Cook, turning frequently until they are browned and crispy and most of the fat has rendered off. Watch carefully, as they cook flare ups will become likely, even on medium heat.

While the wings cook, combine and heat the sauce ingredients. Simmer and reduce to desire consistency and volume.

When the wings are done, toss them in the sauce until well coated. You may want to reserve some of the sauce for dipping if you like.

Rotisserie or Spatchcocked Chicken

Ridley and I have found that cooking a chicken on our BBQ rotisserie is and easy and delicious mid-week meal. Usually we have one meal direct from the grill and use the leftover chicken in a second meal later on. The basics of this recipe also work well on a spatchcocked chicken. Some great suggestions of using the leftovers follows my procedure for making the chicken.

   4 – 4 ½ pound Whole Chicken

Right now there is a degree of controversy whether to clean raw chicken. My personal opinion is that anyone who would eat the leftover juices inside and on the surface of a commercially packed chicken should just not eat chicken at all. While I understand there is a degree of risk of cross contamination, careful rinsing and clean up afterward should mitigate most of this risk. In 40+ years of cooking chicken, not once has anyone fallen ill from my chicken or kitchen. In fact I believe the reason for the terrible results people sometimes complain of when roasting chickens or turkeys a big part of it is failure to properly clean the bird.

I have decided that when it comes to your run of the mill supermarket chicken brining does help add flavor and at least in this case, longer is better when it comes to brining. I have settled on three days as a reasonable length of time.

   Brine
      ½ cup Salt
      ½ cup Brown Sugar
   1 cup Cider Vinegar (or ½ cup Lemon Juice / ½ cup Vinegar)
      5 Star Anise
      7 Allspice Berries
      10 whole Black Pepper
      4 Bay Leaves
      1 Quart Hot Water

Put all the brine ingredients in a seal-able container and mix until all the salt and sugar is dissolved. Clean and add the whole chicken, push down to make sure the internal cavity is filled with brine and submerge as much as possible add enough water to just cover chicken. Refrigerate 3 days.

Rotisserie-

Drain and mount the chicken securely on the spit, truss with twine to make a compact bundle as possible. Arrange an aluminum foil lined pan on grate under chicken, fill ½ full with reserved brine. Turn the rotisserie on continuously throughout the cooking except when checking the temp. If your grill is equipped with an IR rotisserie burner, use that for even crisper skin.

Carefully remove the spit from the grill, and transfer the chicken to a platter and remove the spit and trussing. The bird can now be carved up and enjoyed.

Cook the chicken until skin is crispy and internal temperature passes 150°F. This is a slow cook process so the FDA 165°F safety temperature is ridiculous, see the FDA food temp chart to the right, I guarantee you that if you hit 150°F in the center of your chicken, it will be at 145°F or more for more than 8 minutes and therefor as safe as if you had heated it to 165°F for 10 seconds.

FDA Pasteurization Chart for Cooking Poultry

Temperature	Chicken Times	Turkey Times
136°F/58°C	63.3 minutes	64.0 minutes
140°F/60°C	25.2 minutes	28.1 minutes
145°F/63°C	8.4 minutes	10.5 minutes
150°F/66°C	2.7 minutes	3.8 minutes
155°F/68°C	44.2 seconds	1.2 minutes
160°F/71°C	13.7 seconds	25.6 seconds
165°F/74°C	<10.0 seconds	<10.0 seconds

Spatchcocked-

Drain the chicken and using sharp kitchen shears, remove the backbone. This will allow you to unfold the chicken and press it very hard to make it as flat as possible. While you are at it, remove any loose fat or skin that will just cause flare ups on the grill,.

Cook the chicken until skin is crispy and internal temperature passes 150°F. Flip the bird occasionally for even cooking About one hour cooking time on a medium fire.

Once done, carefully transfer the chicken to a platter. The bird can now be carved up and enjoyed.

Often, we will reserve the carcass/bones of the chicken and use them for stock (page 106).

Chickies, Chuckies, and Porkies

Alan- The next section of barbecue or grill recipes has some of our favorites. In contrast to the previous recipes, all of these marinate the meat before cooking. direct grilling method, after marinating. Baste with marinade during grilling.

Grilled Chicken Breasts with Sandy's Marinade(Chickies)

Use direct grilling method on chicken which has been marinated.

We usually just do chicken breasts, but you can do thighs, drumsticks, etc. as well. It's more difficult to do a mixture of parts because they cook at different speeds. The cooking times in this recipe are for breasts which have been cut in half. You can grill chicken breast with bones still in the chicken or not, and with skin still on the chicken or not. A boneless and skinless breast is a little harder to grill because it is smaller, cooks faster, and tends to stick to the grate. It does have less fat on it, however. I prefer to grill the "natural" kind with skin and bones--and at least some of the fat does drip off during the cooking. Sandy says a lot of the fat is still there--but I say it tastes better!

Whatever kind of chicken you are using should be marinated before grilling. Sandy will often take two whole breasts which have been cut in half (four pieces total), put them in a shallow glass baking dish, sprinkle dried thyme leaves over them, turning to get some on all sides--about a tablespoon total, and pour into the dish about a cup of vermouth mixed with 1 tablespoon of good mustard. We use Grey Poupon. Turn the breasts until they are wet on all sides and allow to marinade for a half hour at room temperature. Marinating longer is good, but we are more nervous about leaving chicken at room temperature so we refrigerate if longer than an hour. Turn each piece several times during the marinating. Be sure there is enough liquid that about a half cup is left for basting during the grilling.

For the grilling, use the direct method but be very careful not to cook too long on the first side. Using a kettle the way I do, the fire is much hotter at the beginning since the cover has not been on it. Once the cover is on, the fire tends to die down and get cooler. As a rule of thumb, turn the chicken after two minutes. Baste after turning. The cooking time for the second side is much less critical because the fire has gotten cooler, but I would probably turn again after another 4 minutes or so. Baste after every turning or until you run out of marinade. I keep turning every 3 or 4 minutes until the chicken is brown all over and completely done. I HATE raw chicken. It usually takes 18 minutes on my kettle, but I am pretty sure the chicken is actually done earlier. Since the fire has gotten cooler, and I am turning them frequently, and maybe moving them from the center to the edge of the grate if they seem to be getting too brown, I don't usually burn them! Not like the good old days of cooking chicken over an uncovered grate when you usually got to eat chicken burned on the outside and raw on the inside!!

This chicken is quite good--it has a smoky-mustardy- + taste that is hard to describe but which is delicious. It needs no additional sauce at the table.Menu suggestions with grilled chicken are Sandy's homemade potato salad or baked potatoes or boiled potatoes, a green cooked veggie, and ripe tomatoes if they are in season. Corn on the cob is also great, although we don't grill corn, we just boil it.

VARIATION: Use dried tarragon in place of the thyme. Actually you can use either fresh tarragon or fresh thyme if you have it.

Chuckies (Grilled Chuck Steaks)

Alan- As always, it is important to use good quality meat. You start with a choice chuck roast. Today, it is hard to find a good chuck roast. Nearly impossible to find a bone-in one. So buy whatever you can, and have the "butcher" split it—that is cut them in half by slicing them horizontally. You end up with two steaks which look like the chuck roast, but are half as thick.

Marinate the steaks for at least 2 hours before grilling. For two typical chuck steaks, use a shallow roasting pan which will hold both flat. Peel and chop 6 garlic cloves and press into the chuck steaks. Salt both sides, and pour a 50:50 mixture of red wine and red wine vinegar over the chuck steaks. The liquid should come up about half way on the steaks, and there should be some leftover for basting. Turn the chuckies at least once, covering with plastic wrap.   Turn them several times during the time they are marinating.

Use the direct method for grilling. Grill 3 minutes on the first side, and 5 minutes on the second side, and continue turning until they are done, about 18 minutes. Baste with the leftover marinade after every turning. We like them well browned, but not burned and well done but juicy inside.

A good menu with chuckies would be boiled new potatoes with fresh parsley, green beans, and a good tossed salad. The chuckies have a piquant smoky taste, so something rather bland like potatoes is a good choice.You would not need another highly seasoned dish. One chuck roast split into two chuck steaks will feed four hungry chuckie lovers--but won't leave a lot of leftovers in our house.

Porkies. (Grilled Pork Steaks)

Alan- Pork steaks are hard to find at many supermarkets. Often we buy country ribs (pork) as a substitute. They are bonier, but can be cooked the same way. Marinate the porkies before grilling as follows: sprinkle each porky with salt, and paprika, turning so to do both sides. Crush 4 cloves of garlic and spread over both sides of porkies. Cover with dry sherry, and cover with plastic wrap and allow the porkies to marinate for 2 hours. Grill using the direct method. Turn after two minutes, then after 3 or 4 minutes. Don't let them get too brown on the first side. Baste each time. Keep turning and basting until they are done. Use a meat thermometer and cook to 170F. You may need to move them around to get them evenly browned.

They should not be burned, but should be fairly brown and well done inside. During this period you may need to move the pork steaks which were in one part of the grate to another in order to get them to cook evenly and all finish at the same time.

In recent years, I seldom use a barbecue sauce on pork steaks on the grill, indeed we often eat them without any sauce at all! However, a well-made sauce or salsa is good. If using barbecue sauce, when you are about 2 minutes from being done, brush the top side with some of the barbecue sauce and turn over.Allow to cook no more than one minute, brush the other side with barbecue sauce, turn over, and grill for about another minute--not too long or the sauce will burn. Remove the porkies from the grill and serve with the barbecue sauce.

Barbecued pork steaks are a real treat. They are one of the most unusual meats we cook on the grill because of the sauce which is used at the end of the grilling.The only other meat which we baste with a heavy barbecue sauce is pork ribs.Pork steaks are available in most supermarkets and butchers.We prefer the ones the butcher sells, but they are only stocked fresh during the summer when most people are barbecuing.

(We tend to grill all year unless the weather is really bad!) Our butcher usually has frozen pork steaks; even in the winter, but fresh are better. However, we do use frozen--you just have to be careful not to let them overcook and get too dry.

Beef Fajitas a la Poblano

Beef fajitas has become a staple of everyday dining around here. It is pretty easy to set up and much of it can be done a bit ahead of time. I often buy enough steak for 4-5 meals and do the marinade and vacuum seal and freeze all but one. I think, without real evidence, that the freezing helps tenderize the meat even more.

1 pounds (900g) trimmed skirt steak (about 1/2 whole steak; see note), cut crosswise into 5- to 6-inch pieces

For the Skirt Steak marinade:(this is enough for several batches)

1/2 cup (120ml) soy sauce
1/2 cup (120ml) lime juice, from 6 to 8 limes
1/2 cup (120ml) canola oil
1/4 cup (55g) packed brown sugar
1 tablespoon chili powder (see note)
3 medium cloves garlic, finely minced (about 1 tablespoon)
2 teaspoons ground cumin seed
2 teaspoons freshly ground black pepper

For Sauteed Vegetables

½ bell pepper sliced into strips
½ medium onion, slides vertically

For a la Poblano

1/3 medium onion sliced vertically
1 poblano sliced into strips
½ lb mushrooms sliced
½ cup heavy Cream
½ cup chicken stock or white wine

Mix all marinade ingredients together and add to steak in a 1 gallon zip lock bag. Make sure meat is fully coated with marinade,

Allow to rest in refrigerator at least overnight or as long as 4 days.

Cook bell pepper and onions in a small amount of olive oil until softened slightly

For the Poblano sauce, saute onions and mushrooms until they gain a bit of color. Add the poblanos and cook for a bit. Add cream and stock and a tablespoon of reserved marinade. Simmer until thickened

Preheat BBQ until very hot

Grill steak over high heat until well crusted on both sides. (~90 second per side)

Remove from grill immediately to tinfoil and seal. Allow steak to rest for 5 to 10 minutes.

After resting, slice steak across the grain into thin strips (¼ to ½ inch)

I often serve this a la Mexican restaurants:

Before grilling meat, partially cook the onions and peppers in a 10-12 inch cast iron pan.

When the meat is resting after the grill, start heating the pan on high heat. By the time you have the meat sliced, the onions and peppers should be sizzling.

Arrange the sliced steak on top of the onions and pour the sauce over the top.

Bring to the table and warn your guests about the red hot cast iron.

You can also set this un as a Fajita bar:

Warm platter with sliced steak and onions and peppers
warmed tortillas
Poblano sauce

As desired
Pico de Gallo (page 49)
Red or Green Salsa
Guacamole (page 49)
Grated cheese
Sour cream
Taco sauce

Grilled Fish

Alan- Use direct grilling method.

We grill any kind of firm fleshed fish.Some favorites are salmon, swordfish, and tuna.Red snapper is also very good, but a little harder to keep together.The problem with soft fleshed fish is they fall apart (flake) when they stick to the grate.I am trying to learn how to use a grill basket to avoid this problem. Anyway, it's no problem with salmon or swordfish.

Fish is not hard to grill, but is a little tricky to get done just right.It all depends on the kind of fish and how thick it is.We usually use steaks of salmon or swordfish --about 1" thick I think.To minimize sticking to the grate, be sure to clean it well and oil it before putting on it.This requires a glove to prevent scorching your hand.Take a paper towel and some peanut oil and wipe it on the part of the grate you will put the fish.Do this rapidly to prevent your glove from burning!

You can put a little oil on the fish if you want, but it doesn't really need it.Don't use olive oil or anything that burns easily.I would cook 1" salmon steaks about 3 minutes on the first side and 4 minutes on the second side, turning only once.I would probably look at them before these times since I am more nervous about the cooking times for fish.If you have thin fillets, they will take a lot less time.

While we don't marinate or sauce fish before or during the grilling, you may want something to put on it on the table.Lemon juice is nice.I think we have also had various sauces based on oil and vinegar or lemon juice with dill--I will have to try these again.However, a good fresh fish doesn't need anything.

Deserts

We don't eat much in the way of deserts outside the holiday season, it's always nice to have some dark chocolate on hand. See the Holiday section for the traditional deserts of the holidays, Apple pie for Thanksgiving; cookies, mincemeat, and fruit cake for Christmas.

Chocolate Crinkle Cookies

1 cup All-purpose Flour
½ cup Unsweetened Cocoa Powder
1 teaspoon Baking Powder
¼ teaspoon Baking Soda
½ teaspoon Salt
1 ½ cup Brown Sugar, packed
3 large Eggs
4 teaspoon Instant Espresso Powder
1 teaspoon Vanilla Extract
4 ounces Unsweetened Chocolate, chopped
4 tablespoons Butter
½ cup Granulated Sugar
½ cup Confectioners' Sugar

Wisk flour, cocoa powder, baking powder, baking soda and salt together in a bowl and set aside.

Beat Brown Sugar, Eggs, Espresso Powder and vanilla extract together until light in color.

Meanwhile melt Butter and chocolate in the microwave, stirring often.

Beat the mixture into the sugar and eggs.

Fold in the flour mixture until mixed completely.

Allow the dough to rest for 15 minutes.

With a medium (about 2 ounces) scoop portion the dough and roll into balls.

Roll each ball in granulated sugar followed by confectioners' sugar.

Bake at 350°F for 15 minutes

Malted Milk Chocolate Chip Cookies

I really like the rich taste that the malted milk gives to these cookies. I often make them at Christmas because who doesn't like chocolate chip cookies? These are the go-to chocolate chip cookie for me.

  2 sticks Unsalted Butter, softened
  3/4 cup golden Brown Sugar
  3/4 cup Granulated Sugar
  2 Whole Eggs
  2 teaspoons Vanilla Extract
  1/2 cup (rounded) Malted Milk Powder
  2 cups all-purpose Flour
  1 1/4 teaspoon Baking Soda
  1 1/4 teaspoon Salt
  One 12-ounce bag Chocolate Chips (I like semi-sweet)

Preheat the oven to 375°F.

Cream the butter, then add both sugars and cream until fluffy. Add the eggs and beat slightly, then add the vanilla and beat until combined.

Add the malted milk powder and beat until combined.

In a separate bowl, sift together the flour, baking soda and salt.

Add to the butter mixture, beating gently until just combined.

Add the chocolate chips and mix until just combined.

Drop by teaspoonfuls on an un-greased baking sheet, leaving plenty of space between the cookies (they spread out quite a bit).

Bake for 9 to 11 minutes.

The cookies will be very flat and very chewy. Allow to cool slightly before removing from pan with a spatula. Reduce the amount of butter to make a higher less flat cookies

Ultimate Killer Chocolate Chip Cookies

Yes, I know the title is a cliche, but that is what Sharon who shared the recipe with me called them. I have made slight changes over the years, but generally making chocolate chip cookies is hard to mess up. Sharon also made Ridley and I a carrot cake that was out of this world, I wish we had the recipe for that as well.

1 cup Butter, melted and cooled
1 cup Sugar
1 cup Brown Sugar
2 Eggs, beaten
1 cup Rolled Oats
1 cup Corn Flakes, Crushed
2 cup Flour
1 teaspoon Baking Powder
1 teaspoon Baking Soda
¼ teaspoon Salt
2 teaspoons Vanilla

Options
¾ Sweetened shredded Coconut
1 cup Raisins
1 cup Chocolate Chips
¾ cup Toffee Chips
¾ cup Walnuts, chopped

Preheat oven to 375°F

Combine oats, corn flakes, sugars, raisins and coconut in a large bowl.

Add eggs, vanilla, and melted butter. Mix until well combined. Stir in chocolate chips.

In a separate bowl, whisk together flour, salt, baking powder, baking soda.

Add dry mixture to wet and fold to combine completely.

Drop spoonfuls of dough onto greased cookie sheet and bake for 12-15 minutes.

Cool on a wire rack.

Oatmeal cranberry walnut cookies

1 cup butter, room temperature
¾ cup granulated sugar
1 cup brown sugar packed
2 eggs
1 ¾ cup AP flour
1 ¾ cup rolled oats
1 tsp baking soda
1 tsp salt
¼ tsp nutmeg
¼ tsp cinnamon
1 ½ cup dried cranberries
¾ cup chopped walnuts

Cream butter and sugars together until light and fluffy, scarping down bowl occasionally, about 5 minutes in a stand mixer. Beat eggs in one at a time until well blended, about 3 minutes.

Combine flour, oats, baking soda, salt and spices in a separate bow, add cranberries and toss to coat completely.

With mixer on low Slowly add flour mixture to butter mixture.

Add walnuts and mix until everything is just incorporated evenly

Cover and rest in refrigerator overnight

Pre heat oven to 350F

Drop dough in ¼ cup sized balls and slightly flatten.

Bake for 20-22 minutes until cookies are golden brown on edges, they will still be a little soft in the center, do not over bake..

Crispy Gingersnap Cookies

I started making these cookies when we could not find gingersnaps in the store during the covid pandemic. They are now Ridley's favorite cookie

- 3/4 cup (170 gr) unsalted butter, room temperature
- 1/2 cup (105 gr) dark brown sugar, packed
- 1/2 cup (100 gr) granulated sugar
- 2 TBSP (11 gr) grated fresh ginger
- 1/4 cup (80 gr) un-sulphured molasses
- 1 large egg, room temperature
- 1/2 teaspoon pure vanilla extract
- 1/2 teaspoon (3 gr) baking soda
- 1/4 teaspoon kosher salt
- 2 tsp ground ginger
- 1 1/2 teaspoons (3 gr) ground cinnamon
- 1/4 teaspoon (1 gr) ground cloves
- 2 cups + 2 Tbsp (255 gr) all purpose flour
- ~1/2 cup granulated sugar for rolling

In the bowl of a stand mixer fit with a paddle attachment, or in a large bowl with a hand mixer, cream together the butter, brown sugar, granulated sugar, and fresh ginger on medium/high speed until light and fluffy. This will take about 2-3 minutes.

Add the molasses, egg, and vanilla extract into the bowl and mix until incorporated.

Add the baking soda, salt, ground ginger, ground cinnamon, and ground cloves into the bowl. Mix until incorporated. Use a rubber spatula to scrape down the sides of the bowl and mix a few turns again to make sure the ingredients are evenly distributed.

Add the flour into the mixing bowl and mix until just incorporated. This shouldn't take longer than about 30 seconds. The more you mix, the dryer your cookies will become.

Cover the bowl and place in the refrigerator to chill for at least 45 minutes - 1 hour until firm enough to be rolled, overnight is better.

Preheat the oven to 325 F (160 C). Line two sheet pans with parchment paper.

Scoop dough balls about 1 teaspoon each. Roll between palms into a ball and then roll in granulated sugar. Space the cookies out evenly between the two sheet pans and use the bottom of a glass to flatten them out to about 1/4" thick, press the bottom of the glass into the sugar each time to prevent sticking.

For cookies that are crispy all the way through, bake at 325 F (160 F) for 15 minutes.

Allow the cookies to cool on the sheet pans for 5 minutes before transferring to a cooling rack to cool completely.

Store cooled cookies in an airtight container at room temperature for up to two weeks, or frozen for up to 3 months.

Mincemeat

Alan, and Sandy- This recipe we also adapted from one of James Beard's newspaper columns. The mincemeat will last in the refrigerator for a long time--months and even years! It is excellent, particularly in little pastry tarts.

If you don't want to use the quantities of liquor in this recipe, I would advise not doing it at all. Maybe find another recipe!! At least don't try to keep it for very long.

I don't think you have to use the best quality Cognac however, because all of the fruit and spices will over power a subtle flavor of Remy Martin VSOP. I think a California brandy or a good quality bourbon can be used. And YES, mincemeat does have meat in it!

3 pounds Brisket or lean rump of Beef
1 fresh Beef Tongue (about 3 pounds)
1 and 1/2 pounds Beef Suet
2 pounds seeded Raisins
2 pounds sultana Raisins
2 pounds Currants
1/2 pound Citron
1/4 pound Orange Peel
1/4 pound Lemon Peel
1 pound dried Figs and Dates
2 cups Sugar
1 pint Strawberry or Raspberry Preserves
1 tablespoon Salt
2 teaspoons Nutmeg
1 teaspoon Allspice
1 teaspoon Mace
A dash of Ground Cloves
1 fifth Sherry
2 fifths Brandy or Bourbon

Boil brisket and tongue in water until they are done and very tender.

Cool them in the broth, and skim off the fat. Remove all fat from the meat and chop fine or grind coarsely by hand.

Chop suet very, very finely.

Shred and dice the citron, orange peel, and lemon peel.

Cut figs and dates into small pieces.

Put meat, fruit, and peels in a deep crock.

Add sugar, preserves, salt, and spices. Add the sherry. Add half of the brandy, and mix loosely by hand.

274

Continue adding brandy and mixing until it is well mixed and rather loose.

Cover the crock and let stand one month in the refrigerator.

Check it every week, and add more brandy if it has all been absorbed.

You can now put in sterile jars add a small amount of bourbon or brandy to cover the top and seal-- we usually store this in the refrigerator. It will keep for a very long time preserved by the alcohol.

Mincemeat Tarts

I love these little treats, but they are a specialty item, making mincemeat is a time consuming and challenging project, and store-bought mincemeat is not a substitute. I prefer to temper the mincemeat by mixing 1 to 1 with diced apple. This cuts the extreme richness of the mincemeat.

You can use either homemade or store-bought pie crust. Homemade is always better, but with the strong flavors and richness of the mincemeat, it is not as noticeable.

Roll out pie dough to about 1/8 inch thick, approximately a 12 inch circle for a single batch.

Cut out small circles of rolled-out rich pastry dough (about 4 inches in diameter).

Using either all mincemeat or a 50/50 mixture of mincemeat and diced apples, put 2 or 3 spoonfuls of mincemeat in the center, fold over, and seal well.

Bake at 375°F until nicely browned and crisp.

Christmas Pudding or Fruit Cake

I found and adapted this recipe while doing research on fruit cakes. My parents have a recipe which they use which is a replication of a fruit cake my dad remembers from his Uncle Heath. Based on his new recipe and the descriptions, I suspect that it may have started as an English "figgy" pudding.

I found and made this recipe which I like the results of. The problem is that it makes a lot; luckily this booze soaked creation has a virtually unlimited shelf life.

1½ cup Pitted dates, coarse chopped
1½ cup Candied Lemon Peel, coarse chopped
1½ cup Candied Orange Peel, coarse chopped
1½ cup Candied Mixed Peel, coarse chopped
1½ cup Candied Red Cherries
1½ cup Candied Green Cherries
15 ounce package dried Currants
15 ounce package Seedless Raisins
15 ounce package Golden Raisins
1 cup ground Almonds
2+ cups Apricot or Peach Brandy

2 cups sifted All-purpose Flour
1/2 cup light Brown Sugar
1 teaspoon ground Cinnamon
1 teaspoon ground Ginger
1 teaspoon ground Nutmeg
1/4 teaspoon of ground Cloves
1 teaspoon Salt
1 cup dry Bread Crumbs
1 lb. chopped Beef Suet
6 large Eggs, well beaten
¾ cup Red Currant Jelly (not jam)

Butter (to grease the pudding molds)
Splashes of Cognac or Brandy to keep the pudding moist while it ages

Pre-soak: Days 1 through 4:

Soak the fruits and ground almonds in apricot brandy, so that the fruit absorbs the brandy. Place the dates, lemon, orange, and mixed peel, red and green cherries, currants, seedless raisins, and ground almonds in a very large metal or ceramic mixing bowl. Add the apricot or peach brandy. Mix all these

ingredients thoroughly (taking care not to crush the cherries). Once everything is mixed, cover the mixing bowl with clear plastic wrap, and let soak for 4 days. Every day or so during this time, take the plastic wrap off, and mix up the ingredients. If the mixture looks a little dry... sprinkle on more apricot or peach brandy.

Mixing the cake: Day 4: Place the flour, brown sugar, cinnamon, ginger, nutmeg, cloves, salt and bread crumbs into a large mixing bowl. Mix these dry ingredients well, before adding the next ingredient. Now add the beef suet into the dry ingredients. Mix well. When the pudding cooks, the suet melts, so it must be well distributed or else it will look clumpy. Add the dry ingredients. Next add the beaten eggs, and currant jelly. Mix all this thoroughly, taking care not to crush the cherries if you can.

Molding and cooking: Next grease up molds with butter, so that un-molding the puddings later on will be easier. This recipe makes 2 large puddings and 2 small ones.

Press the mixture into the bottom of the bowl/mold gently. The bottom of the bowl will be the top of the pudding once it is cooked and unmolded. Pressing the mixture down ensuring you have a solid pudding with no holes or gaps. Don't fill the pudding bowls all the way to the top. The pudding tends to expand when it cooks. Once you have all the pudding mixture in the bowls, press down with the back of a spoon to smooth out the pudding.

Cover each pudding mold with silver foil, and seal each covered bowl with a heavy duty elastic band or several. It is important to do this, as you don't want any water to get into the pudding when it's cooking, in the water bath.

Make sure you don't get water in the pudding!

The puddings are now ready to be cooked, in a water bath. A crock pot is perfect. Fill up the crock pot bowl with boiling water. Leave the water about 1 inch short of the top of the pudding mold, so that water does not get into the pudding molds. Cook the pudding for 10-12 hours on medium or high setting. It's virtually impossible to burn something in a water bath. So over cooking the pudding at low temperatures is hard to do. Check the pot every few hours or so and top up the water to the correct level.

Un-molding: Be careful handling the puddings once they come out of the slow cooker. Allow to cool down for a few hours, before attempting to un-mold it. When one pudding is taken out of the slow cooker, place the next one in, and start the long cooking process all over again. It is an ordeal but it only comes once a year at the most. After un-molding the puddings (once they are cool). Cover each pudding in cheese cloth and sprinkle cognac on the puddings. Then wrap the puddings in aluminum foil to seal. Store it in a cool place, the fridge is OK but a cool closet/cabinet is better

Weekly maintenance: Once a week take the foil off, and the cheese cloth, and sprinkle the pudding with brandy or cognac. Then wrap it back up again (in the same cheese cloth and foil). Sometimes you might have to replace the foil if it tears. Keep up the weekly maintenance on the puddings until Christmas or three months has elapsed.

A good time to start making puddings, is early or mid-October. There is a reason for this. As the puddings age, they develop more flavor. Smell the pudding once it's first cooked. Then smell the pudding on Christmas Day. You can smell and taste the difference in an aged Plum Pudding.

Just remember in October to check your supply and start making pudding...

Pie Crust

Pie Crust if you choose to make it yourself, many times I prefer to just buy the refrigerated version as I think they are nearly as good for the amount of effort.

1 1/2 cup Flour
1/2 teaspoon Salt
1/2 cup cold Shortening (butter or lard)
2 Tablespoons vodka
Ice Water

Sift flour and salt. Add shortening and mix it in with a pastry cutter, until it looks like cornmeal. Sprinkle vodka and then water, one tablespoon at a time over the mixture and lightly toss, until it comes together in a ball. Let rest in the refrigerator for an hour or longer. It can be frozen at this point and used later.

Remove from fridge and roll between two pieces of parchment

If blind baking.,..

Chill rolled out crust for one hour or more before baking. Dock the pastry by poking all over with a fork to allow steam to escape. Place a piece of parchment in the empty crust and fill with dried beans or pie weights to weigh down to prevent bubbles.

Bake at 400°F for 12 - 15 minutes. Allow to cool before filling.

Mom's Apple Pie

I (John) learned to make this pie directly from my Grandmother. She was not at all interested in how pretty it looked; it was all about the flavor. I like to add a tablespoon of lemon or lime juice to offset the sweeter apples. I also substitute brown sugar for half of the sugar. My most important note is that you need to pile the apples as high as possible; they will cook down more than you think. I pile them up until they are literally falling off the sides, four or five inches above the pan is NOT too much. I should rename this one to the Grandma's Award Winning Apple Pie! In November of 2008 I won a desert contest with this recipe.

I (John) like to use 2/3 granny smith and 1/3 Gala or Honeycrisp as I have trouble finding Jonathan around where we live.

Recipe by Alan

My mother makes great pies.This is the recipe she gave us, and it works.It makes a 10 inch double crust pie.Whenever we make this pie, I (Alan) think of all the great pies I had as a kid. MMMmm!

10-11 medium Jonathan Apples(see note)
1 cup Sugar(see note)
1/2 teaspoon Cinnamon(see note)
1/8 teaspoon Nutmeg(see note)
pinch Salt
1 tablespoon All-purpose Flour
large lump of Butter

Peel and thinly slice the apples. There should be enough to be piled high above the rim of the pie pan.Mix with other ingredients.Line a 10 inch pie pan with your favorite pie crust.We use the basic pie crust from the Gourmet II cookbook.

Pour into bottom crust, divide butter into bits and sprinkle over top of apple mixture, then put on the top crust.Bake at 425-450°F for 10 to 15 minutes or until light brown, then reduce heat to 350°F and bake for 1 and 1/2 hours.

NOTE: The kind of apples is important.We like Jonathans, we don't like Delicious for this pie. kinds of "pie apples" may be OK.Mom says if you like a sweet pie, add a 1/2 cup of brown sugar in addition to the cup of granulated white sugar.We like our pie semi-sweet.I like nutmeg better than cinnamon so we skimp on the cinnamon and are generous with the nutmeg.Some people have the opposite opinion, if you like cinnamon you might wish to emphasize it.

Single Apple Pie

As the holidays approach often you may find really big apples in the store. Some are just big and not particularly good, but the Honeycrisp apples retain their crisp flavor and smooth flesh. This is a quick recipe I cooked up to make a quick dessert. The flavor profile is based on Grandmother's pie recipe.

1 large apple
1 tablespoon Lemon or Lime Juice
1/3 cup Brown Sugar
¼ teaspoon Cinnamon(see note)
¼ teaspoon Nutmeg(see note)
pinch Salt
½ tablespoon Butter
1 pie crust (optional)

Mix sugar, cinnamon, nutmeg and salt together in a small bowl. Butter a small glass pie plate or line it with parchment. Core and peel the apple and coat in the citrus juice to prevent browning. If using pie crust lay the pie crust in the pan. Place the apple in the center of the pie plate. Stuff the center of the apple with the sugar and spice mixture, sprinkling any remaining along with any leftover citrus juice over the apple. Put pat of butter on top of the apple. Bring the pie crust up around the apple, and sealing the edges. If not using a pie crust, tent some aluminum foil loosely over the apple, crimping the edges around the pie plate and bake in a 375°F oven for about an hour and a half until apple is completely tender.

Apple Crisp

I made this after Ridley asked me to. It turned out to be a favorite desert.

Topping
½ cup Flour
½ cup rolled oats
½ cup light brown sugar
½ teaspoon baking powder
¼ teaspoon ground cinnamon
Dash of salt
1/3 cup butter, cut into small pieces

Filling
1-4 large apples, peeled, cored and sliced thin
3 Tablespoons butter, melted
2 Tablespoons flour
1 Tablespoon lemon juice
3 Tablespoons milk
½ teaspoon vanilla extract
¼ cup brown sugar
½ teaspoon ground cinnamon
Dash of salt

Preheat the oven to 375 degrees F

Prepare filling

In a large bowl, whisk together the melted butter and flour. Add lemon juice, milk, vanilla, brown sugar, cinnamon and salt and stir until well blended.

Add the apples and toss until the apples are well coated.   Transfer into a baking disk using a spatula to get as much of the coating mixture as possible.

Prepare topping

Combine all topping ingredients and using a pastry cutter or your fingers combine the mixture until you have small crumbs.   Cover the apples evenly with the topping mixture.

Bake for at least 45 minutes, it may take up to 90 minutes depending on the geometry of your pan. Shallow wide pans will cook faster, but I like it better in a taller pan.

Adel's Sweet Potato Pie

By Ridley and Adel

3 cups Sweet Potatoes
2½ cups Sugar
2 Eggs
1 teaspoon Cinnamon
1 teaspoon Nutmeg
8 tablespoons Butter
½ teaspoon Vanilla
½ teaspoon Lemon Extract
½ cup Sweet Milk
1 tablespoon Flour

Preheat oven to 350°F

Steam or Boil Sweet Potatoes. Mix all in mixer

Cook from 1 to 1½ hours

Lemon Pie

As inspired by Alton Brown on the Good Eats program. I thought of this as a nice way to use up lemons until I realized it only uses one or two lemons.

Pre-baked Pie Crust (see previous recipe)

4 large Eggs Yolks
1/3 cup Cornstarch
1 ½ cup Cold Water
1 1/3 cups Sugar
¼ teaspoon Salt
3 tablespoons Butter cut into ½ inch cubes
Zest of one large Meyer Lemon
½ cup Meyer Lemon Juice (1 large Lemon)

Beat egg yolks in a medium bowl until light in color.

In a sauce pan combine cornstarch, cold water, sugar, salt. Heat until boiling and simmer for **exactly** 1 minute.

Remove from heat. Add beaten eggs by tempering.

Simmer for exactly one more minute.

Remove from the heat and add the butter, zest, and lemon juice.

Pour into pre-baked pie crust and allow to cool, unless topping with meringue.

4 Egg Whites
1/2 t. cream of tartar
1/3 C. sugar

To make the meringue, beat the remaining egg whites with cream of tartar.

Gradually add sugar. Beat till the egg whites are stiff and shiny.

Mound meringue on top of warm filling, spreading to the edges.

Bake for about 20 minutes at 325°F until the meringue is golden. Cool pie 1 hour and then refrigerate it.

Lemon Upside-Down Cake

This is our take on a recipe by Cal Peternell, originally appearing in Food & Wine - April, 2005. Ridley and I tried this one spring Sunday afternoon when trying to use up the last of our lemons

¾ cup Butter, softened
3/4 cup plus 2 tablespoons Brown Sugar
2 Meyer Lemons, sliced paper-thin crosswise, seeds discarded
1 1/2 cups All-purpose flour
2 tsp Baking Powder
1/4 tsp Salt
1 cup granulated Sugar
1 tsp Vanilla extract
2 large Eggs, separated
3/4 cup Milk
1/4 tsp Cream of Tartar

Preheat the oven to 350°F.

In a medium sized cast-iron skillet melt 4 Tb of butter over medium heat. Add the brown sugar and heat stirring until a syrup forms. Remove from heat and arrange the lemon slices in a decorative pattern in the melted brown sugar.
In a separate bowl, whisk the flour with the baking powder and salt.

Beat the remaining butter with the sugar until light and fluffy. Beat in the vanilla and the egg yolks, one at a time. At low speed, beat in the dry ingredients in thirds, alternating with the milk. In a non-reactive bowl, beat the egg whites with the cream of tartar at high speed until firm peaks form. Fold the beaten whites into the batter by thirds as well. Pour the batter gently into the prepared pan and bake for about 30 minutes, or until a toothpick inserted in the center of the cake comes out clean. Let cool in the pan for 10-15 minutes, then invert it onto a plate.

Classic Carrot Cake

After a couple of attempts over several years this recipe, adapted from "Flour" is the best I have found.

 2 eggs
1 cup brown sugar
¾ cup canola oil
3 Tbs buttermilk
½ teaspoon vanilla extract
1 cup + 2 Tbs AP flour
½ teaspoon baking powder
½ teaspoon baking soda
½ teaspoon salt
½ teaspoon ground cinnamon
½ teaspoon ground ginger
2 cups packed shredded carrots
½ cup raisins
½ cup chopped pecans

Preheat oven to 350

Butter and flour an 8 inch cake pan

In a stand mixer with whip, beat together eggs and brown sugar until light and thick

In a small bowl wisk together oil, vanilla and buttermilk. With mixer on low slowly incorporate this into the egg mixture.

In a separate bowl, wisk together flour, salt, baking soda and powder, cinnamon and ginger.

Using a rubber spatula, fold the flour mixture into the wet ingredients. When mostly incorporated, add raisins and pecans. Fold until no dry flour is present.

Pour batter into baking pan and bake for 1hr 20 minutes, until golden brown and the cake springs back when lightly pressed with a finger tip.

Citrus Carrot Cake

This is a good variation on carrot cake for a more bright spring option.

Cake
1 pound carrots, peeled and finely grated (about 4 cups)
3 ounces dried apricots, chopped (about 1/2 cup)
2 ounces candied orange peels, finely chopped (about 1/3 cup)
2 ounces raw pistachios, chopped (about 1/2 cup)
1 1/2 cups canola oil
2 cups packed dark brown sugar
4 large eggs, at room temperature
1 1/2 tablespoons grated orange zest plus 1/2 cup fresh orange juice
2 cups all-purpose flour
1 1/2 teaspoons baking powder
1 teaspoon ground green cardamom
1 teaspoon ground ginger
1/2 teaspoon baking soda
1/4 teaspoon kosher salt
Glaze
1/4 cup cream cheese, at room temperature
2 tablespoons unsalted butter, at room temperature
1 1/2 cups powdered sugar, divided
1/4 cup sour cream
1/2 tablespoon grated orange zest plus 3 tablespoons fresh orange juice, plus more orange zest, for garnish

Preheat oven to 350 0 F. Spray a tube or Bundt cake pan with a generous amount of baking spray.

Combine carrots, candied apricots, orange peels, and pistachios in a large bowl. Combine oil, brown sugar, eggs, and orange zest and juice in a high-speed blender or the bowl of a food processor. Pulse on high speed until mixture is emulsified (about 10 pulses).

Fold oil mixture into carrot mixture in bowl.

In a separate large bowl, whisk together flour, baking powder, cardamom, ginger, baking soda, and salt. Make a well in center of flour mixture; add carrot mixture, and fold to incorporate until there are no visible flecks of flour left behind.

Spoon mixture into prepared pan; shake pan lightly to even out the batter and release any air bubbles.

Bake in preheated oven 55 minutes to 1 hour, rotating pan on rack halfway through baking time. (The cake is done when a skewer comes out clean when inserted in center of cake and top of cake is firm to the touch and golden brown.) Let cake cool in pan on a wire rack 10 minutes. Invert cake onto wire rack. Let cake cool completely.

In the bowl of a stand mixer fitted with the whisk attachment, beat cream cheese and butter on medium speed until mixture is light and fluffy, 4 to 5 minutes. Scrape down sides of bowl, and add 3/4 cup powdered sugar.

Beat on low speed until mixture is smooth, about 1 minute. Add sour cream and orange zest and juice, and beat on low speed 1 minute. Add remaining 3/4 cup powdered sugar and beat on low speed until sugar is completely incorporated, about 45 seconds. Scrape sides of bowl, and increase speed to medium-high;

whisk until mixture is well combined.

Drizzle glaze on cooled cake; garnish with orange zest

Double-Layer Vanilla-Buttermilk Cake with Raspberries

For the Buttermilk Cake:

For each of 2 cakes

Nonstick vegetable oil spray
2 cups cake flour
1 teaspoons baking powder
1/2 teaspoon baking soda
1/4 teaspoon kosher salt
12 Tbs (1½ sticks) unsalted butter, room temperature
1 3/4 cups granulated sugar
4 large eggs, separated
1 teaspoon vanilla extract
1 cups buttermilk

For the Vanilla Syrup:

1/4 cup granulated sugar
1 vanilla bean, split lengthwise

For the Orange Cream-Cheese Frosting:

4 (8-ounce) packages cream cheese, chilled
1 1/4 cups (2 1/2 sticks) unsalted butter, room temperature
2 teaspoons finely grated orange zest
2 tablespoons fresh orange juice
2 teaspoons vanilla extract
1 1/2 cups powdered sugar, sifted

For the assembly:

15 ounces raspberries

Place a rack in middle of oven; preheat to 350°F. Lightly coat cake pans with nonstick spray and line bottoms with parchment paper. Whisk 2 cups flour, 1 tsp. baking powder, 1/2 tsp. baking soda, and 1/4 tsp. salt in a medium bowl; set aside.

Using an electric mixer on medium-high speed, beat 3/4 cup butter and 1 1/2 cups granulated sugar in a large bowl, scraping down sides of bowl as needed, until light and creamy, about 5 minutes. Add 4 egg yolks in 2 additions, scraping down bowl after each. Beat in 1 tsp. vanilla.

Reduce mixer speed to low, then add dry ingredients in 2 additions alternately with 1 cup buttermilk in 2 additions, scraping down sides of bowl as needed.

Using electric mixer on medium speed, beat 4 egg whites in another large bowl until soft peaks form, 2–3 minutes. Slowly add 1/4 cup granulated sugar and continue to beat until stiff, glossy peaks form, about 3 minutes more. Fold half of the egg whites into flour mixture, then gently fold in remaining egg whites.

Scrape batter into prepared pan; smooth surface. Bake, rotating pan halfway through and covering with foil during the last 15 minutes of baking, until golden brown, firm to the touch, and a tester inserted into the center comes out clean, 45–50 minutes. Transfer pan to a wire rack and let cake cool.

Repeat steps with second prepared pan and remaining cake ingredients to bake the second layer.

Make the Vanilla Syrup:

Combine granulated sugar and 1/4 cup water in a medium saucepan. Scrape in vanilla seeds, add pod, and stir to combine. Bring to a boil, cover, and steep at least 15 minutes. Set aside to cool. Discard pod before using.

Make the Orange Cream-Cheese Frosting:

Using electric mixer on medium-high speed, beat cream cheese and butter in a large bowl until smooth, about 1 minute. Beat in orange zest, orange juice, and vanilla. Reduce mixer speed to medium and beat in powdered sugar, scraping down bowl as needed, until light and fluffy, 2–3 minutes.

Assemble the cake:

Spread 1 Tbsp. frosting in the center of a platter. Place 1 cake layer, top side down, in the center. Using a pastry brush, brush 3 Tbsp. vanilla syrup over top of cake. Using an offset spatula, spread 1 cup frosting evenly over top. Arrange 6 oz. raspberries in a ring around perimeter of cake, pressing to adhere. Fill interior of ring with 6 oz. raspberries. Spread 1 cup frosting over raspberries inside of ring (do not frost raspberries at the perimeter).

Carefully place second cake layer, top side down, on frosted raspberries, gently pressing down to secure. Brush 3 Tbsp. syrup over top of cake with pastry brush. Spread 2 1/2 cups frosting evenly over top and sides, carefully covering raspberries. Chill at least 30 minutes to let frosting set.

Remove cake from refrigerator. Frost top and sides, swirling decoratively, making sure to cover bottom of platter; reserve remaining frosting for another use. Chill at least 30 minutes or up to overnight to let frosting set. Before serving, top cake with remaining 3 oz. raspberries and edible flowers, if using.

Do Ahead

Cake can be made 3 days ahead; wrap tightly in plastic and chill, or freeze up to 2 weeks. Syrup can be made 5 days ahead; store in an airtight container and chill. Frosting can be made 3 days ahead; cover with plastic wrap, pressing directly on surface, and chill. Bring to room temperature before using.

Bananas Foster

A recipe I make for particularly showy occasions, or an indulgent weekend breakfast. The original version calls for banana liquor, however I have not tried a banana liquor that didn't taste at least a little like fake banana to me. I prefer rum.

2-3 very ripe Bananas, peeled and sliced in half length wise
2 tablespoons Butter
¼-½ cup Brown Sugar
¼ cup rum or Brandy, or other high proof Liquor
Cinnamon to taste

Combine butter and brown sugar over medium heat.

Cook, stirring until sugar is dissolved, add the bananas.

Cook, gently scooping butter mixture over bananas until the bananas begin to brown.

Move the pan off the burner, add the rum and allow to ignite over the burner or use a stick lighter.

When the flames die down, serve immediately with ice cream or as a sauce over waffles or pancakes.

Ice Cream

Basic Ice Cream Base (French style)

6 egg Yolks
2 cups Heavy Cream
1 cup Milk or ½ and ½
¼ teaspoon Salt
3/4 cup Sugar

Heat milk and cream with salt and about ½ of the sugar until almost boiling. Meanwhile, whip the egg yolks with ½ cup of sugar until pale. When cream is hot (175° F), remove from heat and allow to cool slightly. Temper the cream into the eggs, beating all the while. Return to pan and cook until mixture thickens enough to coat a spoon (180° F). Pour through a fine mesh strainer into a glass bowl, refrigerate until thoroughly cold, overnight is best.

Freeze per instructions for your ice cream maker.

To make vanilla ice cream, stir 1 ½ teaspoons vanilla extract into the base right before straining.

Coffee Ice Cream

Reduce milk by ¼ cup. Add ¼ cup of coffee extract to cream mixture during finally cooking step. Optionally, add chocolate chunks after ice cream is nearly frozen.

Mango Ice Cream

Peel and seed two ripe mangoes. Puree one and dice the other. Stir pureed mango into ice cream base just before straining. Add diced mango after ice cream is nearly frozen.

New Orleans Style Bread Pudding

Ever since visiting New Orleans the first time, bread pudding has been one of my desert cravings. Although there is nothing like going to the Palm Court Jazz Café and enjoying a desert while listening to classic jazz music. This recipe was adapted from one by Emeril Lagasse.

12 to 14 cups 1-inch cubes Raisin Bread
1 tablespoon Butter
2 cups Heavy Cream
4 cups whole Milk
6 large Eggs
1 3/4 cups plus 2 tablespoons Light Brown Sugar
4 1/2 teaspoons pure Vanilla Extract
1 1/2 teaspoons ground Cinnamon
1/2 teaspoon freshly grated Nutmeg
1/4 teaspoon Salt
Confectioners' Sugar, for garnish
1 recipe Whiskey Sauce, recipe follows

Place the bread in a large bowl. Combine the heavy cream, milk, eggs, brown sugar, vanilla, cinnamon, nutmeg, and salt, whisk until well combined. Pour the cream mixture over the bread, and fold until all the bread is coated. Allow the mixture to sit at room temperature for 30 to 45 minutes.

Preheat the oven to 350°F.

Grease a 9 by 13-inch casserole dish with the remaining tablespoon of butter. Transfer the bread mixture to the casserole dish and bake until the center of the bread pudding is set, 50 to 60 minutes.

Garnish the bread pudding with confectioners' sugar and serve warm with warm Whiskey Sauce.

Whiskey Sauce

2 cups Heavy Cream
1/2 cup Whole Milk
1/2 cup granulated White Sugar
2 tablespoons Cornstarch
3/4 cup Bourbon or other Whiskey
pinch Salt
2 tablespoons Unsalted Butter

In a 1-quart saucepan set over medium heat, combine the cream, milk, and sugar. Place the cornstarch and 1/4 cup of the bourbon in a small mixing bowl and whisk to blend and make a slurry. Pour the slurry into the cream mixture and bring to a boil. Once the sauce begins to boil, reduce the heat to a gentle simmer and cook, stirring occasionally, for 5 minutes. Remove the sauce from the heat, add the salt, and stir in the butter and the remaining 1/2 cup of bourbon. Serve warm.

Christmas Cookies

Baking cookies during the holiday season became a tradition for me when I moved away from home and wanted to create a holiday feeling. At some point I began giving small boxes of cookies away as Christmas presents. This quickly became a big deal as there are a few colleagues who start looking forward to my holiday offering. I usually end up making something like 20 dozen cookies by the time New Year's rolls around.

Holiday Biscotti with Cranberries and Pistachios

I started making this on a whim when perusing Christmas cookie recipes in Gourmet magazine. I had no idea it would be a hit and become one of the most requested cookies I make.

2 1/4 cups All-purpose Flour
1 1/2 teaspoons Baking Powder
3/4 teaspoon Salt
6 tablespoons (3/4 stick) unsalted Butter, room temperature
3/4 cup Sugar
2 large Eggs
1 tablespoon grated Lemon Peel
1 1/2 teaspoons Vanilla extract
1 teaspoon whole Aniseed
1 cup dried sweetened Cranberries
3/4 cup shelled natural unsalted Pistachios

Preheat oven to 325°F. Line a large baking sheet with parchment paper.

Sift first 3 ingredients together and reserve. Beat butter and sugar to blend well. Beat in eggs 1 at a time.

Mix in lemon peel, vanilla, and aniseed.

Beat in flour mixture just until blended. Stir in cranberries and pistachios (dough will be sticky). Turn dough out onto lightly floured surface.

Gather dough together; divide in half. Roll each half into 15-inch-long slightly flattened log (about 1½-2 inches wide).

Bake logs until almost firm to touch but still pale, about 28 minutes. Cool logs on baking sheet for about 10 minutes. Maintain oven temperature.

Carefully transfer logs still on parchment to cutting board. Using a **very sharp**,!! serrated knife and **VERY** gentle sawing motion, (The cookies are very prone to crumble at this point so take your time.) cut logs crosswise into generous 1/2-inch-thick slices.

Place slices, 1 cut side down on baking sheets.

Bake until firm and pale golden, about 9-15 minutes per side. Don't be afraid to toast longer, because you want them dried out and crunchy with minimal browning, just don't burn them. Transfer cookies to racks and cool.

Ma Monson Cookies

Alan- This recipe came from one of Sandy's Scandinavian cookbooks.

  1 pound Butter
  2 cup Sugar, granulated
  4 Eggs
  2 cup Flour, all purpose
  1 teaspoon Vanilla
  Almonds, sliced
  Currents, dried

The butter and sugar are creamed together until light and fluffy. The eggs are then beaten in one at a time followed by the vanilla. The flour is then blended in, but not over mixed.

The batter is spread into a well-greased 9x13 jelly roll pan. The almonds and currents are then sprinkled on top.

The bars should be baked at 375°F for 20-25 minutes until just beginning to brown.

Cool well before attempting to slice and then keep under lock and key because these will disappear fast.

Brandy Rings

Alan- These are one of our favorite Christmas cookies. Sandy discovered them in a Scandinavian cookbook which she had borrowed from the library. We make them every Christmas; this past year Karen and Doug added food coloring to part of the batch to make a parts of some cookies green which is a nice touch.

> 1 and 1/3 cups Butter
> 3/4 cup Sugar
> 1 Egg yolk
> 4 tablespoons Brandy (see note below)
> 3 and 1/4 cups All-purpose Flour

Cream butter with sugar until smooth and fluffy.

Beat in egg yolk and brandy.

Sift flour separately and then blend in. Mix well.

Chill dough thoroughly. It should be quite cold for easy handling so we suggest you work with small portions of the dough at a time, keeping the rest in the refrigerator.

With floured hands, pinch off small pieces of dough and roll on lightly floured surface into thin lengths slightly thinner than a pencil and about 5 inches long.

Make ropes by twisting two of these pieces together like a twine.

Shape each rope into a ring.

Bake on a buttered cookie sheet in 375°F oven until golden yellow, about 10 minutes.

Makes 5 dozen cookies.

NOTE: The choice of brandy may be important--I plan to experiment on this point. Since we only make brandy rings once a year, memory is likely to be misleading, but I thought that they were less tasty the year we used cheap brandy than the years when we used Remy Martin VSOP.

Mexican Tea Cakes

These also have become a favorite as they are addictive and must be hidden if you want any left on Christmas morning.

  2 sticks (1 cup) unsalted Butter, softened
  3 cups confectioners' Sugar
  1 teaspoon Vanilla
  2 1/4 cups All-purpose Flour
  3/4 cup very finely chopped Pecans (2 1/2 ounces)
  3/4 teaspoon Salt

Beat together butter and 1/2 cup confectioners' sugar in a large bowl with an electric mixer at moderately high speed until pale and fluffy, about 4 minutes. Beat in vanilla, and then add flour, pecans, and salt and mix at low speed until just combined.

Chill, covered, at least 2 hours, more is better, overnight is good.

Preheat oven to 375°F.

Let dough stand at room temperature until just pliable, about 15 minutes.

Roll level teaspoons of dough into 3/4-inch balls and arrange about 2 inches apart on lightly buttered large baking sheets.

Sift remaining 2 1/2 cups confectioners' sugar into a large shallow bowl.

Bake in batches in middle of oven until bottoms are pale golden, 8 to 10 minutes. Immediately transfer hot cookies to confectioners' sugar, gently rolling to coat well, transfer to a rack to cool completely.

Caramel Pecan Cookies

Crust
2 cups All-purpose Flour
1/2 teaspoon Baking Powder
1/2 teaspoon Salt
1 1/2 sticks (3/4 cup) unsalted Butter, softened
1 cup Sugar
1 large Egg
1/2 teaspoon Vanilla

Caramel pecan topping
1 1/2 cups Sugar
1 cup Heavy Cream
3/4 stick (6 tablespoons) unsalted Butter, cut into bits
1 teaspoon Vanilla
1/2 teaspoon Salt
2 cups Pecans (1/2 pound), toasted, cooled, and coarsely chopped

Grease a 13- by 9-inch metal baking pan, then line with foil, leaving a 2-inch overhang on both ends, and grease foil.

Whisk together flour, baking powder, and salt in a small bowl. Beat together butter and sugar in a large bowl with an electric mixer at medium-high speed until pale and fluffy.

Beat in egg and vanilla. Reduce speed to low, then add flour mixture and mix until just combined.

Press dough evenly onto bottom of baking pan and chill until firm, about 20 minutes.

While crust chills, put oven rack in middle position and preheat oven to 375°F.

Bake crust until golden brown, about 30 minutes. Cool in pan on a rack 20 minutes. (Leave oven on.)

While crust cools: Cook sugar in a 2 1/2- to 3-quart heavy saucepan over moderate heat, undisturbed, until it begins to melt. Continue to cook, stirring occasionally with a fork (do not make the mistake of using a whisk, you will end up with a ball of hard candy in a cage.), until sugar is melted to a deep golden caramel.

Tilt pan and carefully pour in cream (caramel will harden and steam vigorously). Pouring slowly is important.   If you have a third hand, then stirring fast that this time will help a lot.

Cook over moderately low heat, stirring, until caramel is dissolved. Remove from heat and stir in butter, vanilla, salt, and pecans.

Immediately spread topping over cooled crust and bake until bubbling, about 20 minutes.

Cool completely in pan on rack, about 2 hours. Run a heavy knife under hot water, then wipe dry and cut confection into 2-inch triangles, diamonds, or squares.

Molasses Crinkles

Alan- These are cookies that my Mom made--not just at Christmas, but that is now the only time we seem to make them. I believe she got the recipe from a cookbook, but it's not one of the common ones that we use.

3/4 cup Shortening (See Note)
1 cup Brown Sugar
1 Egg
1/4 cup Molasses
2 and 1/4 cups All-purpose Flour
2 teaspoons Baking Soda
1/4 teaspoon Salt
1/2 teaspoon powdered Cloves
1 teaspoon powdered Cinnamon
1 teaspoon powdered Ginger
Granulated Sugar (Turbinado) and (separately) Water for topping

Mix first four ingredients together, beat until fluffy. Set aside momentarily.

Sift flour and remaining ingredients together and blend with shortening mixture.

Chill dough for at least one-half hour in freezer, overnight is fine.

Roll into balls about the size of large walnuts.

Dip tops of the cookie balls into the granulated sugar (coarse turbinado sugar works particularly well) and place on greased baking sheet, sugar side up, about 3 inches apart.

Sprinkle each cookie with 2 or 3 drops of water-(Sandy prefers to dip 2 fingers into the water and then just touch the top of a cookie)-this will produce a crackled surface after baking.

Bake in a preheated 375°F oven about 12 minutes or until medium brown (note dough is brown to begin with) and crackles are apparent.

These cookies should be chewy, not hard--and they are GOOD!

Note: Butter is not as good in this recipe as solid shortening because the cookies tend to be too soft. But if you want, you can substitute 11 tablespoons of butter.

Cranberry Shortbread

1 cup Fresh Cranberries, thinly sliced
1 cup Butter, softened
½ cup Sugar
2 cups All-Purpose Flour
½ tsp lemon zest

Using a Food processor with a slicing blade chop the cranberries.

Cream the butter and sugar until fluffy. Add zest.

Slowly add flour followed by the sliced cranberries. Mix only enough to combine.

Using plastic wrap, form the dough into logs approximately 1 ½ inches wide.wrap tightly in the plastic wrap and refrigerate overnight.

Slice into rounds ¼ inch thick and bake in 350 oven for 20 minutes, rotating the cookie sheet once to insure even baking.

Chinese Chews

By Alan

This is Sandy's mother's recipe. I have no idea where she got it, or even the origin of the name. I can vouch for the delicious taste and texture. We wouldn't dream of having Christmas without these!

2 Eggs
3/4 cup Flour
1 teaspoon Baking Powder
1 cup Sugar
1/4 teaspoon Salt
1 cup freshly chopped Dates
1 cup chopped Walnuts
Granulated or Powdered Sugar for dipping

Beat 2 eggs well with 1 cup sugar until fluffy. Add remaining ingredients and blend thoroughly.

Grease a shallow 8 inch square baking pan and spread the dough smoothly over it.

Bake in a preheated 350°F oven for about 30 minutes or until medium brown. The cake should be soft and squishy, but not runny. Sometimes Sandy cuts the edges off and sticks the center portion back into the oven to bake a few extra minutes.

Immediately cut into one inch squares and roll into a cylindrical shaped cookie.

Dip into granulated sugar. Be careful, this is hot work and hard on the fingers, but the cookies are worth it. A trick to do this is to have cold water running and rinse your fingers in the water when too sticky.

Meyer Lemon Cranberry Scones

These are another recent favorite at all times of the year. I make them cookie sized at the Holidays and larger scones sized at other times.

2 tablespoons freshly grated lemon zest (from about 3 lemons; preferably Meyer)
2 1/2 cups All-Purpose Flour
1/2 cup sugar plus 3 tablespoons additional if using fresh Cranberries
1 tablespoon Baking Powder
1/2 teaspoon Salt
3/4 stick (6 tablespoons) cold unsalted Butter, cut into bits
1 1/4 cups fresh Cranberries, chopped coarse, or 1 1/4 cups dried Cranberries or Dried Cherries
1 large Egg
1 large Egg Yolk
1 cup Heavy Cream

Preheat oven to 400°F and line a large baking sheet with parchment paper.

In a food processor pulse flour, 1/2 cup sugar, baking powder, salt, butter and zest until mixture resembles coarse meal and transfer to a large bowl.

In a small bowl toss together fresh cranberries and 3 tablespoons sugar and stir into flour mixture. If using dried fruit, add to flour mixture.

In another small bowl lightly beat egg and yolk and stir in cream. Add egg mixture to flour mixture and stir until just combined.

On a well-floured surface with floured hands pat dough into a 1-inch-thick round, it does not have to be an even shape. Cut scones to desired shapes, some like circles, I like triangles. For Christmas, I make them small.

Arrange scones about 1 inch apart on baking sheet and bake in middle of oven 15 to 20 minutes, or until pale golden.

Finnish Bread

Alan- Warning: these are addictive! They are also one of my (Alan) all-time favorite cookies. Sandy also got this recipe from the Scandinavian cookbook where it claims these are really a Swedish cookie.

    1 cup Flour
    1/4 teaspoon Salt
    1/4 cup Sugar
    1/3 cup ground Unblanched Almonds
    1/2 teaspoon Vanilla extract
    1/2 cup Butter

    For the topping
    1 Egg White
    1/4 cup finely chopped Almonds (optional)
    3 tablespoons Sugar

Sift flour and combine with salt, sugar, and almonds in a bowl.

Using a stand mixer with paddle blade, mix vanilla and butter in until just blended and a soft dough is formed.

Flour hands and roll out a fist sized lumps of dough on floured surface into a long strips the diameter of your index finger. Don't worry if they break a part, just do the best you can.

Place the strips parallel to each other and cut through the 4 strips at 1.5 inch intervals.

Place on buttered cookie sheet about 1/2 inch apart.

Slightly beat the egg white and brush each cookie with it.

Sprinkle with sugar and finely chopped almonds if you like.

Bake at 350°F for 10 minutes or until golden yellow.

Leave on cookie sheet until cool, remove with a sharp knife.

Makes 50 small cookies.

Meyer Lemon Madeleines

The ingredients are from newspaper they adapted from a Julia Child recipe. This was another recipe I adapted to use up the hundreds of lemons my trees produce every fall.

2 large Eggs, lightly beaten in a 2-cup measure
2/3 cup Sugar
1 cup All-purpose Flour, plus 1 tablespoon extra for preparing molds
5 ounces (1 1/4 sticks) unsalted Butter, cut into 6 pieces
Pinch of Salt
Grated rind of 2 Meyer Lemons
1 tablespoon of freshly squeezed Meyer Lemon
Confectioners' Sugar for sprinkling

Preheat oven to 375°F and set the racks in the middle.

Measure 1/4 cup of eggs into a bowl, then, using a wooden spoon, beat in the sugar and cup of flour. When thoroughly blended, let rest 10 minutes. Meanwhile, melt the butter in a 6-cup saucepan, bring it to a boil, and let it brown lightly.

Blend 1 tablespoon flour and 1½ tablespoons browned butter and reserve for preparing pans.

Allow butter to cool until cool but liquid. Blend it and the last of the eggs into the batter along with the salt, lemon rind, and juice.

Paint the Madeleine pans with the reserved butter-flour mixture. Drop tablespoon sized lumps of batter into each Madeleine cup.

Bake 15 minutes until the cakes are lightly browned around the edges, humped in the middle, and slightly shrunken from the cups.

Un-mold the cookies on to a rack. When cool dust with powdered sugar.

Love Letters (Szerelmes Level)

I remember these cookies from my childhood; we make them rarely because even though they are wonderful, they require quite an effort and are only good for a short time after baking.   The day after baking, these are only half as good.

First prepare the dough:

> 2 cups sifted Flour
> 2 tablespoons Sugar
> ½ teaspoon Salt
> ¾ cup Butter, chilled and cut into pieces
> 4 Egg Yolks, slightly beaten

Sift together dry ingredients into a large bowl. Work butter into dry ingredients by pressing against bottom and side of bowl with a fork.

Add gradually to butter flour mixture, blending ingredients with a fork. (Mixture will be crumbly)

Gather dough into a ball. Turn out onto lightly floured surface. Work with hands, squeezing dough until well blended. Shape into smooth ball with palms of hands. Divide dough into halves; wrap in waxed paper and place into refrigerator for about 1 hr. Shape dough in a very cool kitchen.

After 45 min prepare filling:

> ½ cup coarsely chopped Walnuts
> 1 teaspoon grated Lemon Peel
> 2 Egg Whites
> ¼ cup Sugar
> ½ tsp Cinnamon

Mix together walnuts and lemon peel and reserve. Beat egg whites until frothy. Mix together sugar and cinnamon and add gradually to egg whites, beating well after each addition. Beat until rounded peaks are formed. Gently fold nut mixture into the egg whites. Set filling aside.

To form Love Letters – Remove one-half of dough from refrigerator. Place dough on lightly floured surface and roll into rectangle 1/6 inch thick.

Work quickly to prevent dough from becoming too soft. With knife or spatula gently loosen dough from board wherever sticking occurs; lift dough slightly and sprinkle flour underneath. Trim off uneven edges of rectangle. Gather trimmings into a ball; wrap in waxed paper and place into refrigerator.

Cut rectangle into 3in squares. Place about 2 teaspoons of the filling into center of each square. To make "letters", bring opposite corners together, overlapping slightly at center. Repeat with other two corners.

Place on lightly greased baking sheet. In this way, continue to make letters and place 1 in apart on baking sheet. Brush Love Letters with slightly beaten egg

Bake at 350°F 20 to 30 minutes or until lightly browned. Carefully remove from baking sheet to cooling racks.

When cooled sift over a mixture of

  2-3 Tb Powdered Sugar
  ½ tsp Cinnamon

Makes about 2 ½ dozen

Canning, Freezing and Preserving

This section began with my efforts to save some of my many lemons for the rest of the year. But I can remember as a child my mother would Can and preserve all number of things from tomatoes to plum jelly, remember the sticky stuff? Also, down here in Houston, basil grows like a weed in the summer, so we always have massive quantities. We like to make pesto and freeze. Also I have infused olive oil with fresh basil to preserve that wonderful aroma beyond the summer months.

Preserved Lemons

Preserved lemons are one of the indispensable ingredients of Moroccan cooking, recipes for chicken with lemons are found elsewhere in this volume.
I found this method when living in Houston I was searching for a way to preserve the hundreds of lemons produced by my two lemon trees every year. Normally I use quart size jars, but pint size work fine and would be nice for gifts.

Meyer Lemons
Rock Salt; more if desired
Freshly squeezed lemon juice

Optional spices
1 Cinnamon stick
3 Cloves
5 To 6 Coriander seeds
3 To 4 Black Peppercorns
1 Bay Leaf

Place thin layer of rock salt on the bottom of a sterilized Mason jar. Pack in 2 lemon halves and pack them down, adding more salt, and the optional spices, between layers. Press the lemons down to release
their juices and to make room for the remaining lemons. (If the
juice released from the squashed fruit does not cover them, add
freshly squeezed lemon juice

It is important to be certain the lemons are completely covered with salted lemon juice.

Let the lemons ripen at room temp, shaking the jar each day to
distribute the salt and juice. Let ripen at least 30 days.

To use, rinse the lemons, as needed, under running water, removing and
discarding the pulp, if desired - and there is no need to refrigerate
after opening. Preserved lemons will keep up to a year or longer if refrigerated after ripening

Lemon Marmalade

When we lived in Texas, it was a tradition to make at least one batch of lemon marmalade each season. We had two Myers lemon trees which each produce a limb straining bounty, which ripens around Thanksgiving time and last through around March of the following year. A little cold weather does not seem to faze the lemons, the only year we had issues was when it was well below freezing for more than a day. The lemons are one of the few things we miss about Houston.

15-20 Meyer Lemons
8 cup Granulated Sugar

Slice the lemons to between 1/8 and ¼ inch. Discard ends. Remove all seeds and tie them in a square of doubled cheesecloth. Put lemons and seed bag in a non-reactive (stainless steel) pot with enough water to barely cover. Let stand overnight. Add an equal volume of sugar and cook over low heat until sugar is dissolved. Raise heat to medium-high and cook stirring frequently and skimming off the foam as it rises until temperature reaches 220°F about 1/2 hour. Remove marmalade from heat. To test for consistency drop a little marmalade on a saucer and put the saucer into the freezer until marmalade is cold about 5 minutes. Tip the saucer: the marmalade should just barely run. If too thin, return the marmalade to medium-high heat and cook testing often until it has reached the right consistency. Can marmalade as per normal jellies, keeps for several years.

Recipe adapted from Cook's Magazine November/December 1987, however this same recipe is found all over the place.

Candied Lemon Peel

I created this recipe from the results of various online sources combined with some trial and error.

8 large Mayer's Lemons
Water

1 cup Boiling Water
4 cups Sugar

Wash the lemons. Cut into halves and squeeze out the juice. Use the juice for some other purpose, of course. Place the lemons into a large saucepan and cover with cold water.

Place over high heat and heat to a boil. Drain. Add cold water to cover again. Repeat this process five times in all. Drain well and scoop out the pulp. Cut the lemons into 1/4 inch wide strips.

Combine 1 cup of boiling water with 2 cups of the sugar. Heat until the sugar is dissolved. Stir in the lemons strips. Place over medium heat and boil for about 30 minutes, until all the liquid is evaporated. Watch carefully so the peels don't scorch. Cool. Roll the strips in the remaining 2 cups of sugar. Place on wire rack to dry. Package and store in airtight containers, a mason jar is recommended and if you are not sure that they are totally dry store in fridge to prevent mold

Chili Sauce

This is something we always made when I was a child, it was used as both a BBQ sauce fr basting ribs or pork steaks or a condiment for things like burgers. It cans well if you make a big batch.

2 large (28 ounce) cans whole tomatoes, chopped plus 2-3 fresh tomatoes, peeled and chopped
3 medium onions
1 ½ cups chopped Poblano peppers
2 cloves garlic, crushed
2 ½ teaspoon salt
½ teaspoon cinnamon, ground
½ teaspoon whole cloves, ground
½ teaspoon mustard seed, ground
½ teaspoon allspice, ground
½ teaspoon nutmeg, ground
1/2 cup brown sugar, packed
1 cup cider vinegar

Sauté onions and peppers in a tablespoon of olive oil until the onions begin to brown. Add all the rest of the ingredients and simmer for about 1 hour. Can be canned according to established guidelines or frozen in small containers.

Artichoke Pickle

This spicy condiment took me awhile to track down a recipe. Ridley told me about this one and I was able to piece together several recipes into one that we quite like. It is very strong so may be something too strong for many.

1½ - 2 lbs cleaned and diced Jerusalem artichokes (sunchokes)
2 cups diced celery
1½ cups diced carrots
2 cups diced cauliflower
1 cup dice onions
1 cup each diced and jalapeno peppers
1 cup pickling salt
2 tablespoons white vinegar

1 cup dry mustard
½ cup flour
2 teaspoons celery seed
2 teaspoons mustard seed
2 tablespoons Turmeric
½ tsp ground allspice
1 cup sugar
4 cups apple cider vinegar

Dissolve the salt in 2 quarts of water and 2 Tb white vinegar and add chopped vegetables, allow to soak overnight or at least 8 hours.

Wisk together flour and mustard in a bowl

In a large pot combine the celery seed, mustard seed, turmeric, allspice, sugar and cider vinegar. Bring to a boil

Dip a couple cups of the liquid into the flour mixture and wisk until no lumps remain, add back to the pot with the rest of the liquid. Simmer for 10 minutes.

Turn off the heat and add all the vegetables.

Stir to combine well.

The pickle can now be water bath canned or kept in the refrigerator

Vintage Recipes

Collections of recipes handed down from generations past.

Recipes from
My Grandmother's and Grandfather's Cookbook

Transcribed and annotated by Alan.

Grandfather and Grandmother Meriwether (my mother's parents, whose names were Franklin Montgomery Meriwether [F.M.M.] and Ethel Grant Nelson) built a log cabin on land they owned on US highway 61, just south of the town of Eolia, Missouri in about 1932.

They lived there the rest of their lives--she died in 1941 and he died in 1948. My uncle Heath (Nelson Heath Meriwether) inherited the log cabin and its contents. (My mother inherited some of the land away from the cabin.) Sometime before the log cabin was vandalized and its contents ruined, Heath removed some of the contents of the log cabin to his home in Columbia Later Heath and his wife Agnes moved to Hannibal.

Shortly after the death of her father, Heath , my cousin Annie Laurie Hulen was sorting through his personal property and came across an old weather-beaten book.It was originally a book of blank pages, but my grandparents had made it into their cookbook by writing recipes in it, pasting recipes which had been cut from newspapers or magazines in it, and decorating it with a photograph or two, and a letter or two.

My grandparents were very poor, but prided themselves on how they lived, including what they ate. They had strong opinions on how to cook a steak, or make an eggnog. I am particularly interested in the recipes which they wrote in this book in their own handwriting, and have copied them exactly in the following pages.I am in possession of this book because Annie Laurie gave it to Annie Laurie (my mother) who gave it to me.Isn't it an interesting coincidence that I am writing a cookbook about 60 years after my grandparents wrote theirs!

Mulligan Stew(My Grandmother's Recipe)

This recipe was typewritten on a piece of stationary with a printed heading "THE CABIN -- TAKK-A-LOKK . . . Eolia, Missouri"

Typed under the heading was, including the quotation marks: "When the Frost is on the ...And the Fodder in the ....."

Then the heading: M U L L I G A N S T E W

A chicken, a piece of beef, fat, a piece of pork, a squirrel, and a few slices of bacon if handy, Irish potatoes, corn-on-the-cob, onions bear down strong on these and the potatoes, small head of cabbage, beans, carrots, turnips, 2 or 3 green peppers with the seeds out, same of red, these are sweet peppers, a few nice ripe tomatoes and whatever else you have around the camp handy, slice these all together, pour in say a gallon of H20, hang on the totem pole over a slow fire, salt, pepper, and red pepper--cayenne--to taste.Keep an eye on the beast for say four - five hours, don't go way, stir occasionally, add water as it evaporates, you can read a short-short in between but no Somerset Maugham's, after it cooks awhile stir in say 2 tablespoonfuls chili powder, act indifferent but keep your eye on it, remembering the Imp-that-sits-on-your-left."Remembering Laughter"- - it will cheat if it can.After it thickens and the frequent "samplings" fails to appease, and your rage waxes unbearable, is the time to have all hands in the camp out with the forked sticks and make the 5-6-7 loafs (Ha?) into toast, assemble all the pans, the knives-forks-spoons, as a precaution to personal safety....When the Hunters from the Chase sniff the scene from afar and break from Sniff-to Gallop-to-Run it will be just as well, as far as you are concerned to seek places of safety without Finagling.....be sure to have plenty.....Old Friends of a Lifetime have grown Cold and scornful over the question of Apportionment.....Go along on the Idea that Too Much is Enough....Remember that it may not be Your Fault but you'll be Blamed for it.................
....

[I don't know if ever such a thing was ACTUALLY made.Mother talks about Mulligan,claims to have eaten if, but can't remember any specifics.I think it was mostly conversation but it may have had its basis in history.Also, I was told as a boy that it wasn't any good if it didn't have a peckerwood in it!]

Coffee

To each cup of cold water add 1 full dinner spoon of coffee and 1 spoonful for the pot-boil 3 minutes. By F.M.M.

Hot Biscuits

1 quart of flour- 2 teaspoonful of salt, 2 teaspoonful of yeast powder-1 teaspoonful of soda. 1 tablespoonful of lard Mix thoroughly.1 pint of buttermilk.Work dough well.Oven should be Hot-lard and buttermilk Cold. By F.M.M.

Egg Omelet

3 eggs with salt and pepper. 4 tablespoonfuls of cream. 1 teaspoonful of yeast powder. Beat until well mixed.Cook slowly in buttered skillet until brown on both sides. This portion for 2 persons. By F.M.M.

Scrambled Eggs

Double Boiler-1 teaspoon of butter in the double boiled to each egg. Beat eggs well, salt to taste, and add 2 tablespoons milk and cream for each egg.Then pour in double boiler and cook slowly, stirring constantly. (a little baking powder helps)[This recipe may be grandmother's since the handwriting is different and does not have by F.M.M.]

Beef-Steak. Rare

5 pounds-3 inches thick. Salt and Pepper.Hot skillet; turn in 2 minutes, add strips of bacon after 4 minutes and cook 5 minutes.Enough for 4 persons - F.M.M. To cook quails and rabbits or wild game.Ditto above, only cook game until well done. F.M.M. [Editorial comment: I cook a 2 inch sirloin over a hot charcoal fire for about 27 minutes total and it is rare enough for Sandy and John whom we claim like their steak rare.There is usually enough medium rare meat on the outside edges for me and others. If we have people who like well done, I must cook it longer or they have to suffer. If I understand grandfather correctly, he cooked the 3 inch steak for 9 minutes.It would be raw in the middle, but perhaps he liked it that way.It's also amazing that a 5 pound steak would serve only 4 people- - even a real meat lover like me finds over a pound of steak to be a lot!]

The following series of recipes apparently were my grandparents usual Thanksgiving menu. The dressing recipes referred to are cut from a newspaper. Also out were recipes for cranberry sauce, candied sweet potatoes, and creamed potatoes. After these was a handwritten recipe for baked beans, and then a note in probably grandmothers handwriting. I have included all of these.

Roast Turkey

Dry pluck a 15 lb.s fat young (1 year old) turkey. Plump turkey salt and pepper and place in roaster with 1 pint of water. Put in slow oven and cook about 2 and 1/2 hours. Take out and stuff with onion dressing or oyster dressing(see receipt below) Cook turkey 1/1 hours longer until done.F.M.M.

Bread Stuffing for Turkey (newspaper)

To one cup of bread crumbs add two cups of corn bread crumbled, one egg, salt, pepper, a tablespoon of butter, grated onion to taste, and stock to moisten.

Oyster Dressing with Turkey (newspaper)

Take equal parts of stale bread and cold corn bread; place in a pan, cover with boiling water, drain off a once, crumble the bread fine, add melted butter; salt, pepper and whatever seasoning may be liked; drain off liquor from a quart of oysters; boil, skim and pour over the bread crumbs. Add two eggs and mix thoroughly with the hands. Put a spoonful of this stuffing into the turkey, then three or four oysters, and so on until the turkey is filled; place over the openings thin slices of bacon; sew up and it is ready for the oven.

Sausage Stuffing for Turkey (newspaper)

Make as bread stuffing, substituting sausage for half the bulk of the stuffing, using no butter; the sausage should be cooked and mixed with bread crumbs.

Cranberry Sauce (newspaper)

To a quart of cranberries add a half cup of water and cook until they begin to burst. When they are done, not until then, stir in two cups of sugar; take from the fire as soon as dissolved and strain into a wet mold. Put on ice until firm.

Candied Sweet Potatoes (newspaper)

Boil, peel, and slice a quarter of an inch thick and put into a baking dish.Sprinkle sugar over each layer; add butter and bake until hot through and browned delicately.

Creamed Potatoes (newspaper)

Steam six large potatoes until tender; put in hot sauce pan, mash fine; add lump butter size of an egg and one cup of hot cream; beat until light and serve piping hot.

Baked Beans (handwritten)

4 cups of navy beans and soak overnight in water.Next morning put in kettle with 1 quart of water and small piece of salt or fresh pork. Add salt and cook about 1 and 1/2 to 2 hours.Then place in casserole.Next with salt and pepper to taste add strips of bacon and 1 and 1/2 cups of molasses and sugar.Put in slow oven 2 to 3 hours and to about 10 persons.F.M.M.

Handwritten, probably by grandmother: For a "balanced meal, serve 1 or 2 cans spinach with hard-boiled egg sliced.I never fail to serve this.

This is the end of the Roast Turkey menu.

To Cook an Old or Grown Duck

Parboil in steam cooker, with a large onion on the inside of the duck, a couple of acid apples and a stalk of celery in the liquid.

For dressing use stewed apples put inside the duck and around it on the platter or you can make a dressing mostly of corn bread and a couple of eggs, omitting onion.Be sure you parboil til tender, then transfer to an iron skillet and roast brown.You will know how to really cook a duck!

Sauces for Meats

Mint sauce with lamb or mutton, apple and with pork, cranberries with chicken and turkey, any kind of jelly with duck.Currant or apple preferred or grape and apple.

Cabbage

1 head cabbage, small piece salt pork or good meat.Skim, 1 tablespoon sugar-cook til tender about 20 to 25 minutes.Strew 2 LARGE tablespoons lard or drippings and serve hot.Don't overcook.

French Dressing

1/2 cup sugar
1/2 cup oil
1/2 cup vinegar
1/2 teaspoon salt
1/2 teaspoon white pepper
1/2 teaspoon paprika
1/2 teaspoon dry mustard

Southern Beaten Biscuit (newspaper)

This recipe was clipped from a newspaper, but was marked with an ink X, and also the page with a paper clip, so it may have been a favorite.

1 quart sifted flour
1/2 coffee cup lard
1/2 pint sweet milk
1 level teaspoon salt

Rub flour, salt and lard together until smooth, then add milk.Beat twenty minutes, or until dough blisters and cut with small biscuit cutter and prick each with a fork.Bake twenty minutes in a rather hot oven.This quantity makes about 30 biscuits.The recipe may be doubled when desired.

Buttermilk Biscuit (newspaper)

This recipe was right below the southern beaten biscuit receipt.

Sift together one quart of flour, one level teaspoon of soda, and one of salt and then add two cups of sour buttermilk, three tablespoons of lard; roll to the thickness of three-fourths of an inch; cut small biscuits, bake immediately in hot oven.

Hot Water Corn Bread

This recipe is THE famous one, which my mother always talks about. It is also interestingly written. While I (Alan) was growing up, my mother (Annie Laurie Meriwether Bemis) often talked about "pone". She meant corn pone, and a very specific recipe for it. When my mother was a child, and probably well into adulthood, her mother made "pone" in the proper Meriwether fashion. If you read the recipe, you will immediately realize it was written by my grandmother, Ethyl Grant Nelson Meriwether who was the editor of a Clarksville, Missouri newspaper called the Missouri Piker. My mother's family were very fussy about cornbread, among other things any sugar in it was anathema!

Anyway, long after I was grown, I inherited a cookbook from my mother with recipes written in it by her parents. After reading the Hot Water Corn Bread recipe, I asked my mother how it was done and she showed me. My mother was 80 years old, and I was 50.

Mother made them for me. She followed the recipe, but added 1 tablespoon of grease to the pone mixture after she had mixed the hot water with the meal.

We used bacon fat and lard for cooking, the lard because we ran out of bacon fat! She said to use stone-ground cornmeal, a coarse grind. The pone mixture was very stiff. She cooked them on a medium-hot fire until browned, then she turned them, and cooked them until they were brown on the other side.

They were good, but will probably not appeal to those who are used to sweet cornbread!

2 cups corn meal, 1 teaspoon salt (level).Mix.BOILING water, steam coming out of tea kettle spout and pour on and mix and stir well, make it just thick enough to make wet pones.

Have grease (fried meat grease if you have it) HOT so it will sizzle, dip hands into COLD water, make out a "pone", then again into cold-water, til you have it all in.DON'T TRY to cheat!It can't be done.FOLLOW COPY.

Home Made Baking Powder

12 oz. tartaric acid, 16 oz. bicarbonate of soda, 2 # cornstarch.Sift together 8 times and tuck away in sealed jars.

Lazy Daisy Cake

This handwritten recipe was on a separate piece of paper, tucked into the cookbook.I don't know if it is grandmothers or not.Judging from the spelling and grammar, I think not!

2 eggs beaten with 1 cup of sugar. 1 cup flour and 1/2 teaspoon B powder.half cup of scalded milk with one tablespoon of butter, 1 teaspoon of vanilla and pinch.beat this all with eggbeater and when done put on tab while it hot 8 tablespoon B sugar, 2 tablespoon butter, and a little cream and spread on tab and but coconut on tab and but back in oven for a few minutes.

Egg Nogg

12 egg yellows.add 12 tablespoonfuls of sugar.beaten to a cake flufme(?). Pour 4 wine glasses of whiskey, slowly at first into yellows.12 glasses of milk or cream. Beat the whites of eggs and add. Grate nutmeg. Put in cold place.By F.M.M.[Editorial note: sounds a lot like my recipe, depending on the size of the wine glasses]

Holiday Fruitcake(Dark)

This recipe was printed on slick paper and pasted into the cookbook, probably from a magazine. However, it had writing at the end of it which was initialed by my grandmother, the ONLY place in the cookbook she initialed. It's interesting to compare it with Aunt Agnes fruitcake and also the recipe attributed by Charlotte Griffith to Rebecca Terrel.

1 pound (2 cups) butter
2 cups dark brown sugar, sifted
1 cup dark molasses
1 cup dark jam
6 eggs
4 cups all-purpose flour
1/2 teaspoon soda
1/4 teaspoon salt
2 teaspoons cinnamon
1 teaspoon allspice
2 teaspoons nutmeg
1 teaspoon mace
1/2 teaspoon clove
1 cup coffee, triple strength
1/2 cup orange juice
2 tablespoons lemon juice
2 cups currants, chopped
2 cups raisins, chopped
1 cup dates or figs, chopped
2 cups citron, chopped
1 cup each candied cherries, lemon rind, orange rind, chopped
1 cup each almonds, walnuts, chopped

Cream butter; add brown sugar gradually, creaming. Stir in molasses and jam, and add egg yolks, beaten slightly.Beat until creamy and smooth.

Reserve 2 cups flour for nuts and fruit and sift remainder with soda, salt, and spices.

Stir in flour mixture alternately with coffee and fruit juices, and beat thoroughly.

Whip egg whites until they shape, almost stiff, and fold them in. Stir in floured fruit, rind, and nuts.Bake in cake pans lined with thin waxed paper.

Bake 3 hours in a very slow oven (250°F) for the large cakes, 2 to 2 and 1/2 hours in a slow oven (300°F) for the small ones.

This will make 2 large or 4 small cakes.Add any desired decorations before baking.

(Handwritten): To this I add 1 cup wine or whiskey, preferably the latter. EGM

328

Notes

Index

334

355e5c49-1def-4b3e-866b-e18dd13725b5R01